£6.99 8A

CU00822360

£6.99 8A

Coast Lines Limited

1913-1975

S.S. "SOUTHERN COAST." - 2500 tons
Summer Coastal Cruises between Liverpool and London and vice versa,
calling at Intermediate Ports.
COAST LINES, LIMITED, Royal Liver Building, Liverpool 3; and
London House, New London Street, E.C 3.

Nick Robins

COAST LINES LIMITED, 1913-1975

Nick Robins

Contents

First published October 2019 by
Coastal Shipping Publications, 400 Nore Road, Portishead, Bristol, BS20 8EZ, England
Tel: +44 (0)1275 846178
email: bernard@coastalshipping.co.uk   website: www.coastalshipping.co.uk
ISBN: 978-1-902953-95-3
Copyright © Nick Robins

The rights of Nick Robins to be identified as author of this work have been asserted by him in accordance with the Copyright, Design and Patent Act, 1988. All rights reserved.

No part of this publication may be reproduced, stored in a retrieval system or transmitted in any form or by any means (electronic, digital, mechanical, photocopying, recording or otherwise) without prior permission of the publisher.

All distribution enquiries should be addressed to the publisher,

PREFACE

Although there have been a number of fleet lists published for Coast Lines Limited in recent years an accurate account of the company's activities has not previously been recorded. There are excellent accounts of some of the major subsidiary companies, for example, the Belfast Steamship Company history by Robert Sinclair, which touch on a number of facets of the parent company's dealings. The history of Coast Lines is complicated by its evolving relationship with its owners until the mid-1930s, and with its various subsidiary companies throughout its tenure. It had its lows, serious lows, and its highs, for example, the design of the closed shelter deck motor vessel **British Coast** was innovative in the extreme.

The difficulty in compiling this book was not what to put in it, but rather what to leave out. The result is a book that describes the core activities of Coast Lines Limited in detail and includes some of the major events in the history of the other companies in the Coast Lines group. However, a lot of the minor incidents which befell Coast Lines' own activities have been omitted in order to constrain the size of the text. The spotlight, as always, falls not only on the key activities and the ships, but also on the people such as Sir Alfred Read and Sir Arnet Robinson, who made the company almost a monopoly in the coastal shipping trades. Coast Lines Limited reached its zenith in the late 1950s, thereafter releasing its hold in the face of the unit load and roll-on roll-off technologies.

I am grateful for dialogue with Ian Ramsay regarding various details, particularly about Harland & Wolff and the Ardrossan Dockyard Company, and to Malcolm McRonald for guidance with the preparation of the fleet list. Ian Ramsay also kindly reviewed and edited the text.

Photographs are credited to their rightful source where this is known, including those taken by the author, and otherwise come from the author's own collection. I am particularly grateful to Malcolm Cranfield for sourcing a number of rare images, and to John D Hill, custodian of the Richard Parsons collection, for kindly allowing the scanning and publishing of a number of images. I also thank Gerald Drought, Linda Gowans, Jim McFaul, and David Whiteside for access to their maritime photograph collections. I wish to record my thanks to Gil Mayes and Marilyn Sykes for their sterling work in proof reading.

The team at Coastal Shipping Publications, as always, have been a pleasure to work with and have again produced a finely manicured book.

Dr Nick Robins
Crowmarsh

FOREWORD

It is appropriate that the experienced author Dr Nick Robins has finally produced the definitive history of the much admired Coast Lines. This is the last in a series of four books, all published by Coastal Shipping, together fully covering the history of Coast Lines' constituent parts. Dr Robins' first book in the series was on M Langlands and Sons, the second on Powell, Bacon and Hough and the third on Burns and Laird.

During the four decades since the death of Coast Lines' former Chairman Sir Arnet Robinson in May 1975 containerisation has transformed both deep sea and coastal dry cargo transport. Many of the ports which Coast Lines had served now accommodate the network of container feeder ships operating from deep sea hubs including Southampton and Antwerp. However, several ports which had received Coast Lines' ships in the past, including Bristol's City Docks, have inevitably closed to commercial shipping. While air travel has become for many people an attractive alternative to sea passages, the legacy of Coast Lines is apparent in many of the passenger services which continue in operation around the United Kingdom today.

Malcolm Cranfield

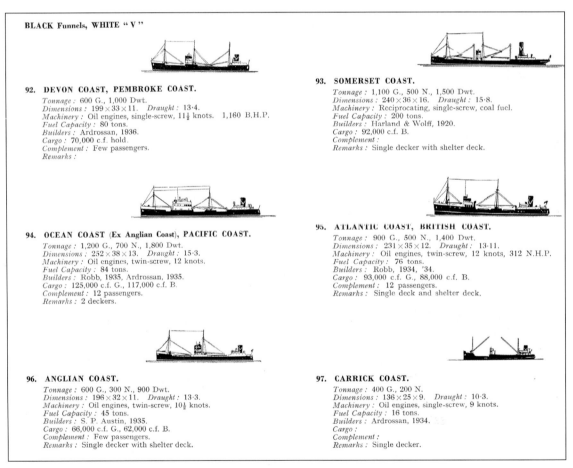

Above : A sample of Coast Lines pre-war fleet.

[from Talbot-Booth The British Merchant Navy 1937-38]

Front cover : **Cambrian Coast** (1957) arriving at Preston Dock, 2 May 1969.

(Jim McFaul)

Back cover : Ports served by Coast Lines Limited in 1956, from Coast Lines Seaway Traders' Guide and Diary 1956.

Title page : The **Southern Coast** (1913) was built as **Dorothy Hough** and used on the prestigious Liverpool to London passenger and cargo service.

CHAPTER 1

FORMATION OF COAST LINES LIMITED

Coast Lines Limited, with its tag line the Coast Lines Seaway, was the largest and most successful coastal shipping company of the twentieth century. Its success lay at the door of its Managing Director, and from 1931 its Chairman, Sir Alfred Read. He was a visionary, a dynamic and energetic man, who fully understood the need to expand and modernise without undue risk to the group of companies that Coast Lines encompassed. Legend has it that Read knew every man in the company by name, certainly in the early days: shore staff, office staff and seafarers.

The company was innovative in many ways, having introduced the door to door parcels service at an early stage: road – sea – road. Read bought Kirks Cartage Company in Liverpool in 1913. Being tied in with the Royal Mail Group, Coast Lines was also exposed to the benefits of the marine motor engine, through Royal Mail subsidiary Harland & Wolff and its association with Burmeister & Wain of Copenhagen. The motor ship was a far more economical unit than the steamer with its conventional triple expansion engine. Coast Lines even owned its own hotel in Liverpool, the Atlantic Hotel, which it bought in the late 1930s to give passengers accommodation between the service to London and the various Irish cross-channel routes.

The main competitors of Coast Lines were the railway companies, which offered cheap freight rates by rail, with connecting sea services across the Irish Sea and elsewhere. The railway companies were tied in to coal-fired steam propulsion by lucrative haulage contracts with the colliers that included the provision of steam coal for the railway engines and the ships. The motor ship was one key economic advantage Read had over the railways, but his empire was small beer compared with the massive freight transport by rail around mainland Britain. Nevertheless, a principal achievement of the Coast Lines Group was to moderate rail freight rates which would otherwise have become a monopoly.

Coast Lines was encouraged to expand in the early days of Royal Mail ownership. Ostensibly this was in order to provide a comprehensive network of coastal feeder routes for the parent company's deep-sea traders which worked largely from west coast ports and the Thames. In reality it was a systematic and comprehensive programme of takeovers that absorbed competition and increased coverage of the overall group around the British Isles. With the demise of the Royal Mail Group, Read was able to buy his independence in 1935, his business reputation was the collateral that supported various promises of loans, significantly one from the Irish Government although this was not fulfilled. Thereafter, the company flourished.

The geographical coverage of the Coast Lines empire was immense. By 1933 regular calls were made by ships within the overall group, from Liverpool, Belfast, Leith and London to: Aberdeen, Bristol, Cardiff, Dover, Dundee, Falmouth where cargo was discharged over the side into company steam lighters, Glasgow, Greenock, Inverness, Kirkcaldy, Llanelli, Leith, London, Middlesbrough, Newcastle, Penzance, Plymouth, Poole, Portsmouth, Shoreham, Southampton, Stornoway, Swansea, Teignmouth and Weymouth. Other ports were served as inducement.

The Coast Lines group came through World War Two to rebuild its various business interests as trade once again picked up. The business of the Coast Lines group spanned the whole of the British and Irish seaboard and included Scotland, the Channel Islands and near Continental ports. By 1951, the Coast Lines group had a fleet of 109 ships which carried four million tons of cargo, more than half a million head of livestock and over a million passengers per year. By the late 1950s the company was at its zenith.

In 1960 George Chandler wrote in his book *Liverpool Shipping*:

> The principal shipping line operating on the oldest of the sea routes from Liverpool – the coastal – is Coast Lines Limited, stated to be, with its associates, the world's largest coastal shipping line, with a fleet in 1958 of 173 steamers, totalling 114,737 tons, excluding five vessels totalling 5,373 tons under construction. Coast Lines carries close on a million passengers and transports over half a million head of cattle each year to various parts of the United Kingdom…

Between 1917 and 1961 Coast Lines acquired a controlling interest in a number of British coastal shipping companies. Among the important and better known acquisitions were: the British & Irish Steam Packet Company Limited in 1917, City of Cork Steam Packet Company Limited in 1918, Belfast Steamship Company Limited in 1919, Burns & Laird Lines acquired separately as Laird Line in 1918 and G & J Burns in 1920 and merged in 1922, Tyne Tees Steam Shipping Company Limited in 1943 and the North of Scotland, Orkney & Shetland Shipping Company acquired in 1961. All of these were allowed to retain their own identity, while many others, such as, for example, M Langlands & Sons, were merged into the core Coast Lines' fleet. There were many other acquisitions, both shipping companies as well as road haulage interests, insurance, docks and wharves and even the Ardrossan Dockyard Company.

Alfred Read's one mistake was to ignore the arrival of the roll-on, roll-off ferry at both Preston and Stranraer in the early 1950s, preferring instead to focus on the unit load system of transport. That decision was ultimately the destruction of the entire group of companies when the remnants were sold to P&O in 1971.

So how did it all begin? Three major coasting companies became Powell, Bacon & Hough Lines Limited in 1913, under the Chairmanship of the former Powell Line leader, Alfred Read (see Robins & McRonald, 2017). Of the three constituent companies F H Powell & Company traded from Liverpool to Bristol, and to London via south coast ports; John Bacon Limited traded from Liverpool and Preston to the Bristol Channel and to Wexford, and Samuel Hough Limited from Liverpool to London via south coast ports. Powell had also an interest in colliers dedicated to supplying the crack transatlantic liners lying in the Mersey with quality high calorific Welsh coal for their bunkers, as well as deep sea tramp ships. Hough also had tramp ship interests while Bacon developed trade to and from the near continent.

The steamer **Augusta** was, in 1862, the first ship to carry the famous black funnel and white chevron adopted by the Powell ships and later, of course, by its successors, Powell, Bacon & Hough Lines Limited and Coast Lines Limited.

The three companies traded independently until the early 1880s when elements of collaboration began. In 1879, Powell and Hough operated the service between Liverpool and London and advertised the route jointly, initially with Powell's steamer **Truthful** working with **Mary Hough**. The Great Victorian Depression then persuaded the Powell and Bacon interests to share the trade on offer rather than compete. Closer collaboration followed during the subsequent twenty years to a degree that a merger of the three companies was a likely outcome. Nobody in the shipping industry was surprised when the proposed new company was announced in 1913.

At that time the new company owned 16 ships and 4 steam lighters, the latter based at Milford on the Bristol Channel and one, the **Enniscorthy**, maintaining the link to the namesake port from Wexford and the Liverpool steamer. The **Enniscorthy** transferred to Milford when the Dublin and South Eastern Railway took over the Enniscorthy link in 1914. She was sold two years later for £625.

The **Sir Edward Bacon** (1899) was originally the **Birker Force** owned by W S Kennaugh & Company of Whitehaven. She was the first ship to be disposed of by Powell, Bacon & Hough Lines when she was sold in 1914. She had not been given a Coast name.

There were two major passenger units, the **Dorothy Hough** which was renamed the **Southern Coast** and the **Powerful** which became the **Eastern Coast**; both were retained on the Liverpool to London service. By 1917 the company acquired another steam lighter and three cargo ships, the **Stonehenge**, **Kentish Coast**, ex-**Hinderton**, and **Irish Coast**, formerly **Rosslyn**. The **Stonehenge** and **Irish Coast** were sold in 1916, replaced earlier by the newly-completed **Wexford Coast**, and the big steamer **Welsh Coast**, both delivered in 1915.

Read applied for membership of the Irish Railway Clearing House in 1914. This was a shrewd move which promoted an element of collaboration between the steamers and destinations inland by rail. Another innovative move by Read was the introduction of a statistical department at Liverpool to track and monitor the finances of all the component parts of Powell, Bacon & Hough Lines. This in due course founded a comprehensive mechanism to track the profitability of each department so that corrective action, if needed, could be instigated.

The *Kentish Coast* (1908) was bought from Mann, MacNeal & Steves Limited of Liverpool after she had been stranded, refloated and repaired in 1919.

[David Whiteside collection]

Launch of the *Welsh Coast* on 11 March 1915 from the yard of Charles Hill & Sons, Bristol.

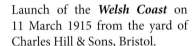

Book-keeping of all component companies was centralised at Liverpool in 1918. In 1914 James W Ratledge was appointed Company Secretary; Ratledge later became an important advisor to Read, especially in the financially troubled years of the 1920s. But next, the company had to cope with the rigours of the Great War.

In mid-May 1915, it was announced that Powell, Bacon & Hough Lines Limited jointly with the Furness group, had purchased a large number of shares in the British & Irish Steam Packet Company Limited.

B & I had operational difficulties, having sold the *Lady Martin* and *Lady Roberts* in July 1914, the *Lady Hudson-Kinahan* in October 1914 and the *Lady Wolseley* the following year, and was no longer able to sustain its weekly Dublin to London passenger and cargo service.

The British & Irish passenger steamer *Lady Wolseley* (1894) at Plymouth. She was one of four major passenger units formerly on the Dublin and London service that were sold during the Great War.

The first casualty of the Great War was the **Suffolk Coast**; she was captured at sea by **U17** on 7 November 1916 and sunk. The **Suffolk Coast** had been on passage from Glasgow to Fécamp with general cargo. Her crew was cast adrift in the ship's boats and later picked up and landed safely. In December 1916, Powell, Bacon & Hough Lines Limited accepted the big three-island cargo steamer **Western Coast** from her builders the Dublin Dockyard Company. W Harkess & Son Limited delivered another machinery aft cargo steamer, with bridge amidships, the following spring. Her triple expansion steam machinery sustained a service speed of 10 knots. She was christened **Suffolk Coast** at her launch on 22 March 1917; recycling names was a ploy to confuse the enemy.

In January 1917 the steamer **Gower Coast** was sold to the Ford Shipping Company Limited (Messrs Mann, MacNeal & Company) of Glasgow. Powell, Bacon & Hough Lines then owned 15 ships and two steam lighters:

Eastern Coast, ex-**Powerful**

Gloucester Coast, ex-**Sir Walter Bacon**

Kentish Coast

Lancashire Coast, ex-**Annie Hough**

Monmouth Coast, ex-**Faithful**

Devon Coast, ex-**Graceful**

Norfolk Coast

Northern Coast

Pembroke Coast, ex-**Sir Roger Bacon**

Somerset Coast, ex-**Graceful**

Southern Coast, ex-**Dorothy Hough**

Suffolk Coast

Welsh Coast

Western Coast

Wexford Coast

and the Bristol Channel lighters **Harfat** and **Pennar**.

In February 1917 Alfred Read persuaded his directors to accept a takeover bid from the Royal Mail group of companies. Read was conscious that Powell, Bacon & Hough Lines might not have the resources to sustain it within the post-war economy. He was also conscious that the political situation in Ireland did little to promote trade across the Irish Sea.

The *Journal of Commerce*, 26 February 1917, reported:
Messrs Elder Dempster & Co., and associated companies have acquired the business of the Coast Line (Powell, Bacon & Hough Lines Ltd.). The Coast Line is one of the oldest and largest shipping companies in the kingdom and maintains regular services for both passengers and cargo on the west and south coasts, particularly between Liverpool and London calling en route at all the chief English Channel ports, where the line has its own branch offices; also maintaining services between Liverpool and South Wales. The fleet consists of some of the finest steamers trading round the British coast. Apparently, no change is to be made in the service.

Under the new ownership the Chairman of the Royal Mail Line, Sir Owen Philipps was appointed Chairman of 'The Coast Steam Packet Company' with effect from 1 March; Alfred Read was retained as Managing Director. Elder Dempster was chosen to liaise with 'The Coast Line' during the take-over proceedings as there was a long-standing relationship between that company and F H Powell & Company, latterly also with Powell, Bacon & Hough Lines. The Elder Dempster African service into Liverpool relied on Powell for transhipment of imports, many of them being tropical hardwoods in long stands, to the south of England and in particular to London. In June 1917 Owen Philipps confirmed at a public meeting in Bristol, that 'We have acquired an interest in Coast Lines Limited, which business is likely to prove a useful auxiliary as providing connections with our own ocean services'.

Pembroke Coast (1912) was originally commissioned for John Bacon Limited as **Sir Roger Bacon**.

Board meetings were then held in London. This suited Alfred Read as he was then domiciled in London.

The relationship between Philipps and Royal Mail began in 1901 when Owen Cosby Philipps started to buy shares in the Royal Mail Steam Packet Company, which was in financial difficulties. Philipps and his financier brother John gained control in 1904 and Philipps became chairman. William J Pirrie of Harland & Wolff offered to build modern tonnage for the company at cost-price, in return for receiving all repair work and subsequent contracts. Thus began a fruitful 20 year relationship during which Royal Mail became the majority shareholder of Harland & Wolff in 1917.

The Royal Mail Steam Packet Company then pursued an expansive programme culminating in 1927 with the purchase of the White Star Line from the American-owned International Mercantile Marine Company:

1907 Acquired David Jenkins & Company to form the Shire Line of Steamers Limited, with the ships repainted in Royal Mail colours. The Brocklebank share was purchased in 1911.
1909 Acquired Elder Dempster and Company which was restructured. The company continued to trade under its own name.
1911 Jointly with the Elder Dempster Line purchased the share capital of the Pacific Steam Navigation Company, and a large interest in the firm of Lamport & Holt.
1912 Acquired Union-Castle Mail Steamship Company.
1913 Acquired the Nelson Line.
1916 Acquired Moss Steamship Company and Robert MacAndrew
1917 Acquired Coast Lines and Argentine Steam Navigation Company
1919 Acquired David MacIver, Sons & Company.

The shipping lines retained their separate identities but Philipps began to treat all the associated companies as an integrated Royal Mail Group which was structured through a network of cross-shareholdings. Thus, Coast Lines, as it became in 1917, very quickly became entangled in a financial web linking it with other parts of the Royal Mail Group.

The British & Irish Steam Packet Company (see Smyth, 1984; McRonald 2005) joined The Coast Line (Powell, Bacon & Hough) almost immediately that company was formed, the takeover being announced in mid-May 1917. All but one of the shares were owned by Coast Lines by July. The key business of the company was a weekly service between Dublin and London calling at South Coast ports. Alfred Read had been on the board of British & Irish from 1915 when Powell Bacon & Hough and Furness Withy jointly proposed a takeover of the company. British & Irish became wholly owned by Coast Lines when Furness Withy & Company wanted to dispose of its interests in the coasting trades and sold its share to Coast Lines Limited two years later.

Lord Pirrie (Harland & Wolff) was appointed to the British & Irish board in 1918. In due course Coast Lines bought Kirkcaldy, Fife & London Steam Shipping Company Limited from Furness in 1918 and the Furness owned London, Welsh Steamship Company Limited in 1924. Unlike the latter two companies B&I was retained as a wholly owned Coast Lines group member but with its own identity, livery, ship names, marketing and staff. The ships were registered at Dublin.

At the time of the takeover the B&I fleet comprised just two ships: the steamers *Lady Cloé* and *Lady Wimborne*, each with accommodation for 70 passengers. In theory they allowed a weekly service from Dublin to London with calls at Cork, Falmouth, Torquay and Southampton. In practice the service was greatly disrupted by wartime demands.

The negotiations for the next acquisition were successfully completed later in 1917 with Rogers & Bright Limited, Liverpool, trading as the Volana Shipping Company Limited. This company was founded in 1886, and served Llanelly, Cardiff and Burry Port loading at both Liverpool and Birkenhead. An attempt was made to run a service between the Mersey and Cork in 1893, but there was insufficient trade on offer and the new route was abandoned. The ships all had the prefix 'Vol...' and were of just 400 to 600 tons gross, a size limited by the approach to Burry Port.

Coast Lines now had access to South Wales ports, and with the goodwill and assets of the company came four ships: *Volpone*, *Volhynia*, *Volturnus* and *Volana*. Due to the war Coast Lines could not rename and integrate the ships with its main fleet and the company essentially maintained its own identity for the next couple of years. Besides, the *Volturnus* had been requisitioned as a stores carrier in 1914 and was not released to Coast Lines until 1919. The *Volhynia* and *Volana* eventually adopted the names *Gower Coast* and *Cornish Coast* in 1920.

The *Volana* (1913) adopted the name *Cornish Coast* after the war and served Coast Lines for a further 15 years.

Navigation, particularly in wartime blackout, could be hazardous. On a voyage from Bristol to Liverpool, the **Somerset Coast** collided with the **Sound Fisher** on 22 April 1917 in a position roughly 1½ miles south west by west of the Bardsey Light. The **Sound Fisher** was on passage from her home port of Barrow to Rouen with pig iron. The **Somerset Coast** foundered, but the crew of fourteen was safely landed at Milford. The **Sound Fisher** had her port anchor and hawse-pipe damaged and the poop and forecastle decks were also damaged, but was able to proceed on her voyage.

In May 1917 the wartime Shipping Controller, Sir Joseph Maclay, appointed Alfred Read as Director of Home Trade Shipping. Until then wartime coastal shipping had not been controlled as had deep sea shipping. The **Norfolk Coast**, **Gloucester Coast** and **Devon Coast** had earlier been requisitioned as auxiliaries, albeit the **Norfolk Coast** only for a period of six weeks.

Powell, Bacon & Hough Limited was officially rebranded as Coast Lines Limited on 7 June 1917. It had already traded under the banner 'The Coast Line' during the Great War. The new company title was used publicly from July onwards; the ships were registered under the new brand name on 12 June and marketing slowly changed to the new name over the next few months, although both old and new names were in use simultaneously for a time.

The 11 month old **Western Coast** was lost on 17 November 1917. The **Western Coast**, Captain Tennent, was torpedoed and sunk by **U40** some 10 miles west south west of the Eddystone Light off Plymouth, with the loss of seventeen men. She had been on passage from Portsmouth to Barry in ballast. On 18 June 1918, the **Norfolk Coast**, Captain H Thomas, was sunk by torpedo fired by **U30**. The **Norfolk Coast** had been on passage from Rouen to the Tyne in ballast and was in a northbound North Sea convoy.

The **Somerset Coast** (1911) in the River Avon wearing an experimental red chevron on her funnel; this ship was sunk following collision off the Bardsey Light on 22 April 1917.

Requisitioned as an auxiliary in the Great War, the **Gloucester Coast** (1913) was built as **Sir Walter Bacon** for John Bacon Limited.

At a point 23 miles east by south of Flamborough Head, at 6.25 pm, the torpedo struck directly under the bridge immediately killing eight men and badly injuring another. Seven survivors were picked up out of the sea by a patrol vessel and later landed at Middlesbrough.

Early in 1918 discussions took place with Furness Withy regarding the purchase of H L Stocks & Company Limited of Kirkcaldy. Furness had bought the company in 1910

changing the trading name from Kirkcaldy & London Steamship Company Limited to Kirkcaldy, Fife & London Steamship Company Limited. Furness also replaced the steamer **Abbotshall**, built in 1890, with **New Abbotshall** in 1912. Purchase was completed in March 1918 and included the steamers **New Abbotshall** and **Kirkcaldy** which had been built in 1902. As with Volana Shipping Company, purchased in 1917, the ships could not be integrated into the Coast Lines fleet until after the war.

The *Norfolk Coast* (1910) in wartime grey; she was sunk by torpedo with heavy loss of life in June 1918.

In July 1918 the Royal Mail board made an offer for the City of Cork Steam Packet Company Limited. Like so many other small independent shipping companies it faced a difficult uphill struggle to retain business during the war and had lost three quarters of its fleet to enemy action. The shareholders readily accepted the offer and the Cork company with its two surviving ships, the passenger steamer **Glengariff** and the cargo-only **Pylades**, became a subsidiary of the British & Irish Steam Packet Company.

The *Glengariff* (1893) was the only passenger ship owned by the City of Cork Steam Packet Company to survive the Great War. The City of Cork company was acquired by Coast Lines in 1918.

The new **Suffolk Coast** was requisitioned in August 1918 and converted into the heavily armed and disguised

'Q' ship HMS **Suffolk Coast**. Her conversion was made under the supervision of Lieutenant Commander Harold Auten. The ship received a 4 inch gun mounted on a lift in No. 1 hatch forward which could be brought rapidly to upper deck level once a U Boat was lulled within range. While many of the 'Q' ships were lost, the **Suffolk Coast** was commissioned too late to be used in action; the Armistice was signed on 11 November 1918.

The company managed five ships for the Shipping Controller at various times during and after the war; none was lost to enemy action. The **Polmina** came under Coast Lines management. She was captured off Rotterdam by HMS **Starfish** on 10 September 1917 as the Dutch coastal steamer **Hermina** – she was found to be carrying a German cargo and was confiscated.

The **Polbain**, formerly the German steamer **Maria Rickmers**, came under Coast Lines' management between 1918 and 1922. The **Clara Zelck** was managed by Coast Lines in 1920 and 1921. She had been mined and sunk in 1918, but was subsequently raised and repaired by the British. The **Stern** was also managed by Coast Lines from 1920 before she was sold to Westcott & Lawrence Line in 1921 and renamed **Gerano**. The fifth and last ship under Coast Lines' management, only for a few months in 1920, was the **Cleopatra**, formerly a member of A Kirsten's Hamburg-based fleet. The **Polbain**, **Clara Zelck**, **Stern** and **Cleopatra** were all substantial ships of between 1,200 and 2,000 tons gross.

The Q ship **Suffolk Coast** was returned to her owners in July 1919. The **Wexford Coast** had also been requisitioned the year before for similar duties but was never converted. A total of four ships had been lost in the war to enemy action: **Western Coast**, **Suffolk Coast**, the new **Western Coast** and **Norfolk Coast**; three other ships were also lost: the **Hampshire Coast** stranded while the **Cornish Coast** and **Somerset Coast** sank following collisions. The **Hampshire Coast** was abandoned to the underwriters, later salvaged and sold back to Powell Bacon & Hough Lines for £24,000 in October 1915, surviving in the Coast Lines fleet until 1936.

The **Cornish Coast** (1904) lying below Woodside Landing Stage after collision with the war prize *Janette Woermann* on 3 March 1915 .

[Booths, New Brighton]

Coast Lines Limited was now left alone to pursue its peaceful civilian business under the expert guidance of its Managing Director Alfred Read. Between 1917 and 1920 Coast Lines absorbed thirteen separate coastal and Irish Sea firms, and another seven during the 1920s. By the onset of the Great Depression the British coastal liner trade was heading towards a monopoly. Those companies within the Coast Lines umbrella were able to survive the Depression due to the buoyant nature of the parent company Coast Lines Limited, whereas coasting companies outside this protection fared less well and some even ceased to trade altogether.

It is notable that as additional companies were bought and put into the Coast Lines group, their steamers were allotted to the most suitable trade and did not necessarily stay on their former owner's routes. Ships often transferred from one company to another, many several times over; management guidance advised that a ship not working profitably for more than three months must be submitted for re-allocation for more gainful employment within the group. This flexibility was a great asset as the company developed and grew.

Michael S Moss, in his biography of Alfred H Read wrote:

He was educated at Liverpool College, and then in Switzerland and Paris, before being apprenticed to the Glasgow-based Anchor Line with services on the north Atlantic and to India. In 1893 at the age of twenty-two he joined the family firm, which then owned four small steamers. He gradually persuaded his partners to acquire more ships and Powell owned nine by the turn of the century. Read began to give all the ships names ending in 'Coast', and like other owners transferred some to single-ship companies to spread his risk.

From the beginning of his career Read was keenly concerned to improve accommodation for crews on his ships, and also to ensure that new recruits were well trained, playing an active role in the management of the Lancashire and National Sea Training Home...

By the turn of the century Alfred Read was a prominent shipowner in Liverpool, and was elected to the Mersey Docks and Harbour Board, on which he served until 1920, and he was chairman of the Liverpool Steam Ship Owners' Association in 1912... Because most coasters were too small to be requisitioned for military service, coastal shipping was not controlled until 1917, when Read was appointed Director of Home Trade Services at the Ministry of Shipping. His contribution to the organisation of coastal services during the unrestricted U-boat campaign and his commitment to training young seafarers were recognised with a knighthood in 1919.

Alfred Henry Read, 1871-1955.

CHAPTER 2

THE MAKING OF AN EMPIRE

In September 1919 the British & Irish Steam Packet Company was empowered to purchase Tedcastle & McCormick Limited, Dublin. The Irish coastal interests of the London Maritime Investment Company (a Royal Mail Steam Packet subsidiary which had earlier bought the five ships of the City of Dublin Steam Packet Company: *Louth*, *Wicklow*, *Carlow*, *Kerry* and *Belfast*) were brought into British & Irish and merged with the activities of Tedcastle and McCormick in October 1919. The City of Dublin Steam Packet Company had already ceased trading between Dublin and Holyhead.

In 1919 two wartime standard coastal ships were bought from the Shipping Controller for the British & Irish Steam Packet Company Limited and given the names *Lady Patricia* and *Lady Emerald*. This pair enabled the twice-weekly London service of the British & Irish company to be resumed with the cargo ships working alongside the passenger ships *Lady Chloé* and *Lady Wimborne*.

So far, Owen Philipps and Alfred Read had caught some of the smaller fish, but their sights were set higher. Four major acquisitions followed in quick succession: M Langlands & Sons; Laird Line; Belfast Steamship Company Limited; and by January 1920 G & J Burns. Having already secured the base at Dublin with the British & Irish Steam Packet Company, Philipps and Read now sought to strengthen their hold on coastal services around mainland Britain with the acquisition of Langlands, secure the position at Belfast and with the Laird and Burns companies ensure a hold on business at Glasgow. In so doing they also took over all the Irish passenger connections that were not in the hands of the railway companies.

Alfred Read's war-time role as Director of Home Trade Shipping had given him a unique perspective of the status of many of the nation's coastal shipping companies. He had full knowledge of the strengths and the weaknesses of many of the more important companies, he was aware of their commercial potential and it was public knowledge what dividends were being paid, if any, to shareholders. There was also civil disquiet in Ireland which was increasingly becoming a disincentive to trade, a factor which brought acquisition costs down in some cases almost to the state of a fire sale. With his new partner Owen Philipps, they were a formidable and persuasive team as they opened a dialogue with each new company they wished to purchase. Philipps clinched the final deals, although at Belfast he ceded this responsibility to his local man, Lord Pirrie; Read was instrumental in setting the deals up.

M Langlands & Sons was a longstanding coastal liner company with passenger and cargo services that encompassed mainland Britain (see Robins & Tucker 2015). It was also renowned for its summer yachting cruises from Liverpool and Ardrossan to the Western Isles of Scotland. However, the war had been extremely costly for Langlands and it had emerged into peace, stunned by its own human and physical losses and now with only half the ships afloat that it had at the start of the war. There was one cargo ship laid down, but not at an advanced stage of construction.

There was no easy way Langlands could resume business at the pre-war scale, nor was there business on offer to warrant this. Resumption of its passenger services was nigh impossible with the loss of four of its five main passenger units including its cherished flagship the *Princess Royal*. It would take time to rebuild the business and for the national economy to recover. It was in this parlous state that Read approached the company making a generous offer to its board to take over its goodwill and assets. The board saw this as a sensible way forward and were given the proviso that the company would retain its own identity under Coast Lines' ownership. M Langlands & Sons was transferred to Coast Lines Limited in October 1919.

A report in the *Aberdeen Journal*, 16 October 1919 stated: Messrs Langlands began business in 1839 with sailings between the Clyde and the Mersey. Later the scope of their concerns was extended to both the east and west coasts of Scotland and in more recent times to all the large English ports. The value of their co-ordination with the Coast Lines will be that there will not be a port of any pretensions in the UK not included in the regular sailings which it is hoped to arrange soon as nearly on pre-war lines as possible. The amalgamation will control about four fifths of the tonnage in the coasting trade.

At first Mr Read allowed the Langlands business to retain its identity and its ships their rightful Princess names and livery. The business was very much as before and included a weekly sailing from Liverpool to Leith, weekly round-Britain and an ad hoc service between Liverpool or Manchester and Greenock and Glasgow. Coast Lines sanctioned the order of three engines-aft cargo steamers. However, in 1920 there was a change of heart and the Langlands fleet was rebranded and the ships given corporate Coast names, for example, the *Princess Thyra* became *Orkney Coast*, *Princess Irma* became *Cheshire Coast*, the *Princess Ena* was renamed *Fife Coast*, and so on. The only surviving major passenger unit in the group, the *Princess Beatrice*, was sold to the Carron Line of Grangemouth to become the *Avon*. The new cargo steamer *Princess Olga* was delivered in April 1920 and renamed *Lancashire Coast*. She took up the old Langlands' service from Bristol along the south coast and up the east coast to Aberdeen.

Langlands' *Princess Thyra* (1909) was renamed *Orkney Coast* in 1920 when the Langlands identity was lost within the main body of Coast Lines.

The only major passenger unit to survive the Great War in the Langlands fleet was *Princess Beatrice* (1893).

This vessel was laid down as *Princess Olga* for M Langlands & Sons but delivered as *Lancashire Coast* (1920) for Coast Lines Limited, as seen here.

Relaxation of wartime restrictions imposed by the Shipping Controller allowed Coast Lines to rationalise its newly acquired fleets in 1919. As a consequence, a number of ships came under direct Coast Lines' ownership, some, albeit registered at strange ports; some of the ships remained in Coast Lines' ownership for only a few months. For example, the **Volpone**, acquired with the purchase of Rogers & Bright in 1917 was registered under Coast Lines' name at Liverpool in 1919 but was sold later the same year.

The **Kirkcaldy**, which had come with H L Stocks & Company, was registered under Coast Lines' ownership also in 1919 only to be sold a few months later. The Langlands ships were all registered under Coast Lines ownership. Most of them were registered at Glasgow, while the **Lady Tennant** retained her Stornoway registration and the little steamer **Silver City** that of Aberdeen, although both were now listed as owned by Coast Lines Limited. Clearly the decision to integrate Langlands into Coast Lines without retaining its identity had already been made. This was not the case with the British & Irish Steam Packet Company which was kept as an independent but wholly owned subsidiary of Coast Lines with ships registered at Dublin. Of this company's acquisitions, the two ships that came with Tedcastle & McCormick were both owned by Coast Lines Limited in 1919 but retained their Dublin registry. However, in 1920 the **Dublin** passed to British & Irish ownership while the **Blackwater** was sold.

Langlands' *Lady Tennant* (1903) was built for the Nobel's Explosives Company Limited and bought by the Stornoway Shipping Company, as seen here, and later acquired by Langlands during the war.

The Laird Line Limited's sphere of operations in the Irish Sea, and the north and west coast of Ireland were complementary to those which Alfred Read already owned, so an approach was made directly by Owen Philipps to Chairman William MacLellan (grandson of Lewis MacLellan, and a founder of what later became the Laird Line). A deal was struck and a price of £933,000 was agreed between the two men for the goodwill, assets and staff of the Laird Line, with a promise that it could keep its identity - for the immediate future. The effective date was 7 October 1919. The price was low for what Coast Lines was getting, but bearing in mind the poor trading conditions in the Irish trades at that time and the equally poor prospects for the foreseeable future, it was probably a fair one. For the time being, nothing changed and the company continued as before, save for a Coast Lines placement into the company board room.

As with all the other companies in this round of takeovers, the Laird Line had a long pedigree (see Robins and McRonald, 2018). It started with steamers on the Clyde extending to Londonderry in the early 1820s. The Glasgow & Londonderry Steam Packet Company was founded in 1835 with its Glasgow agent becoming Alexander Laird in 1867. The Londonderry service soon started to encompass Sligo, Balina, Westport, Coleraine and Portrush. A Dublin to Glasgow service became part of Laird's remit, ultimately trading as A A Laird & Company and in 1885 the various threads came together as the Glasgow, Dublin and Londonderry Steam Packet Company. There were also interests at Morecambe and at Larne. The title Laird Line was adopted in 1907. Among the various acquisitions was the Ayr Steam Shipping Company in 1909. Many of the ships carried upwards of 700 passengers, a popular route being the day service to Portrush.

On 14 November 1919 the board of the Belfast Steamship Company, at an Extraordinary General Meeting, formally elected to accept an offer from Owen Philipps, cleverly made on his behalf by Belfast's own Lord Pirrie of Harland & Wolff, for the goodwill and assets of the company. Robert Sinclair, in his history of the Belfast company recorded:

> The financial details of the offer were that the original £50 shares were to be purchased for £435 each and the £10 (£5 paid) 'A' shares were to be purchased for £43-10 shillings each. A favourable recommendation from the directors was ensured by the offer of £20,000 each for loss of office. This apparently attractive offer was to be financed by a method characteristic of the acquisitions policy of the Royal Mail Group under Sir Owen Philipps, later Lord Kylsant. The deal was to be financed in part by a loan made by the Belfast Steamship Company with its cash surplus of £549, 635.

On the positive side, the Belfast company appeared to be buoyant, having earlier paid its shareholders a dividend of 5% topped by a 2½% bonus. On the downside were the assets, Sinclair again:

> In common with all shipping companies, higher fuel charges and increased wages were threatening increased operating costs. In addition, the *Logic* and *Comic* were both approaching obsolescence and another decade would find the *Graphic* and *Heroic* in the same condition. Then there was the additional uncertainty of the political future of Ireland which was wrapped in obscurity.

Again, the Belfast company had a long history (see Sinclair, 1990). A Liverpool to Belfast steamer service of sorts had been in operation since 1819, with several of the services operated by companies based in the south of Ireland. Irish shipowners had tended to develop separately in the north and the south of Ireland due to social and political differences, but northerners had not yet dominated the Belfast to Liverpool route. In 1852 dissatisfaction led the Belfast Chamber of Commerce to propose a new company to champion the route with the name Belfast Steamship Company. Competitor Langtry & Herdman was taken over in 1859. Thereafter the Belfast company had a monopoly on the route but maintained modern vessels, such as *Magic* of 1893 and the *Graphic* and *Heroic* both completed in 1906. They were fast ships equipped with triple expansion engines that could maintain 18 knots on the overnight passage across the Irish Sea; they were well fitted, being designed principally for the cattle trade as well, of course, for passengers. None of the ships were lost in the Great War.

Belfast Steamship Company's *Magic* (1893) was a fast cross-channel steamer on the Liverpool and Belfast overnight service.

The loss of the *Volturnus* in the Kattegat on 1 November 1919 caused the master, Captain Arthur Hay, to have his certificate suspended and the Chief Officer, Peter Fearn, to be severely censured at the subsequent Inquiry. She carried 'Marconi wireless apparatus' and an operator as well as a standard oil morse lamp for signalling. The ship left Deptford on Monday 27 October bound for Copenhagen, on charter to the Admiralty with a full load of stores. Heavy weather was encountered off the Cross Sands lightship with water entering the chart room damaging, among other papers, various Admiralty notices which became sodden and illegible. These contained detained information about a minefield 5 miles past the Skaw Light at the entrance to the Kattegat and instructions how to safely get around the minefield. The charts had been rolled up and put on a rack where they remained dry. The weather continued heavy until the Skaw light was sighted on Friday 31 October at about 12 midnight.

The lightship signalled the *Volturnus* by morse lamp. The *Volturnus* was reduced to just 6 knots in order to conserve coal. Questions and answers were provided regarding the identity and destination of the vessel and then the *Volturnus* was asked if a pilot was wanted. The master instructed the Marconi operator to reply 'No' and then he went below. A course was laid for Læsø Trindel.

This was the second voyage the *Volturnus* had made to Copenhagen but neither the master nor the Chief Officer had previously been in the Baltic, the earlier voyage being under Captain Walsh. Twenty minutes later, another round of morse signals was received: 'Do you know the minefields?' and 'You cannot steer for Læsø Trindel'. The master was summoned to the bridge and immediately ordered the ship turn about and head for Skaw Point. He sent for the Boatswain who had been on the previous voyage to ask him what course to follow. The reply was to go through Læsø Channel rather than steer the normal course for Læsø Trindel. Ten minutes later the *Volturnus* struck a mine amidships on the starboard side and rapidly started to take on water. The ship had three watertight bulkheads but these were not enough to save her. By 3.45 the crew had successfully launched the port side lifeboat and abandoned the ship shortly before it sank. The report of the Inquiry states:

> In considering the circumstances which principally led to the casualty, viz., the loss of the Admiralty notice to mariners, which the master certainly should have taken greater care of, the presumption being that they were 'knocking about on the chart room table' for two or three days during the bad weather, and which if they had been preserved he might have read before reaching the Kattegat, it is greatly to be regretted that in their absence he did not enquire earlier on the voyage from the boatswain (who was a reliable man and acted as mate of the vessel in the Home Trade service) if they took a pilot off the Skaw on the previous voyage, or where they took one, and incidentally, information about the route down the Kattegat might have been spoken about. Failing that course, which he might not have wished to adopt, he could have tried to get information by using the wireless.

The Inquiry report states that the Captain should have read the Admiralty notices before leaving Deptford and that the loss of the papers at sea was no excuse for not knowing about the minefield. The First Officer, the report stated, should have immediately responded to the second signals received from the lightship and put about to await further instructions, or better wait till dawn, and accept a pilot.

Alfred Read moved the catering and marine engineering sections of both the Belfast and Dublin companies to Liverpool in 1920 and combined them with those required by Coast Lines Limited. This was a typical sound economy-based idea instigated by the Managing Director. More significantly, on 1 January 1920, Read bought a London cartage company founded by Thomas Allen in the 1850s and based at Hermitage Wharf. The company had long served the interests of the British & Irish Steam Packet Company and the City of Cork Steam Packet Company. Within two years Thomas Allen had opened a new depot at Stanford where a large haulage fleet was domiciled under Coast Lines' ownership.

G & J Burns Limited was acquired next. Protracted negotiations had been taking place between Royal Mail, Coast Lines and G & J Burns since summer 1919. On 16 January 1920, the Burns' directors accepted an offer made by Alfred Read of Coast Lines Limited to purchase the entire holdings of G & J Burns Limited and the associated Burns Steamship Company Limited. Burns, like the other companies that had now come under Coast Lines' ownership, was faced with poor prospects in post-war Britain, prospects that were compounded by the poor state of affairs in Ireland that were fast developing into civil war. As with the Laird Line before it, the sale was something of a fire sale and the true value of the company was not realised. For the moment, G & J Burns Limited was left largely to its own devices under the watchful eyes of its new parent.

J & G Burns interests started back in the 1820s, initially in the Glasgow and Liverpool trade (see Robins & McRonald, 2018). Steamships were placed on the route in 1829. Originally trading as J & G Burns the brothers James and George entered the West Highland trade but ceded their interest to David Hutcheson in 1851. Attention was also focused on Belfast and an overnight mail contract for a Glasgow and Belfast service was secured, at no charge to Government, simply for the prestige and to prevent rivals being awarded the mails. The ships were given animal and bird names, while the daylight service to Belfast from Ardrossan had ships named after snakes. In 1908 the company bought the Dublin & Glasgow Sailing and Steam Packet Company. Ships acquired from that company were registered under the ownership of the Burns Steamship Company Limited.

One week after the Burns takeover had been agreed a replacement for the **Setter**, lost in the war, was launched at Dalmuir. She did not stay long in the fleet; Coast Lines' management transferred her to the British & Irish Steam Packet Company with the new name **Lady Kildare**. The **Lurcher** was transferred with her and was given the name **Lady Meath**. The attraction of a large pool of ships and a complex array of business requirements for them was only now becoming apparent. In 1920 British & Irish themselves purchased the Dublin cartage firm A & C Taylor from Messrs Thomas & Angus Nicoll, whose management services were included in the deal.

Sir Alfred Read was a senior director of all the newly acquired companies serving mostly to the Chairmanship of Sir Owen Philipps. He saw to it that they complied with corporate policy while he ministered to their needs. He was indeed a busy man, but the structure of each board was designed on a reporting system to Alfred Read who in turn reported to Owen Philipps. Each company within the group provided a weekly letter to Read stating where each of its ships were, what capacity they were loaded at and it included any issues as they arose. All bookkeeping, of course, was centralised at Liverpool.

The shopping spree included a number of vital short sea services. Had Coast Lines not been financed by Royal Mail to buy them, some would certainly have found it difficult to become viable after the war. Indeed, the City of Dublin company ceased its core activity in 1919, laid up its two surviving fast cross-channel steamers at Holyhead, and was wound up in 1924.

Two new ships joined the Coast Lines fleet during 1919. These were surplus wartime standard ships built to the order of the Shipping Controller. The first was the **War Shannon** launched on 16 May 1919 by Swan Hunter & Wigham Richardson Limited at Sunderland and completed for Coast Lines as **British Coast** in July that year. The second was an identical sister launched from the same yard on 2 August 1919 without name and completed for Coast Lines Limited as **Western Coast** in September. Both ships had triple expansion engines supplied by Richardsons, Westgarth & Company Limited at Middlesbrough which gave them a service speed of 11 knots.

The *Western Coast* (1919) was a wartime standard coaster ordered by the Shipping Controller and bought by Coast Lines in time to be fitted out to their instructions.

[Basil Feilden]

Another new ship was launched for Coast Lines as the **Somerset Coast** at the Harland & Wolff yard (Royal Mail Group) at Govan on 27 December. She was delivered early in 1920. Her engines were supplied by A & J Inglis at Pointhouse and the ship had a service speed of 10 knots. She was initially deployed on the Kirkcaldy to London service, previously maintained by H L Stocks & Company Limited. Their steamer **New Abbotshall** was renamed **Durham Coast** in 1920 and served between Glasgow and Liverpool.

The *Somerset Coast* (1919) took up the London and Kirkcaldy jute and linoleum run when she was first commissioned.

Powell, Bacon & Hough had disposed of several ships during and after the war while others were transferred to other companies in the group. The *Stonehenge* and *Irish Coast* were both sold in 1916. The *Gower Coast*, formerly *Sir George Bacon*, was sold in 1917, but was mined and sunk only a few weeks later. After the war, in 1919 the one-time *Annie Hough*, renamed *Lancashire Coast* under the Powell Bacon & Hough Lines amalgamation, was sold for further trading, eventually passing into Cuban ownership and only being scrapped in 1950.

In March 1920 a further significant acquisition was agreed. This was the Little Western Steamship Company Limited of Penzance (George Bazeley & Sons, managers) which came under Coast Lines' ownership on 28 May. Three steamers came with the company: the *Mercutio* which stayed in the Coast Lines' fleet without change of name for the next five years; the *Cadoc*, which as *Norfolk Coast* served Coast Lines for a further twelve years, and the passenger and cargo steamer *Cloch* which was promptly resold to the Carron Company and renamed *Grange*. The *Mercutio* was the oldest of the three ships dating from 1879; she was equipped with an obsolescent compound steam engine as was the *Cloch*. The *Norfolk Coast* had triple expansion engines and is believed to have lasted in service under the Italian flag until the mid-1950s when she was some 60 years old.

George Bazeley & Sons' *Mercutio* (1879) came into Coast Lines' ownership when Bazeley's Little Western Steamship Company was acquired by Coast Lines in 1920.

The Little Western Steamship Company served between Bristol and London with calls at Penzance, Plymouth and Torquay and as inducement also at Newport and Dartmouth. There was an important seasonal holiday trade with Londoners coming down to the 'Riviera'. The company always bought second hand ships but looked after them, so that they served the company well. Quite a few ships, the *Cloch* included, came from the Clyde Shipping Company of Glasgow.

In 1920 the big passenger steamer *Eastern Coast* was sold. She had been built for F H Powell & Company in 1903 as *Powerful* for the Liverpool to London passenger and cargo service. The decision was made to sell her and retain the slightly more modern **Southern Coast**, built as **Dorothy Hough** in 1911, to maintain a passenger departure from both Liverpool and London and a cargo only service on alternate sailings. The cargo steamer **Monmouth Coast**, formerly Powell's **Faithful**, was also sold in 1920.

In 1920 the **Northern Coast** was transferred to the British & Irish Steam Packet Company to become their **Lady Martin**. The small steamer **Lady Tennant** also went to B&I but she returned three years later to Coast Lines registry as **Elgin Coast**. Transfers involved a cost to the receiving company at a price that suited both, the one keen to get rid of an asset that was underutilised, the other keen to get new tonnage with which to make revenue. That same year the **Welsh Coast** and the **Wexford Coast** were 'transferred' to the City of Cork company to adopt the names **Macroom** and **Blarney** respectively. This was only the beginning of a complex array of transfers throughout the group that took place repeatedly over the next 50 years. A typical example was the deployment of the Laird Line passenger and cargo steamer **Maple** to the Fishguard to Cork Service of the City of Cork Steam Packet Company between December 1920 and May 1921 after which she was replaced by the Belfast Steamship Company's steamer **Classic**.

British & Irish steamer **Lady Martin** (1913) was built for Powell, Bacon & Hough Lines as **Northern Coast** before transferring her allegiance to Dublin in 1920.

[Andrew Duncan]

The **Welsh Coast** (1915), seen off Avonmouth, transferred to British & Irish Steam Packet Company in 1920 with the new name **Macroom** – she returned to Coast Lines as **Welsh Coast** two years later.

By the end of 1920, little under three years since Owen Philipps acquired Coast Lines, the overall fleet stood at 74 ships, totalling some 81,537 aggregate tons gross. Of this the core fleet registered under Coast Lines Limited at Liverpool comprised 24 vessels with an aggregate tonnage of 23,469 tons gross.

Coast Lines Limited:

Mercutio (1879) 872 tons gross – from Little Western Steamship Company

Clyde Coast (1888) 868 tons gross – from M Langlands & Sons

Fife Coast (1892) 665 tons gross – from M Langlands & Sons

Norfolk Coast (1894) 981 tons gross – from Little Western Steamship Company

Dublin (1904) 711 tons gross – from Tedcastle & McCormick Limited

Moray Coast (1905) 677 tons gross – from M Langlands & Sons

Kentish Coast (1908) 758 tons gross

Pennar (1907) 130 tons gross

Orkney Coast (1909) 781 tons gross – from M Langlands & Sons

Durham Coast (1911) 783 tons gross – from H L Stocks & Company Limited

Gower Coast (1911) 617 tons gross – from Volana Shipping Company Limited

Harfat (1911) 128 tons gross

Highland Coast (1912) 1,094 tons gross – from M Langlands & Sons

Southern Coast (1911) 1,872 tons gross

Pembroke Coast (1912) 809 tons gross

Cornish Coast (1913) 616 tons gross – from Volana Shipping Company Limited

Devon Coast (1913) 672 tons gross

Gloucester Coast (1913) 919 tons gross

Cheshire Coast (1915) 1,122 tons gross – from M Langlands & Sons

Suffolk Coast (1917) 870 tons gross

British Coast (1919) 1,928 tons gross

Somerset Coast (1919) 1,353 tons gross

Western Coast (1919) 1,928 tons gross

Lancashire Coast (1920) 1,104 tons gross

Northern Coast building 1,211 tons gross

The Milford steam tender *Pennar* (1907).

[Malcolm McRonald collection]

The *Volhynia* (1911), formerly of the Volana Shipping Company Limited (Rogers & Bright), was renamed *Gower Coast* in 1920.

British & Irish Steam Packet Company:

Blackrock (1892) 866 tons gross – from Tedcastle, McCormick & Company Limited

Eblana (1892) 824 tons gross – from Tedcastle, McCormick & Company Limited

Belfast (1884) 425 tons gross – from City of Dublin Steam Packet Company

Lady Wicklow (1895) 1,248 tons gross – from City of Dublin Steam Packet Company

Lady Carlow (1896) 1,274 tons gross – from City of Dublin Steam Packet Company

Lady Kerry (1897) 1,277 tons gross – from City of Dublin Steam Packet Company

Lady Tennant (1903) 452 tons gross

Dublin (1904) 727 tons gross – from Tedcastle, McCormick & Company Limited

Lady Meath (1906) 862 tons gross – from Tedcastle, McCormick & Company Limited

Lady Wimborne (1913) 1,532 tons gross

Lady Chloé (1916) 1,581 tons gross

Lady Killiney (1917) 1,145 tons gross – from Tedcastle, McCormick & Company Limited

Lady Martin (1917) 1,189 tons gross

Lady Emerald (1919) 1,389 tons gross

Lady Patricia (1919) 1,391 tons gross

Lady Kildare (1920) 1,217 tons gross

City of Cork Steam Packet Company:

Glengariff (1893) 1,286 tons gross

Bandon (1894) 1,229 tons gross

Cumbria (1896) 627 tons gross

Claddagh (1907) 640 tons gross

Macroom (1915) 1,070 tons gross

Blarney (1915) 423 tons gross

Ardmore building 1,679 tons gross

Kenmare building 1,675 tons gross

G & J Burns:

Grouse (1891) 386

Hound (1893) 1,061 tons gross

Spaniel (1895) 1,116 tons gross

Pointer (1896) 1,130 tons gross

Magpie (1898) 1,227 tons gross

Vulture (1898) 1,168 tons gross

Puma (1899) 1,226 tons gross – formerly Burns Steamship Company Limited

Partridge (1906) 1,523 tons gross

Tiger (1906) 1,389 tons gross – formerly Burns Steamship Company Limited

Woodcock (1906) 1,523 tons gross

Sable (1911) 687 tons gross

Coney (1918) 697 tons gross

Moorfowl (1919) 1,464 tons gross

Redbreast building 772 tons gross – ordered as *Princess Caroline* for M Langlands & Sons

Laird Line:

Dunure (1878) 719 tons gross – registered under Ayr Steam Shipping Company until 1921

Brier (1882) 710 tons gross

Thistle (1884) 803 tons gross

Turnberry (1889) 565 tons gross

Olive (1893) 1,141 tons gross

Lily (1896) 668 tons gross

Rose (1902) 1,151 tons gross

Broom (1904) 626 tons gross

Rowan (1909) 1,013 tons gross

Maple (1914) 1,304 tons gross

Belfast Steamship Company:

Classic (1893) 1,575 tons gross – formerly *Magic*

Comic (1896) 935 tons gross

Logic (1898) 959 tons gross

Heroic (1906) 2,016 tons gross

Graphic (1906) 2,017 tons gross

Patriotic (1912) 2,254 tons gross

An empire had been formed, but the shopping spree was not over yet.

The *Cheshire Coast* (1915) in the River Avon. She was the *Princes Irma*, formerly belonging to M Langlands & Sons and was renamed in 1920; the embossed rings on the funnel reveal where Langlands two white bands once were.

[Richard Parsons collection]

CHAPTER 3

DIFFICULT TIMES 1921-1925

During the 1920s inter-port competition became a valuable morale booster within the group. A key part of this was the Sir Alfred Read Challenge Cup which each year was awarded to the winner of the football challenge. One of the earliest matches was between Dublin and Liverpool at Shelbourne Park in Dublin. These matches were a useful means of bringing shore staff and seagoing staff together both at their home port and at other ports.

The year 1921 was one of consolidation. The **Ayrshire Coast** building at A & J Inglis yard at Pointhouse was launched on 29 November 1920 with the new name **Northern Coast** but she was then completed early in 1921 as the **Lady Valentia** for the British & Irish Steam Packet Company. No further new acquisitions or sales took place in the Coast Lines fleet for the remainder of the year.

Nevertheless, four large single deck cargo ships, with engines and accommodation aft, were ordered from Harland & Wolff in 1920 and destined for other members of the Coast Lines Group. Two were laid down at Harland & Wolff's yard at Govan and two at the wholly owned subsidiary yard of A & J Inglis at Pointhouse. They were designed for what had become known as the Burns-Langlands service between Glasgow and Liverpool. The first ship was ready to launch on 14 October 1920, originally as Langlands' **Princess Caroline**, but with a change of heart was christened **Redbreast** and registered

under G & J Burns ownership. The second Harland & Wolff ship, intended to be Langlands' **Princess Dagmar** was launched on 29 December 1921 as **Gorilla**, again for Burns. They each had one long single hold and one long hatch and as single deck ships were more valuable in the bulk cargo trade than the general cargo trade. These two ships entered service early in 1922. Three years later both ships transferred to Coast Lines' ownership.

So poor had trading conditions become on the Irish Sea that work on the second pair of cargo ships building at the Inglis yard was suspended in 1921. Construction only resumed ten months later much to the relief of A & J Inglis Limited. In the meantime, the plans for the ships had been redrawn so that they were completed as shelter deck ships with 'tween decks along the length of the hold. The first shelter deck ship was launched at Pointhouse on 22 August 1922 as **Ayrshire Coast**, although at one time she had been destined for Dublin as **Lady Olive**. The second, intended to be named **Scottish Coast**, was launched on 20 September 1922 as **Lurcher** for what had now become Burns & Laird Lines Limited. The shelter deck arrangement was a great advantage over the single deck configuration of the **Redbreast** and **Gorilla** and these ships were taken in hand in 1925 at the Ardrossan Dockyard Company and converted to shelter deck ships with two hatches, one forward of the mainmast and one aft. Previously the mainmast was immediately before the bridge front.

The *Ayrshire Coast* (1922) was one of four big single deck cargo steamers ordered in 1920. Plans were changed and she and her sister *Lurcher* were completed with shelter decks.

Also, at this time an increasing shareholding was taken up in the Ardrossan Harbour Company Limited until Coast Lines Limited later gained a controlling interest. This was a useful asset as the port was used both by the Burns and Laird companies and by Coast Lines; ownership enabled potential competitors to be vetted before they were allowed access to the port. It was also an investment that repaid itself many times over because Ardrossan was then the main bunkering port for ships leaving the Clyde. Coal was brought in from the Ayrshire Coalfield by train and discharged over the quay by chutes. The harbour dues from all the visitors amounted to a considerable sum over a twelve month period.

Payment for acquisitions and new ships was arranged through a bank loan established with the Liverpool Bank. This was almost a soft loan, arranged on very favourable terms through one of the Bank's directors, a Mr Owen Philipps. Philipps' ability to expand without digging into his own pocket was remarkable.

The 'Rowan Tragedy' hit the nation on 9 October 1921, the Glasgow Herald 10 October 1921, reported:

> By a double collision in the Irish Channel early yesterday morning during fog a number of lives, estimated at 21, were lost. The Glasgow steamer Rowan on a voyage to Dublin, was struck first by the American steamer West Camack, and then by the Glasgow steamer Clan Malcolm. She was seriously damaged by the first blow, but would, it is thought, have continued afloat until all those aboard had been saved. Ten minutes later, however, she was struck right amidships and practically cut in two, sinking within three minutes. Of those on board 77 were rescued, but two died afterwards. The exact number of lives lost has not yet been ascertained but there are unaccounted for 13 members of the crew including the captain, and also probably eight passengers.

Burns' Rowan left Glasgow on her usual evening departure with passengers and cargo for Dublin and left Greenock about 7pm. Five hours into the voyage the Rowan ran into banks of floating fog off Corsewall Point and the master, Captain Burns, duly reduced her speed to between just 10 and 12 knots. Apparently, she was not sounding her whistle as recommended in fog, nor were any other ships to be heard in the vicinity. Without warning at ten past midnight, the Rowan was struck on the stern by the American cargo steamer West Camack, inward bound from the United States with general cargo. Captain Burns immediately gave orders for lifebelts to be issued and for the boats to be prepared for lowering. Before this could be done, at twenty past midnight, the ship was struck again, this time by the Glasgow steamer Clan Malcolm, outward bound for East Africa. The Clan liner rammed the hapless ship a little forward of amidships on the starboard side. The Rowan was practically cut in two, and sank within less than three minutes giving those still below little chance of being saved. The incident

received international coverage in the media as the ship was carrying an American jazz band that were on tour in Europe.

In February 1921 a new Irish company was established to manage the former twin screw Great Eastern Railway steamer Brussels, which had been bought at auction the previous year for £69,000. The company was the Dublin & Lancashire Shipping Company and its objective was to run its new acquisition between Dublin and Preston in the cattle trade. The inaugural sailing from Dublin took place on 13 September.

The service was successful despite it competing head to head with the British & Irish Steam Packet Company's established cattle service from Dublin to Birkenhead and a declining trend in the numbers of Irish cattle being sent to Britain.

Predictably the larger company successfully bid for the newcomer and the Brussels was retained on Liverpool and Preston cattle runs adopting the British & Irish corporate name Lady Brussels in 1923. Just before the Dublin & Lancashire company was taken over by the British & Irish company in 1922, the Dublin & Lancashire had signed a contract for the purchase of the former South Western Railway Channel Island passenger and cargo steamer Lydia. The plan was that she would join the Brussels on the Preston cattle service. The Lydia was a fast twin screw passenger steamer designed for the Southampton to Channel Isles service; she achieved over 19½ knots on her trials in 1890. The Lydia had had a chequered career up to that point, having being used at one time as an accommodation vessel during major construction work at Southampton and later on Mediterranean ferry duties. But she was now about to become the property of the British & Irish Steam Packet Company.

The Lydia was towed from the Mediterranean to Ardrossan according to the contract of sale, handed over to Coast Lines Limited in September 1922 and laid up at Ardrossan pending resale. In the meantime, she was registered as owned by Coast Lines Limited at Southampton, although technically owned by British & Irish. Eventually the idle vessel was bought for service under the Greek flag in May 1923, accruing a total loss to British & Irish of some £8,000.

A second-hand purchase was made in January 1922 with the big cargo steamer Carmarthen Coast. She had been built at Ardrossan and delivered in 1921 to Norwegian owners. She was deployed by Coast Lines on the London to Kirkcaldy route on which a major portion of the northbound cargo was jute transhipped in London docks and southbound she carried finished linoleum. The Carmarthen Coast had accommodation for ten passengers and this was used mainly by company personnel and others related to the trade.

South Western Railway's fast Channel Islands steamer *Lydia* (1890) came into Coast Lines' ownership in 1922 only to be laid up at Ardrossan until she was sold eight months later.

[Nautical Photo Agency]

In 1922 there was also an element of ship swapping with the fellow Royal Mail group Moss Steamship Company of Liverpool. In essence the **Western Coast** and **British Coast** acquired from the Shipping Controller in 1920 were exchanged, along with some cash, for the almost identical Moss steamer **Limoges**, which confusingly took on the name **Western Coast**.

The new **Western Coast** did have two significant differences to the original pair. One was that she had been built by Caledon Shipbuilding & Engineering Company Limited, Dundee, and secondly, she was equipped to carry twelve passengers and was an ideal partner to work with the **Southern Coast** on the London and Liverpool service.

The original **Western Coast** and **British Coast** were the product of Swan Hunter & Wigham Richardson Limited at Sunderland and were not equipped to carry passengers.

Coast Lines had a clear preference for the Caledon-built ships having also purchased the **War Spey** and **War Garry**, in April and May 1919, both products of Caledon, now the British & Irish **Lady Patricia** and **Lady Emerald**. All the Caledon ships were capable of 11 knots.

Another **Western Coast** (1919), sister to the earlier one, but exchanged for that ship with the Moss Steamship Company in 1922. This ship had accommodation for 12 passengers and worked alongside **Southern Coast** on the Liverpool and London service .

[B & A Feilden]

The large cargo deadweight capacity shelter deck ship *Eastern Coast* (1922) served Coast Lines for 32 years - clearly a suitable design for many of the trades on offer.

The *Lady Valentia* was returned to Coast Lines registry in 1922 and again given the name *Northern Coast*. The new *Eastern Coast* was launched from the yard of A & J Inglis on 10 March 1922; it had been planned to name her *Scottish Coast*, but in the event this did not happen. Both ships were substantial shelter deck vessels with useful deadweight capacity. The small steamer *Mayflower* was bought during the year to maintain the Glasgow to Preston service with calls as required usually at Stranraer. She was allocated the name *Irish Coast*.

A new cargo tender for Falmouth was bought second hand in August 1922. This was the small motor ship *Truro Trader* which had been built in 1912 as *Inniscroone*, one of John Paton's innovative fleet of small pioneer motor ships in his Coaster Motor Shipping Company Limited of Glasgow. She was a useful addition and served at Falmouth for the next sixteen years.

The much-heralded merger of the Laird Line and G & J Burns took place on 25 August 1922 to form Burns & Laird Lines Limited. The ships were registered under their newly branded owner over the next several weeks. The joint company was a logical and sensible move that allowed consolidation of the two companies and disposal of some of the older vessels. The ships adopted the Laird Line funnel colour of white with a black top and a broad red band but flew the Burns company's houseflag of a yellow lion on a blue ground (the Cunard houseflag was the same but on a red ground).

Campbell and Fenton describe the main passenger services:

> The company's major service, the nightly Glasgow-Belfast sailings, was maintained by the *Woodcock*

and *Partridge* which, if not chronologically old, were certainly dated. The Glasgow-Londonderry service was mainly in the hands of the even older *Olive* of 1893 and *Rose* of 1902, whilst Glasgow-Dublin was still worked by the *Tiger*, built in 1906 for Burns' predecessor on the route, the Dublin and Glasgow Sailing and Steam Packet Company Limited.

Other main passenger services in the Coast Lines group in late 1922 were the Belfast Steamship company steamers *Graphic*, *Heroic* and *Patriotic* running overnight between Belfast and Liverpool. The Belfast steamer *Classic* was still operating the Cork to Fishguard overnight service until in 1924 she was transferred to the City of Cork company and renamed *Killarney*. The Cork and Liverpool service was operated by *Kenmare*. The Dublin to Liverpool overnight service was yet to be reinstated but a tidal service was maintained by *Lady Wicklow*, *Lady Carlow*, *Lady Kerry* and *Lady Killiney*; new ships were on order. The *Lady Wicklow* and *Lady Chloé* served on the London route.

Trading conditions were poor due largely to the political uncertainty in Ireland; with the Civil War over in summer 1921, the early months of the Irish Free State, with a Provisional Government formed on 14 January 1922, were at best a difficult time of turmoil. The British military commenced their withdrawal and the Free State Army developed from the Volunteers of the IRA. But the situation was set to worsen with the Irregulars taking charge in some areas during July 1922. A number of ships under the Coast Lines' umbrella brushed with the Irregulars, but none so intimately as the British & Irish Steam Packet Company's *Lady Wicklow* and the Burns steamer *Gorilla*.

On the evening of 31 July, 450 Dublin Guard boarded the requisitioned *Lady Wicklow*, of the British & Irish fleet, at South Wall ready to sail to Kerry. On 2 August *Lady Wicklow* approached the village of Fenit at about 10 am. There was a pier that extended 600 yards from the shore where the 'troop ship' berthed; the troops remained below deck until the ship was alongside the dock, then they rushed up topside and ran along the pier to the shore. Fire was exchanged on both sides but the rebel unit was soon overwhelmed.

On Monday 7 August, *Lady Wicklow* in company with the railway steamer *Arvonia*, formerly the crack Holyhead steamer *Cambria*, embarked 800 men and their equipment for landings at Cork. The *Lady Wicklow* now had sand bags around the gun positions on the bridge while the crew of the *Arvonia*, mainly Welshmen, were extremely nervous about getting involved in someone else's civil war. The transports left Dublin and reached Roche's Point at 10.00pm on 7 August. A pilot from Cork harbour was brought aboard the *Arvonia*, unaware of her mission. A side arm was used to help persuade him to cooperate when he seemed reluctant to provide the necessary aid in navigating the harbour. Initially it had been hoped that the ships could dock at Ford's Wharf, near the city, but the pilot stated that a 'blockship' had been sunk to bar the way. The only other deep water berth that was available was at Passage West. Steering their vessels around another 'blockship', the *Owenacurra*, the Free State flotilla reached Passage West early Tuesday morning, 8 August.

The *Glasgow Herald*, 12 August 1922 reported the brief statement:

> A Lloyd's message states that the following report has been received from the Senior Naval Officer at Queenstown:- The British steamer *Gorilla*, of Glasgow, having completed its discharge at Cork was removed at the instance of the Irregulars and sunk in the river fairway, Lough Mahon. An inspection is now being made of the fairway, which is apparently not blocked. The steamer *Wicklow Head* has apparently just navigated the river from Cork and Queenstown is now normal.

The *Gorilla* was a modern shelter deck cargo ship in the fleet of G & J Burns Limited. It appears she had been sunk to prevent further access of Government vessels. The deck of the ship was awash at high tide, while the bow lay in deeper water. The builders of the *Gorilla*, Harland & Wolff, were entrusted with salvage and recovery; the *Gorilla* was back in service the following year. Meanwhile, ongoing industrial problems at several Irish ports, notably Dublin, hindered the trade of the Coast Lines group.

The *Clyde Coast*, formerly Langlands' *Princess Louise*, was transferred in 1923 to Burns & Laird and renamed *Setter*. She was deployed mainly on the Glasgow to Manchester cargo service. The *Ayrshire Coast* went to Burns for the Burns-Langlands Glasgow and Liverpool service and was given the name *Spaniel*.

An almost fatal blow to the Coast Lines group was delivered late in 1922. A board room clash had occurred between Sir Alfred Read and Sir Owen Philipps.

Read complained about decisions being taken by Philipps without his consulting the Coast Lines' board. He cited the building of ten new ships at a value of £1.2 million that had been ordered from Philipps' shipyards in the previous two years stating that not all the orders were necessary and this activity could place the viability of the group in jeopardy. The ships had all been paid for by long-dated or deferred bills, but payment would come due eventually. Fortunately, Lord Pirrie sided with Read, clearly fearful that a downfall of Coast Lines would take the Belfast Steamship Company with it, a prospect Pirrie could not stomach. Philipps sailed for South America the next day but his retribution was already in hand.

Owen Cosby Philipps (1863-1937) was knighted in 1918 for services to the nation and adopted the title Lord Kylsant.

Robert Sinclair reported:

> A letter to the Coast Lines' board arrived from the Bank of Liverpool and Martins Bank, as it was then styled, requesting that the large loan be cleared forthwith. Sir Owen was a director of this bank.

Worse was to follow. Coast Lines was indebted to the deep sea companies in the Royal Mail Group for inter-company subventions were a feature of Royal Mail Group internal finances. Demands for repayment of these loans flooded in following the letter from the bank. 'It looked like ruin'. And so it might have been had it not been for the financial wizardry of J W Ratledge and the sacrificial determination of Sir Alfred Read.

Salvation was possible because much of the Coast Lines capital of £5 million was unissued and these unissued shares were issued at once to the deep sea companies corresponding to the debt owed them. Sir Owen's absence allowed an artfully drafted letter to be sent to each of them accompanying the new shares and suggesting that this was how Sir Owen wished the matter settled. The stratagem worked.

The bank was not so easily quieted. Sir Alfred sold much of his personal estate to raise cash, including his bloodstock farm in Wiltshire and his London home. But it was not enough. James Ratledge then suggested to the bank that Sir Owen had not said that Coast Lines could not open a new account to settle the old one. Loans could be made on the strength of Coast Lines buoyant freight incomes plus lodging further shares with the bank. In this way Coast Lines Limited was able to create £2 million worth of 5% debenture stock with power to create a further £0.5 million secured by a trust deed. The group was saved. Philipps' callous and spiteful actions had allowed Coast Lines an element of financial independence which would become invaluable in due course when Philipps' colours were eventually disclosed.

The London Welsh Steamship Company was acquired from Furness Withy in May 1923 along with the goodwill of its service between London, Cardiff, Port Talbot, Swansea and Llanelly. The two steamers that served the route, the **Channel Trader** and **Llanelly Trader**, were renamed **Glamorgan Coast** and **Yorkshire Coast** respectively. All the accommodation was amidships and there was a twin stateroom for two passengers aboard the **Llanelly Trader**. She had a small shelter deck in the forward hold but the No 2 hatch was at 'tween deck level but open to the elements, being protected by full height bulwarks. This was a useful area for stowage of chemicals and volatile liquids.

In November 1923 the Grahamstown Shipping Company, operated by T L Duff & Company of Glasgow, was bought and its assets and goodwill thereafter were promoted by Coast Lines Limited. The company operated a cargo service from Glasgow to Campbeltown, Stranraer and Preston with the small steamer **Kelvindale**, originally built for G & J Burns as the **Grouse** and sold at auction to the Grahamstown company after the formation of Burns & Laird Lines in 1922.

She was vested with the Burns & Laird Line for future use, but in 1924 transferred to Coast Lines as **Denbigh Coast** for the Leith and Moray Firth service alongside the **Elgin Coast**, one time **Lady Tennant**. The Glasgow and Preston service was continued using the small steamer **Irish Coast**.

Second hand tonnage was acquired in 1924 when Coast Lines bought the **Reedham**, building at Bristol for Walford Lines Limited of London, and completed her as the **Dorset Coast**. She was a small steamer but suitable for some of the Coast Lines' east coast routes and Bristol Channel to South Coast services.

On 24 June 1924 the **Durham Coast**, originally **New Abbotshall**, was in collision with the oil tanker **Sunoil** in the Mersey. The **Sunoil**, a large tanker for the period of 7,157 tons gross, and completed in 1916, rammed the **Durham Coast** just forward of the collision bulkhead. The **Durham Coast** was promptly beached at Wallasey, her forepeak flooded through a large open gash the full height of the ship's hull.

Damage to the tanker was not critical. The **Durham Coast** was patched up and ready to be refloated on the tide on 10 July. She was taken to drydock for permanent repairs and was back in service a few weeks later.

The **Yorkshire Coast** (1913), formerly **Llanelly Trader**, was one of two ships acquired with the purchase of the London Welsh Steamship Company Limited.

The *Durham Coast* (1911) beached at Wallasey following collision with the tanker *Sunoil* in the River Mersey on 24 June 1924.

Lord Pirrie died at the age of 77 on 7 June 1924. He was aboard the Royal Mail Steam Packet Company's liner *Ebro* while returning to New York following a three month trip to South America on Royal Mail Group business. His body was returned to Belfast aboard the liner *Olympic*.

At his funeral he was heralded as a great captain of industry, and one who would be greatly missed. For the interim, Lady Pirrie was appointed Honorary President of Harland & Wolff.

But the story of Lord Pirrie does not end there, and with it comes the first indication of financial irregularity that would later bring the Royal Mail group to its knees, placing the Coast Lines group in jeopardy.

Ian Ramsay wrote (personal communication):

> When Lord Pirrie died in 1924, Lady Pirrie tried unsuccessfully to take over as Chairman of Harland & Wolff. Owen Philipps thwarted this as he had got access to Pirrie's papers and found that Harland & Wolff were in fact bankrupt, as was Pirrie having outstanding personal loans and doubtful assets totalling almost £1 million. This was a severe shock to Philipps as the various shipping companies within the Royal Mail grouping collectively owned 59% of the voting shares and these shares were shown on their balance sheets to be positive assets whereas they were almost worthless. If this situation had become public knowledge it would have seen the collapse of Harland & Wolff and a number of the constituent shipping companies.

The shipping companies in the Royal Mail family could order their ships from Harland & Wolff on an audited cost of labour and materials basis, plus a percentage to cover overheads and profit. However, when Philipps investigated the finished costs he found that the shipbuilder had lost money on most ships built for the group companies. The saving grace in the relationship was that Harland & Wolff built a very fine ship.

In the event, Philipps was able to keep the problem under wraps while he helped to recapitalise the shipyard at Belfast as well as those that had been acquired on the Clyde. Nevertheless, the financial crisis put a huge strain on the funds that were normally available for development within the Royal Mail Group. The knock-on effect for Coast Lines was lessened by its being ostracised by Sir Owen Philipps following the board meeting in November 1922.

Any new investment made by Read from now on was to use cash generated within rather than cash received from without. Internal cash included loans generated on the strength of the group's own collateral. Inevitably it led to further rationalisation within the Coast Lines' empire and an embargo on building any new ships throughout the group. Fortunately, the British & Irish Steam Packet Company had already taken delivery of its new passenger steamers, *Lady Limerick* and *Lady Louth*, for the Liverpool to Dublin overnight service along with *Ardmore* transferred from the Cork to Liverpool service as *Lady Longford*.

In hindsight the new policy of self-financing and, in due course, loans independent from Royal Mail, were undoubtedly the saviour of Coast Lines and its subsidiaries. They enabled the Coast Lines group to achieve financial independence following the downfall of the Royal Mail Group in 1931 (see Chapter 5).

As 1925 dawned the Coast Lines group of companies faced improved trading conditions on the Irish Sea and a more buoyant economy in Britain. The cargo steamer *Clyde Coast* went to the City of Cork company later to be renamed *Macroom* and the elderly steamer *Mercutio* was sold to T W Ward at Preston for demolition. The Burns-Langlands cargo service between Liverpool and Glasgow was rebranded under the Coast Lines banner in the spring of 1925. As a consequence, the Burns &

Laird ships operating this service were renamed shortly afterwards: the *Redbreast* became *Sutherland Coast*, the *Gorilla* was renamed *Cumberland Coast*, *Lurcher* was renamed *Scottish Coast*, and *Spaniel* once again became *Ayrshire Coast*. It was otherwise a year characterised by consolidation and improved financial returns throughout the group.

On 21 April 1925 the White Star liner *Celtic* rammed the *Hampshire Coast* in the confines of the Mersey; the liner only suffered superficial damage. The *Hampshire Coast* was more badly damaged but managed to dock without assistance. The *Celtic* had been manoeuvring ready to disembark her passengers. This was the same *Hampshire Coast* that had once been written off to the underwriters ashore at Shoreham (see Chapter 1).

The Burns steamer *Redbreast* (1920) was renamed *Sutherland Coast* shortly after the Liverpool and Glasgow route was rebranded as a Coast Lines service in 1925.

The *Lurcher* (1922) was renamed *Scottish Coast* when the four ship Burns-Langlands Liverpool and Glasgow service came directly under Coast Lines management.

[B & A Feilden]

CHAPTER 4

RUNNING A TIGHT SHIP

The core services operated under the Coast Lines name essentially carried on as before. The twice weekly Liverpool and Glasgow cargo service had now joined the fold, having been taken back from Burns & Laird Lines in 1925. Liverpool to Wexford enjoyed a weekly departure from each port, while the triangular service from Manchester to Belfast and Glasgow was also weekly. A service was maintained from Liverpool north about to Inverness and on to London as well as from London to Kirkcaldy, Leith and to Moray Firth ports. Along the south coast were cargo services from Bristol and Cardiff to Penzance and ports to the east, while the direct Liverpool and London passenger service was maintained by *Southern Coast* with a twice weekly departure each way, the cargo service to London called at various ports including Dublin with calls along the south coast including Falmouth, Plymouth, Southampton, and Portsmouth. She partnered the Great War standard ship *Western Coast* which offered twelve passenger berths in twin

berth cabins on the service. The 80 berths offered by the *Southern Coast* were in demand during the summer months but in little demand for the remainder of the year.

Most of the cargo ships were attached to a specific route; for example, the *Hampshire Coast* was for many years on the Liverpool and Glasgow roster along with *Scottish Coast* and *Sutherland Coast*, the little *Irish Coast* remained faithful to the Glasgow and Preston trade, the *Elgin Coast* and *Denbigh Coast* to the Moray ports service and the *Highland Coast* running between the Bristol Channel and Aberdeen via north east ports, Leith and Dundee. Many of the masters had pilotage exemption certificates for one or more of the regular ports. However, as shippers' demands changed so ships moved from one service to another, the *Denbigh Coast*, for example, served between Liverpool and Cork for much of 1928.

The *Highland Coast* (1912), built as Langlands' *Princess Melita*, served on the Bristol to Aberdeen anticlockwise route.

[B & A Feilden]

Neither did any new ships join nor old ships leave the core Coast Lines fleet during 1926 and 1927. Money was at a premium and a number of cost-cutting exercises were implemented. All consumables, including crockery and linen, were bulk purchased for the entire group from Liverpool. Advertising was focussed on London where the young Dr Earnest Reader, the publicity manager, was in charge of marketing and public relations. For example, when the Dublin to Liverpool service was upgraded in

1924, he did the rounds of English convent schools to which Irish children were sent and to hospitals with numerous Irish nursing staff in order to promote the route.

Elder Dempster, on behalf of the Royal Mail Group, had purchased a major shareholding in the Ardrossan Drydock & Shipbuilding Company Limited in 1919. The Ardrossan company was then building a new second shipyard at Ardrossan, the New Yard. Coast Lines had enjoyed a good relationship with the Ardrossan company, working within the Royal Mail Group, when it built the passenger steamers *Lairdscastle*, *Lairdsburn* and *Lairdshill*, formerly *Ardmore*, for its Irish interests. Each was equipped with a triple expansion steam engine built by John G Kincaid at Greenock.

Elder Dempster withdrew from Ardrossan in 1926 and Coast Lines along with John G Kincaid, engine builders, took over the reins. The investment was partly mortgaged and partly funded on a deferred payment basis. Kincaid had received a sub-licence from Harland & Wolff to build diesel engines under that company's arrangement with Burmeister & Wain of Copenhagen in 1922. The company was renamed Ardrossan Dockyard Limited by its new owners. Harland & Wolff, also part of the Royal Mail Group since 1917, was entrusted as manager of the Ardrossan business.

Ian Ramsay, former Secretary of the Institution of Engineers and Shipbuilders in Scotland, wrote of the New Yard (personal communication):

> The New Ardrossan shipyard launched directly into the sea from what was an exposed beach facing into the prevailing south-westerly wind and for the few winters that it was operational it must have been very miserable for the poor unfortunates that were working on hulls on the building berth. George Brown's shipyard at Garvel Point, Greenock was always referred to as 'Siberia' but I think by comparison Ardrossan New would be more like Antarctica. The reason for the New yard was because the existing yard was in a non-tidal basin and the size of ships were restricted to both what could be safely dynamically launched into and across the basin and the width of the entrance at the impounding gates.

The New yard was one of the first casualties who offered themselves to National Shipbuilding Securities for closure [in 1930]. This was a funded scheme set up by government and the shipbuilding industry to reduce surplus capacity but a company had to offer itself for closure and financial compensation with among other conditions that the shipyard had to be dismantled and the site not used again for shipbuilding for 40 years.

Although the New Yard was modern and well equipped it was closed. Instead of being able to build ships up to 9,000 tons gross the company could now only build ships up to 2,300 tons with a length of no more than 275 feet. Nevertheless, the yard was productive and innovative despite there being no significant investment under Coast Lines/Kincaid ownership.

There was a long and fruitful association between the Coast Lines group and the Ardrossan shipyard; a succession of motor ships was built for Coast Lines, the first being *Fife Coast*, with 4-cylinder machinery built by Kincaid, the last the *Buffalo* which was delivered in May 1961. Coast Lines sold its share in the Ardrossan company in 1962 to Archie Kelly of Greenock.

In September 1926 the British & Irish Steam Packet Company purchased the shipping interests of Michael Murphy Limited and its associates M J Begg & Company, shipping agents in South Wales, and the Dublin General Steamship Company Limited. Much of the Murphy business had been founded on the coal trade, particularly supplies of South Wales coal for the Irish railways. The Murphy interests retained their own identity into the 1930s; three of the ships later transferred to Coast Lines Limited.

At the end of October, the Dundalk & Newry Steam Packet Company was taken over by the British & Irish Steam Packet Company. The Dundalk Steam Packet Company dated back to 1837 and it absorbed its counterpart at Newry in 1871. Loss of a key steamer in World War I and poor trading conditions thereafter, coupled with serious port labour difficulties, put the company in financial difficulties.

The only steamer involved in the take-over was the *Iveagh*, a passenger steamer with large cattle carrying capacity. But shortly afterwards Irish cattle shipments were suspended and the *Iveagh*, quickly renamed *Lady Iveagh*, was sold. The company continued to trade, its Managing Director was Alfred Read, using British & Irish Steam Packet Company ships as needed. The live cattle trade was reinstated in the early 1930s.

The *Tiger* (1906) at Gairloch on one of her summer cruises in the early 1920s – not the most luxurious of cruise ships but fit for purpose.

Coast Lines had recognised the revenue-earning potential of the former seasonal yachting cruises that had been undertaken by M Langlands & Sons up to the Great War. It reinstated the yachting cruises from Liverpool via Ardrossan or Belfast to the Western Isles under the banner 'Langlands Service' in 1922. From 1922 to 1926 the Burns & Laird Line's *Tiger* was deployed as the summer cruise yacht, although the new Dublin steamer *Lady Louth* stood in for a couple of her cruises in July 1923 when the Liverpool to Dublin ferry service was strikebound.

The last summer cruise operated by Burns & Laird Line's *Tiger* ended on 24 September 1926. For the past three years she had been needed on ferry duties in the early summer and only managed about four or five summer cruises each year. They normally lasted about twelve days allowing two days for storing and cleaning ship in port at Liverpool.

In 1927 the dedicated cruising yacht *Killarney*, released from Fishguard to Cork duties, took over the summer role as cruising yacht. She had been built in 1893 as *Magic* for the Belfast Steamship Company; she was renamed *Classic* in the war and when transferred to the City of Cork company was given the name *Killarney*. In her

cruising role she was based at Liverpool and called at Ardrossan before proceeding to the Western Isles on a set of ten-day round trips. In 1927, the *Killarney* carried out nine cruises to the Western Isles from Liverpool with calls at Belfast for the benefit of Northern Irish clientele. The cruises were of six or thirteen days duration.

After that first season the *Killarney* was taken in hand to convert her from overnight ferry status to cruise yacht, aboard which the entertainment of passengers was paramount. Outwardly it was apparent that the saloon deck house was extended further aft. She was also repainted with an attractive grey hull and her funnels became pale yellow. On the boat deck were 21 single berth cabins, and on the promenade and main decks there were a further 71 twin berth cabins. There was a single deluxe twin berth cabin on the boat deck and a suite aft on the promenade deck with five separate cabins. In all, she could accommodate 190 cruise passengers. The original lower deck cabins were converted for use by crew members, the ship needing an enlarged crew complement as a cruising yacht with additional catering and domestic staff. She was registered at Liverpool and managed by Coast Lines but still owned by the City of Cork Steam Packet Company.

The cruise yacht *Killarney* (1893), with grey hull and yellow funnels, took over the seasonal 'Langlands' holiday cruises to the Western Isles from the *Tiger* which stood down in 1926.

Thereafter, her routine was cruising to the Western Isles with an occasional extension to Kirkwall and Inverness, and a single 'overseas' cruise each year to near continental ports and the Channel Islands. Fares were 8 guineas (£8-40) for a six day cruise in an inside cabin on the main deck to 12 guineas in an outside cabin on the promenade deck. All meals were taken in two sittings. The cruising season started in May and finished in late September; her winter lay up each year was spent in Stanley Dock at Liverpool, occasionally alongside other Coast Lines fleet members temporarily laid up or awaiting sale. In 1931 the *Killarney* was formally transferred to Coast Line Limited for the concession of just £7,000.

The big steamer *Yorkshire Coast* dating from 1913 was in collision on 8 October 1927 in Long Reach off Greenhithe, in the River Thames. She was one of two

steamers acquired with the purchase of the London Welsh Steamship Company in 1923. She collided with the small coaster *Scotsman* which had to be run ashore to prevent foundering. The *Scotsman* was owned by Coppack Brothers & Company of Chester (Connah's Quay) and dated from 1894. The *Yorkshire Coast* received only superficial damage. On 18 November 1928 the *Kentish Coast* grounded at Jennycliff Bay, Plymouth Sound, in a gale. The ship was later salvaged but found unworthy of repair and was scrapped by T W Ward at Lelant. The old *Cardigan Coast*, one time Tedcastle & McCormick's steamer *Dublin*, was sold also in 1928. Despite having been built in 1904, she enjoyed a further twenty four years trading and was scrapped only in 1952.

New tonnage for the London, Midland & Scottish Railway service between Belfast and Heysham (ships commissioned in 1928) prompted Alfred Read to look earnestly at upgrading his own ships on the Liverpool to Belfast overnight service. The question was how was he to pay for them? Three ships were proposed, not steamers as before, but motor ships to be built by Harland & Wolff at Belfast with Burmeister & Wain airless injection, 4-stroke cycle 10-cylinder engines. The two motor ships were intended to provide creature comforts not previously enjoyed on the Irish Sea. Read was able to secure funding from the Bank of Ireland against nine £50,000 and two £25,000 debentures to be repaid by 1936 against an annual interest charge of 6%. A third ship was proposed for the service and this was mortgaged to the Bank. The outcome was the magnificent and innovative trio of twin funnelled motor passenger ships *Ulster Monarch*, *Ulster Queen* and *Ulster Prince*, launched respectively in January, March and April 1929, the last ship championed at her launch by Lady Read in company with Sir Alfred. The displaced steamers from the Belfast service went to the Dublin to Liverpool overnight service in 1930 as *Lady Connaught*, *Lady Munster* and *Lady Leinster*.

Funds were also secured for a fourth motor ship of the *Ulster Monarch*-class to be laid down in 1929. This was the *Innisfallen*, designed for the Cork to Fishguard service, and launched in March 1930, just one year after the *Ulster Prince* and *Ulster Queen*. She was 20 feet shorter in length than the three Belfast boats and sported two funnels adorned in the City of Cork Steam Packet Company Limited colours of white with a black top. She had the same attractive grey hull as the three Ulster ships for the first season but all of them were repainted in a more serviceable black at their guarantee refits. Eventually there were to be thirteen ships of this class all built by Harland & Wolff at Belfast, but no more were ordered for some years until the Royal Mail Group crash and its aftermath had been resolved and Coast Lines had gained independence from its current owner.

Advertisement for Harland & Wolff claiming to have solved 'the problem of cross-channel ship design' featuring *Innisfallen* (1930).

The *Ulster Monarch* (1929) served her owners for 37 years including five years as HMS *Ulster Monarch* during World War II. She is seen in Princes Half-Tide Dock on arrival from Belfast on 20 August 1966 towards the end of her career.

[author]

CROSS CHANNEL TRAFFIC

The problem of cross-Channel ship design is not an easy one. We claim to have solved it, so far as it can be solved, in the three ships of "Ulster Monarch" class and in the "Innisfallen," which in their general conception and accommodation are positively ahead of present-day requirements.

HARLAND AND WOLFF Ltd

INCORPORATED IN NORTHERN IRELAND

BELFAST - GLASGOW - GREENOCK - LONDON - LIVERPOOL - SOUTHAMPTON

Sir Alfred Read's reputation had been greatly enhanced by refinancing the group after Sir Owen Philipps had spited him in 1922. As a consequence, he was invited by Westminster to help with an issue that had arisen in the West Highland services and the cessation of the mail contract. A consequence was that Coast Lines took a 50% share in David MacBrayne Limited, independent operator of West Highland passenger and cargo services in 1928. MacBrayne had lost three of its ships in 1927, two wrecked and the third gutted by fire alongside at Oban (for history of David MacBrayne see Robins & Meek, 2008). The ships were all elderly and claimed little cash from the insurers. MacBrayne, which had been struggling financially for some time, was now seriously undercapitalised. When invited to tender for the renewal of the mail contracts at the end of 1927 the Directors of MacBrayne were forced to decline, placing their family firm in immediate terminal decline. This caused alarm and urgent discussion at Westminster; invitations were sent to the railway companies to step into the breach and there was even talk of Government subsidies.

Ultimately, Alfred Read of Coast Lines, along with his sparring partner Josiah Stamp of the London, Midland & Scottish Railway, agreed to take up the reins. The two companies each took a half share in a newly structured company called David MacBrayne (1928) Limited through a total investment amounting to just £77,000. From 1 November 1928 Alfred Read was appointed both Chairman and Managing Director while Josiah Stamp became Vice Chairman. Government promised 'adequate support' to the new owners in the form of subsidies. The new company was given extensive powers to develop road haulage feeder and connecting parcels services. Interestingly the Directors insisted on a new nomenclature for the fleet; all new or acquired vessels were to be given names with the prefix 'Loch…'. But there were also a number of strictures applied by Government on the new owners of MacBraynes.

Robins and Meek wrote in *The Kingdom of MacBrayne*:
David MacBrayne (1928) Ltd had various strictures placed on its new parents by government. In return

for adhering to these requirements, government promised to maintain a dialogue regarding the need for, and value of, any ensuing operational subsidies due the company. Government, it seems, was primarily concerned about getting the mail through to the islands. Happily, Coast Lines was intent on the business of shipping, and the London, Midland & Scottish Railway, though also a significant shipowner, whose assets included the Caledonian Steam Packet Company, was more concerned about the carriage of people and goods. This combination of interests suited the new company perfectly. Collaboration between Sir Alfred Read of Coast Lines and Sir Josiah Stamp of the LMS Railway soon led to the formation of an Irish Sea cabal, which included all the companies in the Coast Lines Group and the London, Midland & Scottish Railway, but not the London & North Eastern or the Great Western railways. It is said that Sir Alfred Read had a guarded respect for his new ally, the emphasis apparently being on the word 'guarded'!

The strictures of the 1928 deal required that the passenger accommodation on the Outer Isles services be brought up to accepted standards, and that the passenger- and freight-rates be capped, and, in some instances, reduced. This was coupled with an instruction that capital had to be provided to equip the company for the modern age, with four new major units provided within the first two years of operation. In addition, road services were to be provided as feeders for ship and rail in the form of a parcels network and a range of bus routes. However, before even that could be done, the company desperately needed tonnage to support the Glasgow-based cargo services to destinations such as Stornoway, Portree and Tobermory. The Coast Lines' response was to cede the elderly steamer **Denbigh Coast** to the MacBrayne fleet as the **Lochdunvegan**. She was built to the order of G. & J. Burns in 1891 as **Grouse**, but she was able to assist her new owners with the West Highland cargo services from Glasgow until withdrawn for scrap in 1948.

The *Lochdunvegan* (1891) at Tobermory; built as G & J Burns' *Grouse* and latterly named *Denbigh Coast*.

[Linda Gowans collection]

The first new ship delivered under the deal was the steamship **Lochness**. Coast Lines interest in motor ships meant that she was the last major steamship unit in the fleet.

Robins and Meek again:

The first of MacBrayne's diesel passenger ships were the twins, **Lochearn** and **Lochmor**, which were designed for the Inner Isles and Outer Isles services respectively. They were built at the Royal Mail Group's Ardrossan Dockyard, and were launched in April and May 1930. When viewed from the bows, they looked business-like, but abeam and from the stern, they offered a solid central superstructure which, combined with their plump and ungainly cruiser sterns and grey hulls, persuaded Duckworth and Langmuir to liken them to a pair of wooden models in a toyshop window! They had twin sets of direct-drive machinery which required to be shut down and started again, in order to reverse the propellers during manoeuvres, the engine in each case being started by compressed air which was stored in a bottle in the engine-room. Although the compressed air was replenished while

the engines were running, the Master had to plan his ahead starts and reverse starts, to ensure that the bottle would not empty before the ship was alongside! Reversing gears were not yet available to suit the high torque generated by a diesel engine.

The actual design speed for the ships was over 12 knots, but in practice they could manage only just over 9 knots. Their lack of power was famously summed up by one of their masters: 'They canna get oot their ain road!'. In 1931, shortly after taking up service, the two vessels deeply embarrassed their owners by illustrating their lack of power and their clumsy manners before the watching public. The **Lochmor** grounded hard on a sandbank near Kyle of Lochalsh, and the **Lochearn** was summoned north to her assistance. She grounded likewise on the same bank, alongside her twin sister. The two new vessels, conjoined amidships, remained fast until the eighty-five year-old veteran **Glencoe** paddled along to their rescue, and towed both motorships off the sandbank in fine style!

The **Lochmor** (1930) seen at Mallaig after the initial grey hull had been replaced by a more practical black.

[Linda Gowans collection]

The pair was notoriously noisy. There was no escape for passengers from the constant rattle of the engines and thumping of the exhaust discharge. The fourth new ship was the passenger only **Lochfyne**. She had electric drive powered by the motor to overcome the reduction couple between engine and shaft. She too was noisy.

Ian Ramsay wrote:

The **Lochfyne** suffered from horrendous vibration and airborne noise. The vibration was so bad that the

compass bowl in the binnacle in the wheelhouse was mounted on damping springs as were the clock and the barometer, and the foremast continually whipped back and forth like a fishing rod about to cast a fly. The noise was not helped by the fact that the engine room had viewing windows along the length of the main deck and many were open for ventilation which resulted in the whole midship area of the ship being subjected to a deafening roar.

The passenger only *Lochfyne* (1931) was the mainstay of the Greenock to Ardrishaig service connecting at Tarbert East with the Islay steamer at Tarbert West.

[author]

David MacBrayne (1928) Limited was allowed to revert to its former name of David MacBrayne Limited in 1934. During the nationalisation of the railways in 1948 the railway share of MacBrayne came under direct Government ownership, and later when the Scottish Transport Group was formed in January 1969, Coast Lines was obliged to sell its partnership to Government, a transaction that was completed in July 1969.

The British & Irish Steam Packet Company acquired the goodwill of the Drogheda to Liverpool cattle service from the Lancashire & Yorkshire Railway in 1928. Passenger carrying ceased at the outset of the Great War and was not resumed thereafter, but the cattle trade remained lucrative.

In the spring of 1929, at the time the **Ulster Monarch** and **Ulster Queen** were launched at Belfast, rumours were

circulating that the Royal Mail Group was suffering dire financial problems and that the group might need to be restructured. The Royal Mail stocks collapsed later in the year.

The Coast Lines group was once again in jeopardy of at worst failure, or at best sale to another master. Alfred Read and his team set about distancing the Coast Lines group from such an occurrence.

Two of the former Michael Murphy ships came under Coast Lines registry in 1929, the **Enda** being renamed **Anglesey Coast** and the **Patricia** became **Cardigan Coast**. The **Cumberland Coast** passed to the City of Cork Steam Packet Company in January and was renamed **Kinsale**, and the **Dorset Coast** went to Belfast in June to become the **Logic**.

The *Cardigan Coast* (1913) was built as the *Patricia* for Michael Murphy and was acquired by the British & Irish Steam Packet Company in 1926.

Significantly, Coast Lines was able to purchase the shipping interests of the Antrim Iron Ore Company in April 1929. This included its two ore carriers, **Glentaise** and **Glendun**, along with the goodwill of its Belfast to Stockton passenger and cargo service – iron ore to Stockton, general cargo to Belfast. Calls were made at Stornoway, Dundee, Leith, Newcastle, Hartlepool and Middlesbrough if sufficient inducement.

Coast Lines was contracted to maintain the service much as before and the only outward sign of change were new Coast Lines liveries and names for the ships; the **Glentaise** became **Antrim Coast** and the **Glendun** became **Aberdeen Coast**, both ships using their twelve passenger berths which had been marketed under the banner 'The Antrim Line'.

This was the first company acquisition for Coast Lines Limited since the Grahamstown Steamship Company and the London Welsh Steamship Company were bought in May and November 1923 respectively.

The Antrim Iron Ore Company's **Glendun** (1903) was renamed **Aberdeen Coast** and remained on the Belfast and Stockton cargo and passenger service.

Coast Lines also maintained the **Durham Coast** on a service between Manchester northabout via Stornoway to Leith and other ports as required. Her master at this time was Captain Peter Miller.

The 1920s had been a real roller coaster for Alfred Read and his team. They had weathered the financial lows and enjoyed the rare highs and at the end of it they had a buoyant group of shipping and associated companies. They remained under the shadow of the impending collapse of the Royal Mail Group but work was in hand to shake free from that spectre. Any future investments in the group would depend on the financial returns then being generated such that the company was very reliant on favourable trading conditions. The Wall Street Crash of October 1929, just preceded by the London Stock Exchange Crash in September, signalled the start of the 1930s Depression and did little to raise hopes for the future.

There was considerable exchange of vessels within the group in 1930 in an attempt to maximise the use of ships and their capability to earn money. The **Pembroke Coast**, formerly **Sir Roger Bacon**, was transferred into the City of Cork fleet and later renamed **Blarney**. At the same time the City of Cork's old **Blarney** came to Coast Lines and was given the name **Pentland Coast**. The little **Irish**

Coast was converted for use as a barge at Liverpool, her services no longer needed on the Glasgow to Preston route which was discontinued other than on an ad hoc basis as required. The big cargo ship **Sutherland Coast** went to Burns & Laird Lines as **Lairdsbrook** in which guise she became the regular Belfast to Manchester steamer for much of the rest of her career. The third and last of the new motor ferries for the Liverpool to Belfast overnight service, the **Ulster Prince**, entered service in March.

By mid-summer 1930 it was apparent that the Royal Mail Group was in real financial trouble as were the component parts of the Group including Coast Lines and its own subsidiary companies. On 13 November the Court of the Royal Mail Steam Packet Company appointed a committee to investigate what economies could be achieved with speed and then turned its attention to instigating them. A device to safeguard creditors put voting trustees in place with control over finance and management of each company or group of companies within the Royal Mail empire. An outcome of this was that each company was asked neither to commit funds to any capital development, nor return a dividend. They were also asked not to lend or borrow funds without the consent of the appropriate trustee. Coast Lines reluctantly signed on the dotted line.

The *Pentland Coast* (1915) returned to Coast Lines in 1930 after serving as *Blarney* in the City of Cork Steam Packet Company from 1920, but was sold in 1934.

[*Richard Parsons collection*]

The third of the new Belfast passenger motorships was *Ulster Prince* (1929) seen on trials in Belfast Lough.

[*Real Photographs, Liverpool*]

CHAPTER 5

AN INDEPENDENT PUBLIC COMPANY

The Royal Mail Steam Packet Company and its financial debacle slowly unravelled during the course of 1931. It was not long since the company had bought the White Star Line from the ailing International Maritime Marine and it was becoming clear that a degree of false accounting had kept the Royal Mail Group afloat for some time. Rumours were rife, one being that Lord Kylsant, as Owen Philipps was now known, had even pilfered the shipping company pension funds, a rumour given some credence in lunch time conversations between senior management personnel in Harland & Wolff shipyard canteens in later years. If Kylsant did open the pension purses he at least had the dubious distinction of being several generations ahead of Robert Maxwell!

Matters came to a head in July when Lord Kylsant was convicted of making false statements in a prospectus for a new share issue for the Royal Mail Steam Packet Company. The prospectus reported trading profits for the years 1921 to 1927 whereas the Court heard that substantial and consistent annual losses had been incurred during that period. In June, Kylsant had requested 'leave of absence' from his Chairmanship of Coast Lines Limited and other companies within Coast Lines' ownership. Lord Kylsant received a twelve month gaol sentence which he served following an unsuccessful

appeal. In October his resignation as Chairman of Coast Lines and its associate companies was accepted, no doubt without regret by those that remembered his outlandish behaviour in 1922 when he cut off Coast Lines funding, determined to promote business to his shipyards rather than safeguard his own shipping interests. Alfred Read at last became Chairman.

During the year the cruising yacht **Killarney** was finally registered as owned by Coast Lines Limited rather than the City of Cork Steam Packet Company. Coast Lines acquired the former Admiralty barge **Penhallow** for use at Falmouth and the following year she was joined by the **Penpol** and the passenger launch **Ganilly** the latter from the Isles of Scilly Steamship Company Limited. The **Ganilly** was sold in 1937 and stripped down for use as a stores hulk.

The **Gower Coast**, formerly **Volhynia** in the Volana Shipping Company fleet, was sold in 1932 to John Kelly Limited who renamed her **Millisle**, and the **Fife Coast** was sold to Italian owners. The cargo ship **Fife Coast** was the former **Princess Ena** and came to Coast Lines with the Langland acquisition in 1919. The **Norfolk Coast** was also sold, one time **Cadoc** in George Bazeley's fleet.

The *Fife Coast* (1892) originally commissioned for Langlands as *Princess Ena*, was sold to Italian owners and remained in service until 1947 when she was scrapped.

On 13 September 1932 Lloyd's issued the following notice:

Penzance: The steamer **Glamorgan Coast**, Liverpool and Bristol for Penzance, general cargo, is ashore at Cape Cornwall, seven miles west of Penzance. The crew have been landed. The vessel lies in a very exposed and dangerous position, and the captain reports eight feet of water in the ship.

She went aground in thick fog at North Point on Cape Cornwall, apparently coming in closer to shore, to the east, than had been calculated and was head on to the rocks making evasive action ineffective.

The local media later reported:
The wreck of the **Glamorgan Coast** – latest developments from Cape Cornwall.

The wreck of the steamer *Glamorgan Coast* at Cape Cornwall is proving a great attraction to visitors, and large numbers are visiting the scene daily.

The vessel is firmly fixed on the rocks, and lies broadside on to the cliffs. All hope has been abandoned of getting her off, and she has been sold to a Penzance salvage firm as a wreck. Her bottom is so badly holed that the vessel is flooded from stem to stern.

She is unable to float, and when the tide rises the waves wash across her decks, which are almost completely submerged – the stem portion completely. Quantities of her cargo are floating out of her, most of which is coming ashore, but some is being taken out to sea. Local residents are keen on salving whatever is floating ashore and these operations are keenly watched by visitors…

The cargo consists of general merchandise; cases of apples and onions, barrels of grapes, flour, bran and other feeding stuffs, clothing, etc. Two or three tons of

stuff have been salved and taken onto the land at the shore end of Cape Cornwall.

Some surprise has been expressed that no salvage operations were carried out by the salvage company on Thursday. The wind had veered round to the south east and the sea was fairly smooth, though there was a fairly heavy ground swell running. At low water it is possible to reach the *Glamorgan Coast* from the shore, but at some little risk owing to the waves as they rush ashore.

The hatches of the vessel have been blown up [sic]. This occurred not long after she struck. As she bumped on the rocks, these tore a big hole in her side, and when the tide began to rise the pressure of air forced off the hatches and the cargo floated out.

If the wind goes to the north west and blows at any considerable force, there is every possibility that the steamer will quickly break up, and her cargo and remains will be piled up on shore.

The wreck of the *Glamorgan Coast* (1912) lying at the foot of the cliffs at North Point, Cape Cornwall, not far from the village of St Just, in September 1932.

[Wreck Site]

Shortly afterwards she broke her back at the forward end of No 2 hold. Salvage operations continued into the Autumn until they had to be abandoned due to deteriorating weather. The engines and the boiler, what is left of them, still lie offshore at a depth of about 18 feet.

It is noticeable that during 1932 three ships were sold. No new ships replaced these vessels. This reflects the downturn in trade in the early 1930s. More particularly it resulted from acute economic measures brought about by the downfall of the Royal Mail Group. There was a desperate need for Coast Lines Limited to seek an injection of cash to safeguard it from being sold off piecemeal. The Royal Mail Group needed to sell assets and recoup debts in order to salvage as much of the remainder of the shipping and shipbuilding interests as possible. Government was so worried about the damage done to Royal Mail, recognising it as an important transport network and a network doubly important at times of war, that it charged P & O to undertake a thorough

audit to ensure that its capital assets were appropriately valued and that subsidiary companies were not double accounting. This was a precautionary measure to check that P & O was not on the same slippery slope that the Royal Mail Group had descended. The outcome was a small reduction in the value of the company.

Coast Lines returned small profits in both 1931 and 1932. The board was only too aware of the savings to be had from motor ships over steam ships and was determined to re-equip its steam cargo fleet with motor ships with immediate effect. Sale of older ships along with cash in the bank allowed two orders to be placed during the year, both of which were justified to creditors as an essential cost-saving development. The two ships were quite different and intended for different use.

The first motor ship was the *Fife Coast* and she was launched in 18 October 1933 from the company's Ardrossan shipyard. She was a small ship by Coast

Lines standards of just 367 tons gross and was intended to support some of the smaller volume cargo runs such as London along the south coast and London along the North Sea coast. She was equipped with a 4-cylinder oil engine built by fellow owners of the shipyard, John G. Kincaid & Company Limited, of Greenock, under sub-licence from Harland & Wolff for Burmeister & Wain. The engine was intended to provide a service speed of 9 knots at 300 brake horsepower. She could not achieve this target and was re-engined in 1936 with a unit rated at 500 brake horsepower built by British Auxiliaries Limited at Glasgow, after which she could work up to 10 knots.

The innovative motor ship *Fife Coast* (1933) was the first of many such ships built for the company by its associate Ardrossan Dockyard Company.

The *Fife Coast* was very much the test case for the diesel engine and was clearly a success because an identical sister, the *Carrick Coast*, was delivered from Ardrossan the following summer. The *Carrick Coast* was given a more powerful 4-cylinder engine built by Atlas Diesel A/B in Stockholm. Like many of the cargo ships in the fleet the engine was placed aft aboard the two vessels and

there was a small bridge island between Numbers 1 and 2 hatches. No 2 hold included a shelter deck whereas No 1 hold forward had an open well deck, for the carriage of volatile goods, with four large open scuppers on either side to allow water shipped onto the well deck to be displaced.

The second motor ship was in an altogether different class to the *Fife Coast*. This was the highly innovative *British Coast* launched by Henry Robb Limited at Leith on 4 November 1933. The *British Coast* had two oil engines and twin shafts. The engines were built by British Auxiliaries Limited at Glasgow and comprised 5-cylinder, 4-stroke single acting airless injection engines which on trials allowed a recorded speed of 14.2 knots. The cylinders were 13.4 inches diameter with a stroke of 22.4 inches. The ship had two Paxman auxiliary diesel units powering two 60 kW Campbell & Isherwood direct current generators working at 750 revolutions per minute that supported the pumps, electric winches and windlass, and the steering gear.

The *British Coast* was a shelter deck ship with one long hold, served by three hatches, one before and two abaft the bridge island. The shipside of the hold, along with the bulkheads and tank top were lined with timber to protect the cargo. Importantly, she was designed with accommodation for twelve passengers in two berth cabins on the main deck of the bridge island, where the officers were also accommodated. Passengers enjoyed a small lounge/smoking room beneath the bridge with windows facing forward and a small sun deck behind the bridge. The *British Coast* and a second identical ship, *Atlantic Coast*, ordered in February 1934, were designed to replace the aging *Southern Coast* and *Western Coast* on the Liverpool to London service, with calls at intermediate ports on the south coast.

The innovative closed shelter deck motor vessels *British Coast* (1933) and *Atlantic Coast* (1934), with berths for 12 passengers, set the design standard for the coastal liner for several decades – note the passenger sun deck abaft the navigation bridge.

[*Coast Lines Seaway Trader's Guide and Diary for 1934*]

The passenger accommodation on the elderly **Southern Coast**, now reduced to just 40 berths, was rarely used at capacity even in the height of summer. The twelve berths offered by the **Western Coast** were in demand throughout the year. However, the large cargo capacity of the **Southern Coast** was fully utilised on many voyages. The idea of replacing these two ships with two motor cargo ships with limited passenger accommodation was soundly based. The words 'summer coastal cruises' had already entered the marketing literature replacing the phrase 'regular express passenger service' back in the 1920s.

The **Atlantic Coast** was launched from the yard of Henry Robb Limited on 16 May 1934. The **Atlantic Coast** had

the same pair of auxiliary diesel generating sets plus a third smaller Paxman diesel generating set that provided an additional 45 kW output. The two ships replaced the **Southern Coast** and **Western Coast** in the autumn providing a weekly departure with calls at Falmouth, Plymouth and Southampton. The **British Coast** took her maiden commercial voyage from Kirkcaldy to London with a cargo of lino flooring, ready for her first sailing to Liverpool. The **Southern Coast** was kept available for the following two 'cruise' seasons but was sold in September 1936, whereas the **Western Coast** transferred to the Belfast and Middlesbrough route reintroducing a passenger service, albeit at irregular timings. The passenger accommodation on the two new ships was removed after the Second World War.

The **British Coast** (1933) after her passenger accommodation had been removed in 1948.

Meanwhile, Thomson McLintock & Company, a leading firm of accountants, was appointed by the Bank of England to try to unravel the complex finances of the Royal Mail Group. Part of the work included settlement of claims in American courts incurred during the sinking of the Lamport & Holt Line's **Vestris** at the entrance to New York Harbour in 1928, with the loss of 112 lives. The work of the accountants was completed in 1933 and the way was cleared to sell off those parts of the Royal Mail Group necessary to secure the core companies and especially the shipbuilders at Belfast and Glasgow.

Coast Lines was not considered to be a core company. Alfred Read immediately went into discussion with the authorities handling the preparation of parts of the Royal Mail Group ready for sale. It was agreed that if Sir Alfred could raise enough cash to buy himself out of Royal Mail that process would be given priority over an offer from a third party. Fortunately, trading conditions improved immensely in 1933 when a group profit of £359,644 was returned from the diverse trades maintained by the Coast Lines Group. This was achieved by the recession lifting, coupled with what was now a lean and mean shipping group. Coast Lines was large enough to support its weaker departments and adjust its corporate efforts to suit the changing demands of trade. Making a profit was

the saviour of the Coast Lines empire, although as will be seen, there was still a great deal of haggling and argument to settle before appropriate funding could be assured.

Neither the shippers nor the passengers were aware of the delicate position that the Coast Lines' Chairman found himself in. There is no mention of the possibility of a fire sale of Coast Lines and its various assets in the contemporary press. Indeed, the whole business of putting Coast Lines onto a firm independent footing was successfully kept from the public eye with all the actors playing behind the scenes. Had the real position of the group been public knowledge, confidence in its ability as a shipping company could easily have failed and profitability would have fallen. The Belfast Steamship Company and Burns & Laird Lines Limited were the most successful components of the group at that time.

British & Irish transferred the **Monmouth Coast** to Coast Lines in 1933 – one time Michael Murphy's **Grania**. She replaced the **Antrim Coast** which was formerly the **Glentaise** in the Antrim Iron Ore Company fleet acquired in 1929. The **Kinsale** was returned from the City of Cork Steam Packet Company and was renamed **Cambrian Coast**.

The *Cambrian Coast* (1920) was commissioned as *Gorilla*, sunk as a blockship at Cork in August 1922, and at one time had the names *Cumberland Coast* and *Kinsale*.

[B & A Feilden]

The key, but diverse, services of Coast Lines Seaway listed in the *Traders Guide and Diary 1934* were as follows, with numerous other ports as inducement:

From Liverpool

Tuesday to: Milford on alternate weeks, Llanelly, Swansea, Cardiff, Bristol (for Channel Islands)

Wednesday to: Stornoway, Inverness on alternate weeks, Aberdeen, Dundee, Kirkcaldy, Leith (for Cromarty, Buckie and Invergordon), Middlesbrough on alternate weeks

Wednesday to: Falmouth, Plymouth, London

Friday to: Aberdeen, Dundee, Leith, Newcastle-upon-Tyne

Saturday to: Llanelly (as inducement), Swansea, Cardiff, Bristol (for Channel Islands)

Saturday to: Penzance, Falmouth, Plymouth, Southampton, London

Weekly to: Weymouth, Poole, Portsmouth, Shoreham, Dover, Milford Haven

Twice weekly to: Greenock, Glasgow

Main services from Manchester:

Every Monday to: Stornoway (on alternate weeks), Inverness (on alternate weeks), Aberdeen, Dundee, Kirkcaldy, Leith, Newcastle-upon-Tyne

Every Tuesday to: Bristol

Every Tuesday or Wednesday to: Greenock, Glasgow

Every Saturday to: Bristol

Main services from London:

Wednesday to: Swansea, Cardiff, Bristol

Wednesday to: Portsmouth, Southampton, Torquay, Liverpool

Wednesday to: Kirkcaldy

Saturday to: Falmouth, Plymouth, Liverpool

Main services from Newcastle-upon-Tyne:

Monday to: Portsmouth, Southampton, Plymouth, Falmouth, Swansea, Cardiff, Bristol

Wednesdays to: Belfast (on alternate weeks), Liverpool, Manchester

Main services from Leith:

Monday to: Stornoway, Belfast (on alternate weeks), Manchester

Monday to: Dundee, Aberdeen, Buckie, Cromarty, Inverness

Wednesday to: Dundee, Aberdeen, Invergordon, Lossiemouth, Liverpool

Wednesday to: Portsmouth, Plymouth, Falmouth, Swansea, Cardiff, Bristol

Thursday to: Dundee, Aberdeen

Friday to: Liverpool

The diverse network of routes operated by Coast Lines in 1934, from *Coast Lines Seaway Trader's Guide and Diary 1934*.

Plans had been discussed with Henry Robb at Leith for a modified version of the *British Coast*/*Atlantic Coast*, some 20 feet longer and with an extended bridge/ accommodation island. A firm order for one ship was placed in August 1934; the result was the *Pacific Coast* which was launched on 4 April 1935. A near identical sister was built at the company's own Ardrossan Dockyard; she was allocated the name *Anglian Coast*, but was launched on 31 July 1935 as *Ocean Coast*. The ships had exactly the same auxiliary motors and direct current generator array as the *Atlantic Coast*, although the *Pacific Coast* had an upgraded third auxiliary motor that provided 1,000 revolutions per minute to the generator. The key difference with the earlier pair was that the new ships had a deadweight of 1,790 tons whereas the *British Coast* and *Atlantic Coast* offered only 1,395 tons. The newer ships had improved passenger accommodation with a smoking room looking forward beneath the bridge and a small saloon/day room.

The *Pacific Coast* (1935) was designed and built by Henry Robb Limited for the Liverpool and London passenger and cargo service.

[B & A Feilden]

The *Ocean Coast* (1935) sister to *Pacific Coast*, was delivered three months after her sister started work on the London service.

Once commissioned, in the summer of 1935, the **Ocean Coast** and **Pacific Coast** displaced the **British Coast** and **Atlantic Coast** on the Liverpool and London service. The increased cargo capacity of the newer ships was needed on this service and it was found that the earlier sisters, with their smaller deadweight capacity, were not always able to accommodate booked cargo.

The **British Coast** and **Atlantic Coast** were transferred to the Belfast to Stockton service inherited from the Antrim Iron Ore Company, allowing the **Aberdeen Coast** which had passenger accommodation and **Devon Coast**, which could not carry passengers, to be sold, so reinstating availability of passenger berths on every sailing, rather than on alternate ones only. The **Durham Coast** still maintained the Manchester via Stornoway to Leith service. In addition, the two smaller steamships **Moray Coast** and **Cornish Coast**, formerly the **Volana**, were sold out of the fleet.

The time had finally come for Alfred Read to take his group of companies out of the Royal Mail stranglehold. The group had again enjoyed excellent earnings throughout 1935 and during the year it paid an arrears dividend on its preferential stocks. Alfred Read and his board agreed to seek a stock exchange floatation for the two million ordinary shares so that final payments could be made to Royal Mail.

Robert Sinclair neatly summarised the process:

> Hambros Bank handled the issue and two conditions were imposed. First, the Group's debenture stock must be redeemed and a Draft Debenture Stock Redemption and Conversion Scheme was prepared and approved by Sir William McClintock, a Royal Mail Voting Trustee and Coast Lines Director. The second condition was that Sir William McClintock would ask the government of the Irish Free State to take a controlling interest in the British & Irish Steam Packet Company, City of Cork Steam Packet Company, Dundalk & Newry Steam Packet Company and Michael Murphy Limited.

> Negotiations proceeded with the Ministry of Industry and Commerce in the Irish Free State in 1936 and a new subsidiary company was formed to hold the Group's interests in the State, British & Irish Steam Packet Company (1936) Limited. There is evidence that the services it operated were to be marketed as 'Irish Free State Lines' in expectation of the Government's forthcoming controlling interest and Bradshaw's Guide carried an advertisement to that effect in 1937.

Once the new Irish company was established, and vessels started to be reregistered accordingly, the Directors of Coast Lines Limited started to get cold feet. They had long been conscious that their Irish interests were liable to control by the now foreign Government at time of war or political conflict and had always been fearful that control might be wrested from them at some point. As a consequence, they insisted that Coast Lines must retain a controlling interest in the prestigious British & Irish Steam Packet Company; they also insisted that any sale of shares must be strictly on a commercial basis.

This more independent attitude reflected the buoyant financial state the company now found itself in. No shares were sold to the Irish Government and the deal fell through. However, there was recurrent discussion on the disposal of the Irish interests to the Irish Free State and, post-war, to the Republic of Ireland Government but it was to be several decades before a sale was accomplished.

Dealings on the two million Coast Lines Group ordinary shares commenced on the London Stock Exchange on 12 December 1935 and the various mortgages and debts incurred by the Group were duly paid off. Coast Lines had become an independent public company, the fight with the Royal Mail Group was finally over, and Alfred Read and his men could look to the future and focus all their efforts on the development of their network of coastal shipping services and the numerous complementary shore-based activities.

In the meantime, a decision had been made to improve the Burns & Laird Lines' overnight service between Glasgow and Belfast and close the Ardrossan to Belfast overnight service operated by the **Lairdsrock**, formerly **Vulture**, which had been built in 1898. Orders had been placed for two slightly smaller versions of the **Ulster Monarch**-class of ship. Construction of the two new ships was funded by two separate loans from the Midland Bank which were both guaranteed by the Northern Ireland Ministry of Finance. The Northern Ireland Government, of course, was keen to champion its own Belfast-based engineering industry in the form of Harland & Wolff with all its local suppliers.

The ships were known as **Laird of Ulster** and **Laird of Scotia** at the preliminary stage of construction but were launched as **Royal Ulsterman** and **Royal Scotsman**, the one registered at Belfast the other at Glasgow. The pair commenced service in June 1936. In an attempt to reduce the vibration suffered by earlier ships of the class, the twin propellers were placed such that they projected just beyond the beams of the ships. This meant that they could never be used on relief duties at Liverpool as they could not use the entrance lock to the Princes Dock system.

When the **Ulster Monarch**-class ships started on the Liverpool to Belfast overnight service the three existing ships on the route, **Heroic**, **Patriotic** and **Graphic** went to Dublin as **Lady Connaught**, **Lady Leinster** and **Lady Munster** respectively. The Dublin company parted with £25,000 each for the **Graphic** and **Heroic** and £35,000 for the **Patriotic**. The ships were given a smart modern livery and the **Graphic** and **Heroic** received dummy second funnels to give them a more modern appearance.

The Glasgow to Belfast ferry **Royal Ulsterman** (1936) served the route with her consort **Royal Scotsman** throughout long careers.

[author]

The 1921-built **Ardmore** had worked initially on the Cork to Liverpool service before transferring to Dublin in 1923 as **Lady Longford**, where she joined **Lady Louth** and **Lady Limerick**. The latter pair had been built for the service in 1923 and 1924 respectively.

With the arrival of the ex-Belfast trio at Dublin at the end of the decade the three Ladies were released from duty and transferred to Burns & Laird: the **Lady Longford** adopted the name **Lairdshill** and took up the Glasgow and Dublin service while the **Lady Louth** was given the name **Lairdsburn** and **Lady Limerick** became **Lairdscastle**, ready to take over the overnight service between Glasgow and Belfast.

Burns & Laird had revived the daylight passenger service from Ardrossan to Belfast in 1933. They purchased the Southern Railway Company's fast turbine steamer **Riviera**, built by William Denny and Brothers in 1911. She was given an extensive overhaul, converted from coal burning to oil burning and renamed **Lairds Isle**. She maintained a ten hour round trip with two hours ashore, although her voyage time increased in later years.

Deployment of the other Burns & Laird passenger units in the group included the **Rose**, **Magpie** and **Maple** on the Glasgow Londonderry route. They were renamed **Lairdsrose**, **Lairdsgrove** and **Lairdsglen** in 1929 when the corporate 'Laird' prefix was given to all the Burns & Laird ships. The elderly **Lairdsbank**, built in 1893 as **Olive**, had been withdrawn from Londonderry duties in 1930. The **Lairdsvale**, former **Pointer**, was used mainly on the Ardrossan to Belfast route until withdrawn and sold for scrap in 1933, and worked mainly alongside the **Lairdsrock**. The **Lairdswood**, one time **Woodcock**, maintained the Glasgow to Dublin service until she was sold in 1936. She worked alongside the **Lairdsford**, former **Puma** and one time **Duke of Rothesay**, until she was withdrawn for demolition in 1934, and the **Lairdsforest**, formerly **Tiger** and before that **Duke of Montrose**, transferred to British & Irish in 1931 stripped of her passenger accommodation as **Lady Louth**. The Dublin service was then in the hands of the **Lairdsmoor**, built as **Moorfowl** in 1919.

Little by little the old steamers were being weeded out of the various fleets in the Coast Lines Group and replaced by motor ships. There was nevertheless a long way to go before the steamships finally disappeared. Coast Lines was a leader in developing coastal general cargo ships as well as cross-channel ferries and its close links with both Harland & Wolff and the company-owned shipyard at Ardrossan were responsible for innovative, modern and efficient vessels.

47

The *Lairds Isle* (1911) as she looked when first on the Ardrossan to Belfast daylight service before the lounge was extended the full width of the ship.

The *Rose* (1902) wearing the early funnel colours of Burns & Laird Lines before she was renamed *Lairdsrose*.

CHAPTER 6

THE 'FIVE SISTERS' AND OTHER MOTOR SHIPS

Coast Lines was now sufficiently buoyant to be able to continue its search for companies worthy of being purchased. The first acquisition for some time took place in 1936 with the takeover of the Plymouth, Channel Islands & Brittany Steamship Company Limited, J W H Stokes.

This company operated between Plymouth and the Channel Islands and onwards to ports in Brittany with the elderly steamship **New Verdun**, dating from 1905. She was later disposed of and the service was continued with one of the numerous motor cargo ships then on order or under construction for Coast Lines Limited, until the Dutch-built motor ship **Emerald Queen** was available in May 1937 to take over the service.

In October 1936 Coast Lines acquired an interest in the London & Channel Islands Steamship Company Limited, a company incorporated in 1899. Prior to that date Stanley Cheeswright and Matthew Ford operated a weekly service from their rented wharf at East Dock in London to the Channel Islands.

The first big steamer on the route was the **Island Queen** commissioned in 1901, and along with the smaller vessel **May Queen** maintained departure every fortnight from London. From 1912 passengers were carried on the service. By 1916 a new **Island Queen** offered 60 berths on the route, but she was bought by Government in 1917 and was replaced with a cargo only ship in 1921.

Typical of the early London & Channel Islands raised quarter deck cargo ships was the *Island Queen* (1920) which replaced her passenger carrying namesake which had been bought by Government during the Great War.

General cargo was carried to St Helier and St Peter Port, and stone was loaded at St Samsons in Guernsey for London along with seasonal agricultural produce. The passenger service was not reintroduced after the Great War. During the war only one ship was needed in service and surplus tonnage was chartered out; this was valuable experience that was repeated thereafter whenever ships could be spared.

At the time of the Coast Lines takeover, the service required three ships with a departure from London every ten days. The ships each of about 1,100 tons deadweight, were the **Island Queen**, **London Queen** and **Foam Queen** and were joined by an even larger new ship, the **Jersey Queen**, ordered by the company in 1936 and delivered in 1937.

Thus, in October 1936 Alfred Read became Chairman of the company with M W Ford retained as Managing Director. Coast Lines also had J W Ratledge and G A Read on the board. Coast Lines now had services to the Channel Islands added into its burgeoning portfolio.

The London & Channel Islands Steamship Company Limited was retitled British Channel Islands Shipping Company Limited in 1937 with representation on the islands by subsidiary companies British Channel Islands Shipping Company (Jersey) Limited and British Channel Islands Shipping Company (Guernsey) Limited. These companies acquired local cartage companies in 1937 on Guernsey and in 1939 on Jersey.

The recently-acquired Plymouth, Channel Islands & Brittany Steamship Company Limited was vested in the British Channel Islands Shipping Company at the formation of that company in 1937. The goodwill and the steamer **Combe Dingle** running from Bristol to the Channel Islands were also acquired that year, while the **Anglesey Coast**, dating from 1911, joined the company briefly as **Norman Queen**. The **Norman Queen** had insufficient cargo deadweight for the service and was almost immediately sold.

During the course of all the financial shenanigans to free the group from the shackles of the Royal Mail Line, nine new shelter deck motor cargo ships were ordered and commissioned by Coast Lines along with a new cargo tender for Falmouth. This considerable investment in new tonnage reflected both the need to replace aging and inefficient steamships and, more particularly, the confidence gained from the independence from Royal Mail.

The first two were the **Anglian Coast**, launched by S P Austin & Son Limited at Sunderland on 1 August 1935 and the **Pembroke Coast** launched by Henry Robb Limited at Leith on 18 June 1936, each had twin 5-cylinder single acting oil engines and twin screws.

The **Anglian Coast** was deployed on the London to Swansea and Bristol service including other ports as inducement and the **Pembroke Coast** generally ran between Liverpool and Dundee with calls at Belfast, Stornoway and Aberdeen. The old steamer **Durham Coast** ran a similar service from Manchester without calling at Belfast.

The *Anglian Coast* (1935) was the first of a pair of twin screw motor cargo ships that could maintain a service speed of 10½ knots.

The next comprised the 'Five Sisters': **Devon Coast**, **Dorset Coast**, **Antrim Coast**, **Norfolk Coast** and **Welsh Coast**. They were launched by Ardrossan Dockyard Limited on 30 May by Lady Read herself, on 9 September, 23 December 1936, 28 September and 1 December 1937 respectively. The Five Sisters each had a single 4-cylinder oil engine. All five ships had a service speed of between 10 and 11 knots; the single screw ships set the standard for efficient and economical cargo ships in the fleet for some years. They had two hatches, one forward and one abaft the bridge island, each served by two derricks. All of these ships had wireless and direction-finding equipment fitted. Crew accommodation was in the poop and the crew were well provided for with a small mess adjacent to the engine casing. Officers were accommodated beneath the bridge amidships. The new motor ships displaced the steamships **Welsh Coast**, **Hampshire Coast**, and **Cardigan Coast**, which were sold.

The *Antrim Coast* (1936) was the third of the 'Five Sisters', near identical single screw motor ships. She was placed on the Liverpool to Belfast and Aberdeen service.

Fourth of the Five Sisters to be commissioned was the **Norfolk Coast** (1937); note the absence of rigid bulwarks adjacent to the hatches for ease of cargo handling.

The **Devon Coast** served between Liverpool and Bristol, the **Dorset Coast** and **Antrim Coast** worked the service between Liverpool and Aberdeen calling at Belfast, although the **Antrim Coast** was initially on the Liverpool to Glasgow route. The last two of the Five Sisters served as needed on a variety of rosters, including London to south coast and Bristol Channel ports as well as the Belfast and Manchester and the Liverpool and Glasgow routes.

Exactly a week before the **Antrim Coast** was launched at Ardrossan in December 1937, a small motor tender was given the name **Cornish Coast** at her launch. She was just 120 feet long but beamy with a breadth of 20 feet. She was equipped with the engine removed from the **Fife Coast** when that ship received a larger unit at Ardrossan earlier in the year. The **Cornish Coast** took up duty at Falmouth in the New Year. Along with the other company tenders, she used to lie alongside the Liverpool or Bristol to London ships which anchored in the harbour for transhipment of cargo to various local destinations. Passengers were embarked and disembarked via the company's own passenger launches **Ganilly** and **Polperro**, although the **Ganilly** was sold after the 1937 summer season.

Three further identical motor cargo ships, to a different design than 'The Five Sisters', were ordered from a Dutch yard to complement the vessels delivered by the Ardrossan Dockyard. These were the **Denbigh Coast**, **Hampshire Coast** and **Welsh Coast**, although the latter was completed as **Emerald Queen** for the Plymouth, Channel Islands & Brittany Steamship Company Limited, J W H Stokes, London and after the war became **Grampian Coast** for Tyne-Tees Steam Shipping Company.

The trio was built by N.V. Industrieele Maat. 'De Noord' at Alblasserdam. The **Denbigh Coast** was launched on 6 January 1937, the **Hampshire Coast** on 6 March and the **Emerald Queen**, as yet without a name on her bows was launched on 17 April. They were smaller than the **Dorset Coast** and her sisters, being 164 feet in length rather than 200 feet.

The trio was equipped with German-built engines made by Humboldt-Deutzmotoren A.G., Köln-Deutz, which were 8-cylinder single acting oil engines. The ships had a speed of between 9 and 10 knots although their operational capability was rarely above 8 knots. This trio was ideal for the lower capacity runs and the **Denbigh Coast** took up service on the Manchester, Belfast and Glasgow triangle cargo service, also fitting in occasional return trips between Liverpool and Belfast for the Belfast Steamship Company, while the **Hampshire Coast** took over the Liverpool to Plymouth run.

Falmouth in 1937: from left to right: the motor tender **Cornish Coast** (1936) which took up station at Falmouth in January 1937, **Atlantic Coast** (1934), **Penhallow** (1931), **Harfat** (1913) and one of the passenger launches.

The **Denbigh Coast** (1937) was the first of a trio of ships built for Coast Lines in the Netherlands, the first orders the company had placed on the continent.

[B & A Feilden]

The ships were quite unlike the earlier cargo motor ships and had the bridge, engine and accommodation set right aft. They had a mainmast situated between the two hatches with a derrick available to service each hatch. All winches and the windlass were electrically driven from a single auxiliary diesel engine driving a direct current generator.

One of the Coast Lines group's major passenger units operated by Burns & Laird was lost at 3.20 am on the morning of 7 April 1937. The **Lairdsmoor**, built as the **Moorfowl** (not the most attractive of names!) in 1919, was in collision in fog off Black Head, Wigtownshire.

The *Glasgow Herald*, 8 April 1937 reported:

> Two Glasgow men, it is feared, lost their lives early yesterday morning when the Burns-Laird steamer **Lairdsmoor** sank off the Wigtownshire coast after a collision in dense fog with the Shaw, Savill motor liner **Taranaki**.

> Only after the crew and passengers had been transferred to the **Taranaki** and the **Lairdsmoor** had sunk was it discovered that the master of the Glasgow ship (Captain John Campbell) and one of the firemen (Edward M'Bride) were not among the rescued.

> Altogether 41 persons were aboard the **Lairdsmoor** – six passengers, a crew of 31 (including Captain Campbell) and four cattle men who were attending to the three hundred head of bullocks which were being shipped from Dublin to Glasgow.

The report does not dwell on the 300 animals that drowned as the ship went down. The previous day, the almost new cattle carrier **Lairdsbank** had gone ashore on submerged rocks off the Mull of Galloway in dense fog while on passage from Londonderry to Heysham. She was refloated with substantial bottom damage some 20 hours later.

Two more new big passenger motor ferries of the **Ulster Monarch**-class were ordered in 1936, this time for the Dublin and Liverpool overnight service of the British & Irish Steam Packet Company (1936) Limited. Once again, the Midland Bank provided a loan, this time for £380,000, and once again, the loan was guaranteed by the Ministry of Finance in Belfast.

The Ministry was concerned that the ships were going to a 'foreign' company, the British & Irish Steam Packet Company (1936) Limited being Dublin based although controlled from Liverpool by Coast Lines Limited, while there was also a fear that the company be sold to the Free State Government and with it the collateral, the new ships themselves. As a consequence, the Ministry imposed the condition that the two ships should not be transferred to Free State ownership until the loans had been redeemed.

The directors at Liverpool considered ways round this condition. At a board meeting in 1937 the suggestion was made the British & Irish should be merged with Burns & Laird Lines and its ships registered at Glasgow. This suggestion was not well received and Directors in Dublin were not at all impressed that the suggestion had been tabled. In the event the two ships, **Leinster** and **Munster**, which were slightly bigger than the **Ulster Monarch**, were kept in the ownership of Coast Lines Limited and chartered to the wholly-owned Irish subsidiary company.

Thus, both **Leinster** and **Munster** were launched with Liverpool as their port of registry. Each had saloon accommodation for 425 saloon (first class) passengers and were licensed to carry over 1,000 third class passengers. The two ships had no provision to carry cattle but had two holds suitable for general cargo and passengers' cars, the latter loaded into the two upper cargo decks by crane.

Coast Lines new cross channel ferry **Leinster** (1937), showing her home port of Liverpool on her stern but managed by the British & Irish Steam Packet Company.

[B & A Feilden]

The **Leinster** sailed on her maiden voyage on 4 November 1937, the day after the **Munster** had been launched. The pair had an attractive livery of buff hull with green boot topping and white superstructure. The **Leinster** first sailed from Belfast to Liverpool to take up a charter to the Belfast Steamship Company running between Liverpool and Belfast standing in for **Ulster Monarch**. The latter ship was back at her builders having a major refit while also bringing her accommodation into line with the new Dublin ships with a view to her acting as relief during their annual refit season. The **Ulster Monarch** also had new propellers fitted in a bid to reduce the on board vibration problem.

The first class public rooms aboard the **Leinster** and **Munster** were completed in stained oak and mahogany paneling, the 86-seater restaurant, for example, was finished in bleached and limed oak with contrasting walnut and sycamore panels. The after bulkhead was adorned by mirrors and marquetry. Blue leather chairs and coloured and patterned flooring complemented the overall warm appearance of the room.

The main lounge on A deck had gold curtains to contrast with pine paneling and paintwork. The main staircase to the boat deck led to a smoke room and bar with doors to the outside deck at the aft end. The third class accommodation was austere by comparison, but offered a cafeteria and 120 berths in 2- and 4-berth cabins, a general room, smoke room and ladies room.

The new ships started on the Dublin service on 28 March 1938. There was nothing obvious to show that the ships were owned by Coast Lines and not by British & Irish other than the port of registry (the Irish tricolour was not flown at the stern until the war years and so the Red Ensign gave nothing away). An element of relaxation on the part of the Government of Northern Ireland allowed the **Munster** to enter service with her port of registration changed to Dublin while the **Leinster** was also re-registered as 'foreign owned'.

However, ownership remained with Coast Lines and the two ships stayed on charter to their Dublin managers; in the event neither vessel was ever owned by the Dublin company. The possibility of selling the British & Irish Steam Packet Company (1936) Limited to the Free State Government was clearly no longer on the cards and the company name reverted to British & Irish Steam Packet Limited in 1938.

The *Munster* (1937) entered service in March 1938 registered at Dublin but very much owned by Coast Lines Limited.

[B & A Feilden]

Of the three ships previously on the Dublin to Liverpool route, the youngest of the three, **Lady Leinster**, was renamed **Lady Connaught** and retained as spare ship. The former **Lady Connaught** became **Longford** and **Lady Munster** was renamed **Louth**, and both were retired to Wallasey Dock to lay up, **Louth** carrying out four trips to Greenock in July 1938 in conjunction with the British Empire Exhibition at Glasgow, a trip to Dublin and a short charter to Burns & Laird Lines. The **Louth** was in service the following summer on charter to Burns & Laird again, and with war looming once more, her port of registry was changed from Dublin to Liverpool. Meanwhile the **Longford** remained at Birkenhead and Alfred Read was under pressure from his Board to sell her. Read resisted, having an affection for the old ship coupled with the certain knowledge that the likelihood of a second war with Germany would bring her full employment. As it turns out, Read yet again was absolutely right. She too was registered at Liverpool before becoming operational again in 1940.

In May 1937 Coast Lines chartered the **Ulster Prince** for £750 to attend the Royal Naval Review at Spithead. The ship carried 129 guests of Sir Alfred and Lady Read, and only the great and the good were included in the passenger list. The **Ulster Prince** or **Ulster Queen** had carried out a number of short weekend summer cruises since 1933, departing on Saturday afternoon from Liverpool and returning on Monday or Tuesday morning. The cruises passed to the east of the Isle of Man, round the Mull of Kintyre and via Iona and Staffa to Tobermory, thence calling at Oban and Fort William. With an arrival from Belfast on the day of sailing to Scotland, and a departure to Belfast on the day of return, the cruises made life hectic for the crews. Even the **Innisfallen** managed to fit in some day cruises from Cork on summer Sundays.

Also, in 1937, the firm of Henry Burden, Jr., & Company Limited of Poole was acquired by Coast Lines. It operated a cargo service between Poole and London which was commenced with steamships in 1845. As the South Coast Shipping Company it was responsible for distributing flour brought into London from the United States. Various company titles followed until in 1906 what was then the London & Poole Steamship Company failed, and was taken over by its major shareholder, Mr Henry Burden.

Coast Lines acquired the goodwill of the service along with the 30 year old steamer **Palmston** and the small oil tender **Burdenna IV**. Both vessels were rapidly sold and the London and Poole service was then served by one of Coast Line's new motor cargo ships.

Three more motor cargo ships were ordered from N.V. Industrieele Maatschappij 'De Noord' in Alblasserdam during January 1938. Of these the **Mersey Coast** and **Clyde Coast** were essentially modifications of the 'Five Sisters' class, equipped with a 6-cylinder motor built by Humboldt-Deutzmotoren A.G that provided a service speed of marginally above 10 knots. They were delivered during the summer and took up service between Liverpool and Glasgow.

The construction of the third ship was sub-contracted to a neighbouring yard at Alblasserdam, Werf. Jan Smit, Hgn. This was a smaller vessel some 30 feet shorter in length than the **Mersey Coast** and **Clyde Coast** and based on the design of the **Denbigh Coast** and **Hampshire Coast** with engine, accommodation and bridge set aft. During construction the name **Thames Coast** had been allocated but this was changed to **Kentish Coast** by the time she was launched on 4 May 1938.

The *Mersey Coast* (1938) was another Dutch-built ship built to a modified and smaller design than the 'Five Sisters'. She served initially between Liverpool and Glasgow.
[author]

The Dutch-built *Kentish Coast* (1938) was of similar design to the earlier *Denbigh Coast*.

On 19 July 1938 the hazards of navigation in fog in busy sea lanes resulted in the Coast Lines' ferry *Munster* colliding with the American Lykes Line freighter *West Cohas* off the Skerries. The *Munster* was on passage from Liverpool to Dublin and had some 200 passengers on board. She was struck on the starboard side just abaft the bridge. Considerable damage included the destruction of eighteen staterooms; fortunately, only one of these was occupied causing injuries to that passenger. The Belfast-bound *Ulster Queen* stood by the *Munster* until the inbound *Ulster Prince* arrived to escort the *Munster* into Liverpool under her own power. The freighter received damage to her stem, which was badly twisted, but was able to resume her voyage from New Orleans to Liverpool without assistance.

The Lloyd's Law Report cited excessive speed in fog on the part of both vessels, lack of whistle signals from either ship, and inadequate look outs with none at the bows of the American. The two ships approached at six degrees on opposite courses. The *Munster*, taking last minute evasive action, had begun a turn to port, but this only increased the angle of contact to some 28 degrees

so worsening the impact. It was noted that if the impact had been just a few feet aft and abaft of the engine room forward bulkhead, the consequences could have been much more serious. The *Munster* was out of service for two months while repairs were effected by Harland & Wolff at Belfast.

The old British & Irish steamer *Lady Cloé* was transferred to Coast Lines and renamed *Normandy Coast* in 1938. She originally had 70 berths for passengers designed for the Dublin to London service. Her passenger accommodation was little used in the 1930s when the service was reduced in capacity to one cargo only sailing per week. As a cargo ship, the *Normandy Coast* continued to serve from Dublin via Cork to London calling at various south coast ports and occasionally between Dublin and Bristol Channel ports. In 1938 and 1939 the *Atlantic Coast* and *British Coast* forsook their northern service between Belfast and Newcastle and joined the *Ocean Coast* and *Pacific Coast* running between London and Liverpool. They returned to Liverpool via Cork while the *Ocean Coast* and *Pacific Coast* still called at Dublin.

The **Galway Coast** (1915) at Bristol. She was the former **Lady Wimborne**, which with the **Lady Cloé** had for many years maintained the British & Irish company's Dublin - London passenger service.

[Richard Parsons collection]

Passengers enjoying games on the sun deck of **British Coast** while in the English Channel bound for London in June 1939.

[George Robins]

A key appointment made in 1939 was that of Arnet Robinson as Deputy General Manager of Coast Lines Limited. He had been Joint Manager with J W Lester since 1932, having been appointed Commercial Manager at Liverpool in 1931. He was previously the Manager at Bristol and had joined Coast Lines in 1920 as a staff member at London.

Ernest Reader wrote in *Sea Breezes*, February 1949:
> Mr Arnet Robinson... is a man of wide and varied interests with a deep-seated consciousness and faith in the role the coasting liner trade has to play in our national economy. With a fund of human understanding, he is deservedly popular with his staff. He was born in Stanmore, Middlesex in 1898 and educated at Westminster School.

Arnet Robinson married Beatrice Baber in April 1928; they had two sons and one daughter. Robinson went on to become general manager in 1941 and after the war,

in 1948, he was appointed Managing Director and later Chairman.

The **Leinster** was in collision in the Mersey with the Belfast ship **Ulster Monarch** on 6 May 1939. Damage was slight although the pride of the navigation officers aboard both ships was severely dented.

The goodwill and three remaining cargo steamers belonging to Fisher Renwick Manchester-London Steamers Limited was acquired in 1939. Fisher Renwick had built up a considerable road haulage business with an express daily road service between Manchester and London. Although the service by sea had served the route well, since just before the Manchester Ship Canal was opened in 1894, at first using Runcorn as its northern terminal, the company decided to sell its interests in shipping to concentrate on its road haulage and distribution business.

Fisher Renwick's ***Cuirassier*** (1914) was given the new name *Thames Coast* – photographed on 25 August 1939 in the River Avon.

[Richard Parsons collection]

The three remaining Fisher Renwick ships were integrated into the Coast Lines' fleet: the ***Cuirassier*** dating from 1914 was renamed ***Thames Coast***; the ***Sapper***, built in 1922, became ***Avon Coast***; and the ***Sentry***, completed in 1924, was renamed ***Medway Coast***. The three ships were near-sisters of just over 1,000 tons gross, with shelter decks and engines and accommodation amidships. Initially the ships remained on Manchester to London duties although schedules were set for disruption at the onset of war later in the year.

A small motor ship was bought during the year and given the name ***Suffolk Coast***. She had been built at Westerbroek, in Holland, as the ***Marali*** for Newcastle Coal & Shipping Company Limited (Marcel Porn). She was similar in many respects to the ***Denbigh Coast*** and ***Hampshire Coast*** delivered from Alblasserdam two years earlier, and had almost the same hull dimensions although the ***Suffolk Coast*** was slightly narrower in the beam. Her Humboldt-Deutzmotoren oil engine sustained a service speed of 9 knots. The ***Suffolk Coast*** tended to serve between Liverpool and Glasgow in her early years with Coast Lines.

Attrition of the Dublin-registered British & Irish fleet was accelerated in 1939 once the prospect of war was inevitable. In quick succession the ***Lady Wimborne***, formerly on the London service with ***Lady Cloé***, was transferred to Coast Lines and renamed ***Galway Coast*** (she was the sister of ***Lady Cloé*** which had already become Coast Lines' ***Normandy Coast*** in 1938); the Great War standard coasters ***Kerry***, ex-***Lady Patricia***, ex-***War Spey***, became ***Kerry Coast*** and the ***Carlow***, ex-***Lady Emerald***,

ex-***War Garry***, was renamed ***Brittany Coast***. The latter pair still sported their lattice derricks, a device used to save steel when they were built in 1919. In addition, Michael Murphy's last remaining steamer within the British & Irish owned companies, the ***Finola***, was transferred to Coast Lines and renamed ***Glamorgan Coast***.

The Dublin and Cork fleet then comprised the ***Meath***, the brand new ***Dundalk***, the ***Kenmare***, ***Lady Connaught***, the motor ship ***Innsfallen***, and technically also the former Belfast steamers ***Louth*** and ***Longford*** which were laid up at Birkenhead and re-registered at Liverpool in 1939 and 1940 respectively.

At the outbreak of war, 3 September 1939, the remaining British & Irish vessels were encouraged to fly the Tricolour of the Irish Free State, rather than the Red Ensign as before, to indicate their neutrality. There was a dispute with the crews who demanded danger money for sailing in vessels protected only by their neutrality; their demands unmet they then went on strike. As a consequence, the ***Leinster*** moved from Liverpool to lay up at Barrow on 4 October and the ***Munster*** joined her there on 7 October. The ***Munster*** was reactivated on 11 December, the dispute settled, to commence a charter to the Belfast Steamship Company as a replacement for the ***Ulster Monarch*** which had been requisitioned. The ***Munster*** had been repainted at Barrow with a black hull and a large Tricolour amidships. Meanwhile the motor ship ***Innisfallen*** moved from Cork to the Dublin service while the ***Kenmare*** served both Liverpool and Fishguard from Cork.

The **Suffolk Coast** (1938) was bought second hand as a similar unit to the **Denbigh Coast** and her various quasi-sisters.

[Fotoflite]

The **Brittany Coast** (1919) was one of a series of ships that came into Coast Lines ownership from British & Irish, just before the war, to avoid their being owned by a declared neutral country.

CHAPTER 7

WORLD WAR II

Of the 127 ships in the Coast Lines group at the start of the war, 33 were lost or declared constructive losses. A further five ships were sold, mainly for Government service, and the group was able to build ten new ships under licence, while a further seven ships were bought second-hand.

Ernest Reader wrote in *Sea Breezes*, February 1949:

> In almost every major operation undertaken by Britain and her allies – save perhaps those in the Pacific area – the ships of the Coast Lines organisation took a worthy, and often an heroic part. The tragic evacuation of Dunkirk and Brest; the gallant expedition to Norway; the superb gesture to Greece; the freeing of the East African territories; Dakar and Oran; the 'Moonlight Ferry'; the unceasing hazards of the North Atlantic ports; Malta, Sicily, Salerno, Normandy and the Channel ports – all these mighty episodes in the story of victory witnessed the participation of the gallant ships and dauntless personnel of Coast Lines Limited… Of the personnel, 123 received decorations for bravery and meritorious service.

The first two losses both occurred on 9 November, nine weeks into the war and before either the **Leinster** or **Munster** were awoken from their strike-induced slumbers at Barrow. The **Carmarthen Coast** was sunk by a mine off Seaham Harbour. The mine is believed to have been laid by **U24**. The ship was on passage from Methil to London with general cargo, including linoleum from Kirkcaldy and granite kerb stones, and was under the command of Captain John Owen Rowlands. Almost the entire crew, including the master, were from Kirkcaldy.

The *Glasgow Herald*, 10 November 1939 reported under the headline 'Scots vessel sunk':

> Two Kirkcaldy merchant seamen have lost their lives through the sinking of the steamer **Carmarthen Coast** which for the past fifteen years has been employed on the Kirckaldy to London trip with general cargo… The missing men are second engineer Harry King (40)... and John Kerr (38), donkeyman. Six men were taken to hospital with injuries…

> Leslie, a fireman, told this story: 'I was in the stokehold when there was a tremendous bang, and I was blown 25 to 30 feet up the ladder. As I was falling I managed to seize the ladder and hang on. Both my arms and hands were injured in the effort to save myself.

> Mr King, who was near me, was, I think, killed outright. I was very dazed, but I am told I was able to get into a lifeboat unaided. I do not remember anything very clearly after that.

It transpired that Mr King's father, Captain W T King, was a previous master of the **Carmarthen Coast** until he retired.

The same day, 9 November, the **Pacific Coast** was gutted by fire at Brest. She was carrying cased petrol in support of the British Expeditionary Force. Cased petrol was a hazardous cargo as damaged tins leak flammable vapour and sometimes liquid petroleum. While lying at Brest, the cargo ignited and exploded; the ship was rapidly overtaken by fire. Her crew were able to evacuate safely leaving the ship to burn out. The hulk was later towed back to Falmouth and eventually broken up, scrap metal being at a premium during the war years.

In December the **Munster** was chartered to the Belfast Steamship Company and commenced on Liverpool to Belfast work now with a black hull and large Tricolour painted on either side. Her master was Captain W J Paisley, senior master of the Belfast company. Neutrality of the Dublin-registered ship, albeit working between two belligerent ports, did not safeguard her from mines.

Robert Sinclair reports:
> On 6 February 1940, the **Munster** sailed from Belfast with 180 passengers on board. At about 6 am the following day, some twenty miles from the Bar light vessel in a position 20° 36' N by 3° 24' W, there was an explosion which seemed to come from under the port side of the bridge. The fore part of the vessel was lifted into the air and fell back on the water with a thud. Such was the force of the explosion that the compass was torn out of the binnacle on the bridge, the upper deck hatches fell down below and the radio equipment was destroyed, preventing the transmission of distress calls.

> In the accommodation, lights went out and the galley collapsed. In many of the saloon cabins the washbasin, mirror and splash panel were blown off the cabin bulkhead by the force of the explosion. The **Munster** had become the victim of a magnetic mine and sustained a mortal wound in her auxiliary pump room.

> Captain Paisley suffered a broken arm and dislocated shoulder and had to be persuaded to leave the ship by Mr Wrigley, the Chief Officer. Though a sea was running and the **Munster** had taken a list to port and was going down by the head, passengers were got away in the boats safely with surprisingly few injuries reported. Flares burned on the **Munster** were sighted by the collier **Ringwall** at about 7am, and she picked up the **Munster**'s passengers and crew, landing them some five hours later at the Landing Stage.

Two weeks later, in the morning of 28 February, the **Ulster Queen** was almost lost. She had run aground onto sand at Maughold Head, to the north of Ramsey on the Isle of Man, while on passage for Belfast. Her passengers were taken off and transferred to the railway steamer **Duke of Lancaster** which took them to Belfast; the crew remained with the ship. Later in the day a tug arrived to assist in refloating the hapless ferry, but all the tug achieved was

to swing the **Ulster Queen** broadside onto the shore such that as the tide fell her bottom was punctured by rocks. Although the situation then looked hopeless the ferry was eventually refloated on 25 March. Shortly afterwards she was converted into the anti-aircraft ship HMS **Ulster Queen** and in which role she was commissioned on 26 July 1941.

HMS *Ulster Queen* (1930) looking every bit a fighting ship, but was structurally condemned at the end of the war and sold for demolition.

[Imperial War Museum]

The depleted fleet of the British & Irish Steam Packet Company was further reduced during 1940. The **Meath** was lost to a mine off Holyhead in August 1940, the passenger and cargo ferry **Innisfallen** was sunk by a mine while leaving Liverpool for Belfast in December the same year and the **Lady Connaught** was badly damaged by a mine at the Mersey Bar on her way to Belfast just a week later – she was towed back to Liverpool and laid up, for the moment, unworthy of repair.

With the loss of the **Innsfallen** and the **Lady Connaught** laid up, the Dublin service was withdrawn; the British & Irish and Cork fleet now stood at just three ships, the **Dundalk**, **Kilkenny** and **Kenmare**, so leaving the neutral Free State without a viable sea connection between Dublin and Liverpool and precious little from Cork. Coast Lines ships did continue to serve Dublin, the **Galway Coast** and **Western Coast** worked the British & Irish service to Liverpool for much of the early part of the war while the **Carrick Coast**, **Kentish Coast** and **Suffolk Coast** were regular visitors between 1940 and 1942.

Other losses in the Coast Lines' fleet in 1940 were **Pembroke Coast** and **Fife Coast**. The German Fifth Airfleet raided ships lying at Harstad, Norway, on 20 May while they waited to be unloaded. The raid badly damaged the Norwegian steamer **Deneb**, the **Pembroke Coast** and United Baltic Corporation's **Balteako**. The destroyer HMS **Delight** was able to assist and it was found that two crewmen had been lost aboard the **Pembroke Coast** and two also aboard the **Deneb**. Damage to the two ships was such that the **Deneb** and **Pembroke Coast** were towed out to sea the next day and scuttled by gunfire from HMS **Delight**. The **Balteako**, though damaged, was able to proceed with unloading.

The **Fife Coast** was torpedoed and sunk by E-Boats **S-21** and **S-27** on the 8 August, about 12 miles west of Beachy Head, on voyage from London to Falmouth and Plymouth. She had joined convoy CW9, a westbound Channel convoy, code name Peewit, when the ships were repeatedly attacked by E-Boats and German aircraft.

60

Andy Saunders wrote in the synopsis for his book *Convoy Peewit*:

During the morning of 7 August 1940 over twenty merchant ships set sail in Convoy CW9 'Peewit' and edged past Dover, hugging the shore, slowly heading westwards as daylight faded. Under the watchful eyes of the Germans, the large convoy had been seen from Cap Gris Nez and warning messages flashed to the Kriegsmarine and Luftwaffe. At Boulogne E-Boats were readied and left port in the early hours of the 8th to take up station off Beachy Head to watch and wait for the inevitable convoy. With horrendous suddenness the E-Boat flotilla was amongst the convoy as it passed Newhaven. Like a pack of wolves into a flock of sheep, the German boats scattered the convoy and mayhem ensued until the E-Boats called off the attack in the gathering light. The rest would be left to the Luftwaffe. What followed was initially and correctly recorded in history as the first day of the Battle of Britain, and resulted in the heaviest losses witnessed in the war so far.

The *Fife Coast* was one of seven ships lost to the attacks; one, the *Ouse*, sank following collision while trying to avoid a torpedo. Five men lost their lives in the sinking of the *Fife Coast*.

One new ship was delivered by the Ardrossan Dockyard for the parent company Coast Lines Limited in 1940; the *Moray Coast* launched on 6 December. She was from the same stable as 'The Five Sisters' and had a British Auxiliaries 7-cylinder oil engine that provided a sea speed of 11 knots. She went straight into service.

The *Moray Coast* (1940) in the River Avon on 13 February 1954. She spent much of her peace time career as *Jersey Coast* for British Channel Island Shipping.

[Richard Parsons collection courtesy of Ray Perry]

The *Leinster* finally came out of Barrow on 3 May 1940 to serve on the Dublin route. She completed just twelve round voyages and returned to Barrow on 21 June. In September the *Leinster* was stripped of her Free State registry and again had Liverpool painted on her stern. Within a week she was requisitioned for use as a hospital ship and converted at Liverpool. The *Leinster* sailed for north Iceland towards the end of November, British forces having now occupied Iceland, and during part of the winter she was frozen in at Akureyri. On return to Britain in the spring she was modified for use as a troopship and sailed in convoy from the Clyde for Gibraltar. From Gibraltar she joined another convoy bound for Malta, but ran aground soon after leaving port and returned to Gibraltar for repairs. There followed further voyages to Gibraltar and to Iceland.

The small German steamer *Phädra*, dating from 1898, was captured off IJmuiden by a British armed trawler on 15 January 1940. The *Phädra* had been on passage from Königsberg via Emden to Rotterdam. Escorted to the UK she was given the name *Empire Sentinel* and placed under the management of Coast Lines Limited. Although relatively small by Coast Lines' standards she offered useful capacity which was much in demand in support of military activities. The *Empire Sentinel* remained under Coast Lines' management until 1943 when she was converted into the wreck disposal ship HMS *Rampant*.

During 1941 Coast Lines was again the focus of enemy attention. The coastal waters around Britain had become exceptionally hazardous due to mines, both magnetic and acoustic, as well as from aerial and submarine attack.

Fortunately, no ships belonging to the parent company were lost during the year although there were substantial losses to subsidiary company fleets.

The **Ulster Prince** was lost at Nauplion in Greece on 24 April 1941. She was attempting to get to the port of Argos to evacuate Allied troops ahead of the German advance when she went ashore by the mole. After being refloated, the ship went aground on rocks – both groundings took place at night with the local pilot in charge. Her crew evacuated her and the ship was destroyed by enemy aircraft at first light.

The Great War standard ships **Western Coast**, which had served faithfully on the London route for much of the inter-war years, and **Kerry Coast**, were transferred in 1941 to Burns & Laird. After the war the **Western Coast** was given the name **Lairdsvale**, and the **Kerry Coast** reverted to the name **Kerry**. Still as **Kerry Coast** but registered under Burns & Laird Lines, she sank off Princes Landing Stage on 11 March 1944. Six weeks later she was refloated and beached at Tranmere. She was eventually towed to Dublin, arriving in late May 1945 without funnel or masts, where she was later repaired and refurbished.

The *Kerry* (1919) transferred from the Dublin registry to Liverpool in 1939 and was given the name *Kerry Coast*. She sank in the Mersey in March 1944 but was raised and repaired.

(Andrew Duncan]

The British Channel Islands Shipping Company Limited became a full subsidiary of Coast Lines Limited in 1942. Shortly afterwards British Channel Traders Limited replaced the Merchants Line brand, which looked after the coastal charter business, and ships in the fleet were registered accordingly; the **Saxon Queen** and **Coral Queen** being owned by British Channel Traders from January 1943 onwards. The London office of the Channel Islands interests was moved from its premises in Lime Street to join Coast Lines at its offices at 35 Crutched Friars. The company had taken delivery of one new unit built at Ardrossan in 1940, the **Stuart Queen**, significant in that she transferred to Coast Lines shortly after the war was over.

During 1942 the **Lady Connaught**, which had been badly damaged by a mine in December 1940, was taken in hand by the Dublin Dockyard Company and converted into a cattle carrier.

British Traders Company took delivery of the *Stuart Queen* (1940) from the Ardrossan Dockyard Company; she had been ordered in 1939.

A large tranche of nine ships, as part of the new Lend-Lease arrangement with the American Government, was placed under Coast Lines management during 1942. They were requisitioned by the American Government from their civilian owners, some out of lay up, and were gathered into a single small convoy from St John's bound for the Clyde. A tenth ship in the convoy, Convoy RB1, turned back after three days at sea. Some of the vessels were in ballast, others lightly loaded. The ships were registered under the ownership of the Ministry of War Transport and had volunteer crews on board drawn from across the Coast Lines group and elsewhere. Most of the ships were elderly, but were nevertheless welcome tonnage to Britain at that stage of the war despite some of them being essentially river steamers. The ships managed by Coast Lines ranged from the small **Col. James A Moss** of 842 tons gross, to the Delaware river steamers **Northland** and **Southland**, which were to be used as accommodation ships. They were just over 2,000 tons gross and dated from 1908 and 1911 respectively. There was also the even larger twin-screw steam turbine passenger ships **Boston** and **New York**, built in 1924, each of 4,989 tons gross.

Both the **Boston** and **New York** were lost to submarine attack in quick succession in the delivery convoy, code named 'Maniac', on 25 September 1942. The following day the **Yorktown**, which was also managed by Coast Lines, was torpedoed and sunk. It is possible, but has never been confirmed, that the convoy was used as a decoy to allow safe passage of a much larger one carrying American troops and equipment for the North African landings. Nevertheless, of the remaining six

ships, all managed by Coast Lines, the **Col. James A Moss** and the **Southland** were returned to the Americans in 1943, the **President Warfield** and **Northland** in 1944, and the **New Bedford** and **Naushon** not until 1946. The **Naushon** spent much of the war serving between Belfast and Liverpool. She was barely suited to the trade being a former river steamer built entirely of wood above the main deck with light scantlings and tall superstructure.

One other ship was put under Coast Lines' management in 1942, the **Empire Atoll**. She had been ordered by Coast Lines for the refrigerated carcass trade and was completed with several large refrigerated compartments. She was built at Ardrossan and was a near sister to the **Moray Coast** delivered in 1940, complete with the same 7-cylinder British Auxiliaries oil engine. She remained with the Ministry of War Transport throughout the war until she was purchased in 1946 and given the name **Hadrian Coast**.

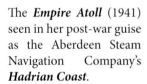

The **Empire Atoll** (1941) seen in her post-war guise as the Aberdeen Steam Navigation Company's **Hadrian Coast**.

Flagship of the Coast Lines' fleet, the **Munster**, stood down from her trooping duties to Iceland and was made ready for the assault on Oran, leaving the Clyde for Gibraltar on 26 October. She successfully landed troops and stores off Oran and returned home for further trooping duties to Iceland, finishing in May 1943. She was then converted back for use as a hospital ship once more and sailed in convoy from the Clyde in June, bound for Sicily.

After the landings at Sicily she served at Salerno and later at Anzio, thereafter she stayed in the region in her capacity as a hospital ship, and spent the remainder of the war in the Adriatic.

A new ship, the **Southern Coast**, was launched on 25 January 1943 to the order of Coast Lines Limited. She was placed on the Liverpool to Belfast service under the management of the Belfast Steamship Company for the remainder of the war. She was of larger dimensions than the **Moray Coast** but of the same basic design. The **Southern Coast** had an 8-cylinder oil engine built by British Auxiliaries Limited, Glasgow, and had a service speed of 12 knots.

A small flotilla of coastal ships was gathered to assist in the assault on Italy as supply ships. Few of the Coast Lines' masters possessed foreign going certificates but most in the British Channel Islands Shipping company did in order to cater for the charter business. Consequently, the **Moray Coast**, **Devon Coast**, **Dorset Coast** and **Atlantic Coast** sailed for the Mediterranean with masters from that company: Captain Lucas, Captain Mastin, Captain Storm and Captain Quail. The ships all came under enemy fire; neither the **Devon Coast** nor **Dorset Coast** returned home and Captain Storm was killed during one of the many attacks on the ships.

The **Dorset Coast** was bombed and sunk while lying off Algiers on 12 May 1943. The bomb exploded just to the stern of the ship but the explosion damaged cased petrol loaded on deck and set fire to the ship. She had been taking petrol, both in small cases and in 44-gallon drums, from Algiers to Bone, there to discharge it into landing craft to be taken ashore. Following the explosion, the crew were able to go over the side and climb aboard a motor launch that they had access to; the entire crew safely made it to the launch and onwards to the shore.

The *Southern Coast* (1943) was delivered from Ardrossan; consideration had been given to converting her into a tanker during construction, but work was too far advanced to make the necessary structural changes.

[Richard Parsons collection]

The **Devon Coast** was destroyed during the massive explosion of two ammunition ships during an air raid at Bari, south-eastern Italy, in the early evening of 2 December 1943. A number of ships were hit including two ammunition ships and a Liberty ship, the **John Harvey**, carrying among other stores a secret consignment of mustard gas 'to be used in the event the Germans used it first'. Large quantities of burning fuel added to the chaos.

The **Devon Coast** was set alight; her crew evacuated into a rain of liquid mustard gas. The fatalities and fatal injuries caused aboard ships in the harbour, within the harbour area and right across the town, were staggering. On top of all that, in Parliament, Churchill denied that mustard gas poisoning had ever occurred at Bari... until the awful truth dawned for everybody to see.

The *Devon Coast* (1936) after the devastating air raid at Bari in which a consignment of mustard gas exploded causing burns, often fatal, to personnel over a large area of the harbour and the town.

Robert Gilchrist & Co, the South Wales and Liverpool Steamship Company Limited, was acquired by Coast Lines in 1943. The company dated from 1824 when Robert Gilchrist started running schooners between Liverpool and Glasgow. The cargo service was extended south to the Bristol Channel in 1882; steamers were introduced in the 1870s. Coast Lines acquired with the business four raised quarterdeck, engines aft, steamships: **Victor** dating from 1907, **Perdita** built in 1910, **Fire Queen** in 1921, and **Portia** completed in 1925. **Fire Queen** was an old Lamont name; Henry Lamont and Company had been purchased in 1910, although it kept its own identity for some years. The venerable **Victor** was sold on almost immediately, while the **Perdita** was kept until 1945. Neither ship was given a Coast Lines name due to wartime restrictions. However, in 1945, the **Fire Queen** became **Orkney Coast** and **Portia** was renamed

Shetland Coast. Coast Lines now had access and the goodwill of trade from a host of small ports in the Bristol Channel.

In December 1943, a larger acquisition was made with the purchase of the Tyne-Tees Steam Shipping Company of Newcastle and Middlesbrough. This company was formed in 1903 by the merger of the Tyne Steam Shipping Company, the Tees Union Shipping Company and Free Trade Wharf Company of London. It also acquired the two steamers owned by Furness Withy running between Newcastle and London. Passenger and cargo services were operated from the Tyne to London, to Rotterdam and to Hamburg and a cargo service was maintained from Newcastle and Hartlepool to a variety of German and French ports. There were also passenger and cargo services from the Tees to London and to Hamburg and

Bremen. In 1912 the new company acquired the Havelock Line and with it the passenger cargo ship *General Havelock* and its twice weekly service between London and Sunderland. Services developed subsequently and included collier work to London and elsewhere (see Robins, 2014).

Coast Lines had collaborated with Tyne-Tees between the wars with cargo trans-shipped at Newcastle to and from the Continent for Liverpool, Belfast and elsewhere. Coast Lines had never had a proper foothold on the east coast of England and acquisition of the Tyne-Tees Steam Shipping Company finally provided this and giae the Coast Lines group a vital opening to the North Sea Continental trades.

Overtures made by Coast Line's Chairman, Sir Alfred Read, were at first rejected by the Tyne-Tees board. However, the board recognised that an independent shipping company could face uncertain trading conditions following the eventual declaration of peace and that it would be more secure as part of a larger group of companies. It was eventually agreed that the Tyne-Tees Steam Shipping Company would become a part of the Coast Lines' empire through purchase of all the share issue recommended by the Tyne-Tees board to its shareholders at a total price of £1.3 million. This sum was to be paid both in cash and shares in the parent group. The deal was completed in December 1943. For the moment the Tyne-Tees directors were left to carry on much as before with one of the Coast Lines' directors appointed to the board as an observer rather than an agent for the new owners. An early consolidation of the two companies was merging the London offices of Coast Lines and the Free Trade Wharf Company under one roof at Seaway House, 338 The Highway, directly behind Free Trade Wharf.

In 1944 Alfred Read and his Vice Chairman, Captain Nutting, were able to conclude negotiations for the purchase of the Belfast, Mersey & Manchester Steamship Company. With it came the two former Clyde Shipping Company steamers *Greypoint* and *Mountstewart*, now converted for cattle carrying. This company had been established in 1891 as a specialist carrier of produce between Belfast and Manchester, developing the cattle trade as a secondary line until the original rope and textile cargoes diminished in the 1920s. It had always been a serious competitor to the Belfast Steamship Company and Coast Lines had wanted to buy it out in the 1930s. The new acquisition was placed under the wing of the Belfast Company where it was allowed to retain its own identity and business clientele.

The *Mountstewart* (1907) was one of two cattle carriers acquired with the Belfast, Mersey and Manchester Steamship Company in 1944. She was originally Clyde Shipping Company's *Pladda*.

[B & A Feilden]

Three ships were lost in the final months of the war. The *Normandy Coast*, formerly *Lady Cloé*, was torpedoed and sunk by German submarine *U-1055* on 11 January 1945 off Point Lynas, Anglesey. She was carrying a cargo of steel plates and was on passage from London to Liverpool; she sank rapidly with the loss of 19 men. The *Kentish Coast* was torpedoed by submarine *U-1302* on 28 February 1945, north west of St David's Head, Pembrokeshire, on passage Cardiff to Liverpool. Six of her crew and one of the two gunners were killed. The other gunner, four crew members and the master, Captain Thomas Humphreys, were picked up by HMCS *Moosejaw* and landed at Fishguard. The *Monmouth Coast*, under the command of Captain Albert Standen, was torpedoed and sunk on 24 April 1945 at about 2.15 in the afternoon, by submarine *U-1305*, some 7 miles north-east of Tory Island. The *Monmouth Coast* was unescorted and was on a routine voyage from Sligo to Liverpool loaded with 840 tons of barytes. The master, 13 crew members and 2 gunners were lost. The sole survivor, messroom boy Derek Cragg, was rescued by an Irish fishing boat and landed at Arranmore Island two days later.

The *Monmouth Coast* (1924), formerly Michael Murphy's *Grania*, was lost at the very end of the war.

The loss of the **Normandy Coast** was particularly galling. Having undertaken exercise in the Bristol Channel with the American army, loading cased petrol at Sharpness and discharging over various beaches, the **Normandy Coast** eventually sailed in convoy to the Solent to await orders to proceed to the Normandy beaches. Her master was Captain Frederick Mara. The convoy sailed on D-Day plus three and was attacked by E-Boats that were seen off by the convoy escorts. On arrival the **Normandy Coast** was ordered to discharge her cargo of petrol alongside the **Atlantic Coast** which was loaded with ammunition. The two ships were beached and as the tide fell away from the ships they were attacked by shell fire from the air. The pair were eventually discharged and ten days later sailed for home, but not until the convoy had ridden out the big storm that nearly destroyed the Mulberry Harbours. The **Normandy Coast** repeated the petrol run for the next nine months getting the process of unloading down to just 16 hours, especially when access was given to the Mulberry jetty at Arromanches, and later still when she was allowed to dock at Caen and finally also at Dieppe.

A rare prewar picture of the *Normandy Coast* (1916) still in British & Irish livery on 21 July 1938, but already registered at Liverpool.

[Richard Parsons collection]

66

Eventually released from American Army control, the **Normandy Coast** returned to the Irish Sea in convoy and then dispersed for Liverpool and home. At that late stage of the voyage she was struck by a torpedo and began to sink by the stern.

Captain Mara is quoted from a letter drafted in 1945, *Sea Breezes*, June 1994:

> She was under water aft to the top of the bulwark and visibly sinking fast. The starboard boat was smashed and blown inboard; the port boat was hanging by the after fall; doors were blown off and the stokehold ventilators down. The wireless room was wrecked and the bridge a shambles, with both telegraphs jammed.

Some of the men got away in the ship's two rafts but 19 of the crew went down with the ship. Eight of the survivors were injured and all were suffering from hypothermia when they were later rescued from the rafts.

Victory in Europe, VE Day, was celebrated on 8 May 1945, although victory in the Pacific arena, was not resolved until August.

HMS **Ulster Queen** had led a long and gallant role throughout the war including the hazardous task of escorting Russian convoys. She was converted into a cruiser in the 15 months following her being requisitioned in March 1940. This involved a great deal of structural work, the removal of her boat deck and the fitting of 4 inch armour-plating onto her original steel hull. She was involved in the occupation of Italy and later ended up in India as a fighter direction ship. Brought back to the UK at the end of the war it was found that electrolytic corrosion between the armour plating and the ship's hull had severely damaged the latter. Any thought of renovating the ship and rebuilding her boat deck was out of the question; she was paid off in 1946 and demolished shortly afterwards.

Both the **Royal Ulsterman** and **Royal Scotsman** were able to return to duties with their owners, Burns & Laird after the war. They too had been involved in many of the landings and evacuations as landing ships and troopships, notably in the North Africa campaign. The **Ulster Monarch** was sole survivor of the three original ships of this class; of the British & Irish contingent only the **Leinster** survived.

The Landing Ship HMS **Royal Scotsman** in the Clyde with her array of landing craft.

[Imperial War Museum]

CHAPTER 8

PICKING UP THE PIECES

In 1945, after the war had ended, Coast Lines was instructed to manage the **Empire Consett** on behalf of what had then become the Ministry of Transport. The **Empire Consett** had been built in 1936 as the German coastal motor cargo ship **Thalia**. Confiscated as a war reparation, she was given to Russia in 1946 and renamed **Akademik Karpinsky**.

The Dutch-built **Hampshire Coast** was sold in 1945 for further service, attracting a high price that reflected the lack of available tonnage at that time. The elderly steamer **Galway Coast**, one time **Lady Wimborne** in the British & Irish fleet, was also sold.

Coast Lines made an initial approach for control of the Aberdeen Steam Navigation Company (see Graeme Somner 2000) once Germany surrendered on 2 May 1945.

Graeme Somner recorded:
> …in May 1945 an approach to the [Aberdeen] company was made by the Coast Lines group of Liverpool as to the possibility of buying out the company. A firm offer was received in June 1945 from the Tyne-Tees Steam Shipping Company of Newcastle (a company within the Coast Lines group) to take the [Aberdeen] company over, and this offer was accepted. It was all part of a move to rationalise coastal shipping in the light of the drift of passenger and cargo traffic from the sea to road and rail…

The [Aberdeen] company had already decided that passenger sailings would not be resumed when peace came because of the changed trading conditions, and the fact that the transportation of livestock at sea was no longer acceptable, further reducing the potential revenue of the company. The age and condition of the three passenger steamers anyway was such that to reintroduce them into service would be expensive, so steps were put in hand to sell them by Coast Lines.

The transfer of control to the Tyne-Tees Steam Shipping Company came about in November 1945, with the [Aberdeen] company then becoming Coast Lines' group agents at the same time. The new managers found that they had taken over an old an uneconomical fleet of four steamers, all heavily worked during the war, and all requiring extensive refurbishment.

The fleet that Tyne-Tees acquired comprised the passenger cargo ships **Aberdonian**, built in 1909, the **Harlaw** built in 1911 as GSN's **Swift** and the **Lochnagar** which was G & J Burns' Ardrossan steamer **Woodcock** when first commissioned in 1906. There was also the venerable cargo steamer **Koolga** acquired by the Aberdeen company in 1918 and built for Thomas Cowan of Leith in 1910. **Harlaw** and **Koolga** were put back into traffic with a new intermediate call at Newcastle as the Aberdeen, Newcastle & Hull Steam Company had then ceased trading.

Coast Lines sold the elderly cargo steamer **Cheshire Coast** in 1946. She had been completed as **Princess Irma** for Langlands in 1919 when Coast Lines acquired that company. The **Durham Coast**, originally H L Stocks & Company's **New Abbotshall**, and dating from 1911, was also sold.

An interesting purchase in January 1946 was the small passenger ship **Robina**, which had previously served the Ulster Steam Tender Company at Belfast. She had been built in 1914 as an excursion steamer to work at Morecambe, and after the Great War she occupied the same role at Blackpool before going to Belfast in 1925. The reason for her purchase was, as it turned out, not really justified. Her new role was that of an excursion ship based at Falmouth, but her draught was found to be too deep for much of the river work she was intended to do. In June that year she was chartered to David MacBrayne Limited and returned to her owners in February 1948.

The **Robina** (1914) was an unlikely purchase by Coast Lines. She was to be an excursion steamer at Falmouth but her draught was too deep for much of the river work.

The *Stuart Queen*, built in 1940, transferred from the British Channel Islands Shipping Company to Coast Lines and adopted the name *Hampshire Coast*. She had a large deadweight and was a useful unit on the Irish Sea routes. She is seen entering the River Ribble at Preston.

In 1946 the *Atlantic Coast* was equipped with radar; her master was sent on a one day radar training course. It was stressed on the course that radar was to be used alongside all the conventional tools of navigating in poor visibility and that normal precautions regarding speed and sounding of the whistle were still mandatory. The outcome of the trial was that all ships in the fleet received radar and their masters received training by the end of the year. Coast Lines also took part in trials with the new Decca Navigation system on behalf of the Ministry of Transport. The company was equally impressed with this equipment and all the ships within the group were equipped with the navigation system once it became commercially available.

At Aberdeen, the *Harlaw* and *Koolga* were displaced in October 1946 when the Tyne-Tees motor ship *Valerian Coast* was transferred from Newcastle to Aberdeen to maintain the weekly round trip between Aberdeen and London. The maiden departure of the *Valerian Coast* from Aberdeen took place on 24 October 1946. She sported a new funnel design with the traditional all yellow funnel of the Aberdeen company defaced by a broad green band.

Two new ships were ordered by Coast Lines from Hall, Russell & Company at Aberdeen to take over the Aberdeen service. The pair was an upgraded successor of the pioneer *British Coast* and *Atlantic Coast* built in 1933 and 1934. The new ships had accommodation for eleven passengers and were expected to take over the service to London by early 1948. Building of the two

new ships was slow as materials in postwar Britain were in short supply. Nevertheless, the first of the pair was launched on 27 September 1946, resplendent with a spotless white hull, and christened *Aberdonian Coast*. The local press reported the launch in the excited tones of heralding a new beginning of the Aberdeen to London service. Fitting out proceeded slowly but the new ship was finally set to take her maiden voyage via Newcastle on 1 June 1947. The *Aberdonian Coast* was built at a cost of £178,072. Her twin 8-cylinder oil engines were designed to provide a service speed of 14 knots.

Completion of the second of the new motor ships built at Aberdeen, *Caledonian Coast*, was seriously delayed when the casting of her engine bed plate was dropped at the iron works and had to be replaced. She was launched on 30 September 1947 but was ready for her maiden voyage south on 21 April 1948, this time with a black hull, the 'spotless' white of her sister having quickly been deemed impractical.

Graeme Somner again:

It was soon found that post-war labour conditions in the port of London made it difficult to maintain a passenger schedule, and when a 15-day strike took place in that port at the end of June 1948, the company decided to withdraw the passenger ships permanently. The sister ships were transferred to the ownership of the parent company, Coast Lines, at the beginning of July 1948, and then employed on the Liverpool - Dublin - south coast - London sailings instead.

The new **Caledonian Coast** (1948) when first commissioned for the Aberdeen Steam Navigation Company in 1948 before transferring to Coast Lines Liverpool to London service.

[W H Brown]

The **Aberdonian Coast** (1947) was renamed **Hibernian Coast** after transfer from Aberdeen to Liverpool.

The **Caledonian Coast** retained her name but the **Aberdonian Coast** was renamed **Hibernian Coast**. The passenger and cargo ships were replaced at Aberdeen by the cargo only ships **Hadrian Coast**, ex-**Empire Atoll** (see Chapter 7), now with her refrigerating machinery removed, and **Valerian Coast**, both from Tyne-Tees Steam Navigation Company.

A third new passenger and cargo ship, **Pacific Coast**, was launched from the Ardrossan Dockyard on 9 January 1947, being a direct replacement for her namesake lost in the war. She was fitted with two 6-cylinder oil engines built by British Polar Engines, a company previously known as British Auxiliaries Limited. The **Pacific Coast** had berths for 12 passengers and on delivery joined the pre-war built **Ocean Coast** to serve from Liverpool to London via Falmouth and Southampton and returning north via Cork. The slightly faster **Caledonian Coast** and **Hibernian Coast** returned from London to Liverpool via Dublin. Meanwhile the other pair of passenger cargo ships, **Atlantic Coast** and **British Coast**, had their passenger accommodation removed and tended to work the Kirkcaldy to London lino trade and occasionally the Newcastle to Belfast service.

Above: The **Pacific Coast** (1947) was a passenger and cargo ship built as a replacement for her namesake which was lost in the war as a petrol carrier.

Right: The **British Coast** (1933) discharging cargo into a lighter at Falmouth before being transferred to the London to Kirkcaldy service in a cargo-only mode.

[George Robins]

70

The Coast Lines group embarked on a major renovation and rebuilding programme to get its cross channel services back up to strength. The compensation for losses did not pay for new ships as postwar prices had escalated considerably during and immediately after the war. The *Leinster* transferred from Coast Lines' ownership to the Belfast Steamship Company for a consideration of £300,000, was refurbished and renamed *Ulster Prince*; she was set to work alongside the *Ulster Monarch*. The pair were well matched having an almost identical saloon class lay out and being of similar deadweight. The Belfast nightly service to Liverpool resumed in December 1945 when the *Longford* was able to join the *Louth* on the service. The *Ulster Prince* started on the service in February 1946 and the *Ulster Monarch* followed in August displacing the older ships.

Burns & Laird Lines' Glasgow and Belfast route recommenced once their *Royal Ulsterman* and *Royal Scotsman* were refurbished.

The Dublin to Liverpool service eventually received two new composite motor ships, again named *Leinster* and *Munster*. They had less saloon passenger accommodation than their predecessors but critically were equipped for the carriage of live cattle providing an all-year-round source of income, while the passenger revenue fell significantly in the winter months.

The Cork to Fishguard route received a smaller version of the Dublin sisters when a new *Innisfallen* entered service in June 1948.

The *Innisfallen* (1948) lying alongside at Fishguard Harbour preparing for her evening departure to Cork.

[author]

At the end of 1946 Sir Alfred Read stood down as Managing Director of Coast Lines and its associated companies and was succeeded by Arnet Robinson.

In 1947 Coast Lines' *Cambrian Coast* and *Ayrshire Coast* went to the Belfast Steamship Company to assist with cargo work between Belfast and the Mersey and Manchester. They adopted the new names *Ulster Merchant* and *Ulster Mariner*. The Dutch-built motorship *Saxon Queen* came from the British Channel Traders Limited fleet into that of Coast Lines as *Dorset Coast*. She was a useful unit although of modest deadweight capacity. The big steamer *Glamorgan Coast* replaced her in the fleet of British Channel Traders Limited and was given the name *Stuart Queen*. Bristol Channel Traders was restyled as Queenship Navigation Limited of London later in the year.

A new *Devon Coast* entered the Coast Lines' fleet in 1947. She was bought from John Stewart & Company (Shipping) Limited of Glasgow. The *Devon Coast* was a large, single deck, engines aft motor ship that had been built in Fife in 1937. She was a useful unit for the bulk trades and was often allocated to the Ford Motor Company charter work from Dagenham to Cork.

The **Devon Coast** (1937) was acquired second hand specifically for the charter service between Dagenham and Cork with cars for the Ford Motor Company.

A new ship was launched at Ardrossan on 27 November 1947 intended for A Coker & Company Limited with the name **Baltic Queen**. She too was a twin screw motor ship equipped with 8-cylinder British Polar oil engines to provide a service speed of 13 knots. She was a raised quarter deck vessel with engines and accommodation amidships – quite unlike any other vessel in the Coast Lines group. In the event, she was completed for Coast Lines as **Baltic Coast**, when delivered early in 1948, and immediately chartered to A Coker & Company Limited, Liverpool. Coker had been acquired by Coast Lines during the war and acted as agents and ship managers, trading largely with chartered tonnage to the Baltic from Manchester.

In February 1947 the Island Shipping Company was created by British Channel Island Shipping Company (Guernsey) Limited, expressly to run a passenger link between St Peter Port and Sark.

Godfrey Ford wrote in *Sea Breezes*, September 1953:
> ...two ex-Admiralty vessels were purchased to inaugurate the service. The smaller one, the **Herm Coast**, a motor fishing vessel, was a good sea boat and suitable for carrying cargo and a small number

of passengers all the year round. The larger one, the **Sark Coast**, an ex-landing craft, was put into the hands of Camper & Nicholson of Southampton for conversion to a passenger carrier. Unfortunately, owing to labour troubles, the conversion took much longer than anticipated and the vessel did not come into service until nearly the end of the summer season...

The next season a determined effort was made to secure the tourist traffic by chartering the passenger steamer **Robina** from Coast Lines Ltd., which with the **Sark Coast** would cater for all passenger requirements and, it was hoped, would discourage a rival enterprise which had just started up. The venture was ill-fated, however, as on June 5, 1948, the **Robina**, after being on the run for a very short time, collided with the **Herm Coast** while approaching Sark in restricted waters, resulting in damage to herself and the sinking of the smaller vessel. No lives were lost and the **Herm Coast** was raised, but the accident crippled the service and after running the **Sark Coast** for the rest of that season the company decided to cut its losses and discontinue the inter-island service.

The former landing craft **Sark Coast** (1945) at her moorings at Creux Harbour, Sark, in 1948. She came into Coast Lines' ownership in 1950, and was sold in 1952.

The **Robina** returned to Plymouth to lay up mid-season and was sold in 1949 for use at Southampton. The **Sark Coast** was sent to Great Yarmouth to lay up. In 1950 her ownership transferred to Coast Lines and it was only in 1952 that she was sold for further service.

A significant threat to the Irish traffic had emerged. The arrival of Frank Bustard's former Landing Ship, Tank **Empire Cedric** at Preston in May 1948 was not initially of concern to the Coast Lines' board. Bustard had been able to charter a number of these redundant ships from the Ministry of Transport for just £500 per week.

Although Bustard had to find the cash to install crew accommodation, attend to bulkheads around the boiler and engine spaces and bring the ships into line with commercial regulations, the ports of Preston and Larne were keen to offer linkspan facilities at little cost to the operator. After a shaky start the new service eventually attracted the shippers, a key feature being lorry-loaded goods taken from factory door to consumer without intermediate handling. Another attraction was that the rate charged depended on the volume of the lorry not on the product, its type and weight as required by the existing Irish Sea Conferences.

One of the Landing Ships, Tank converted for use by Atlantic Steamship Company Limited between Preston and Larne was the **Empire Nordic** (1945) seen here arriving at Preston.   *[author]*

Coast Lines began to watch the development of the new service keenly. A recommendation was prepared for the board that they take the new company head on by starting another roll-on roll-off service from Liverpool directly to Belfast. However, this it could not pursue because such a move would be in direct contravention of the Belfast Conference in which the newly nationalised British Railways was a key signatory. The alternative approach was to buy the company outright; operating from Preston would circumnavigate the Conference rules. In the event, Coast Lines was too slow off the mark and, ultimately, the British Transport Commission invested in Frank Bustard's Atlantic Steam Navigation Company in April 1953 (see Cowsill, 1990) on the premise that it was a logical extension to its haulage operations carried out under the nationalised banner British Road Services. Coast Lines' inability to grasp the new technology and run with it was to be the beginning of the end of the entire group – just as the loss of the **Titanic** in 1912 had been the beginning of the end of the White Star Line.

The **Lady Connaught**, which had been laid up since the end of the war, was earmarked as the successor to the pre-war cruise ship **Killarney**. The **Killarney** had spent much of the war as a depot ship at Rosyth, was no longer serviceable and was sold in 1947. The **Lady Connaught**,

however, was ideally suited for the role given the substantial modifications she received as a hospital ship in the war which promoted one class accommodation, and given her reduced speed subsequent to her being damaged by a mine in December 1940. She was transferred to Coast Lines from British & Irish ownership in 1947.

Robert Forsyth described the conversion:
> She was beautifully fitted out for her new career with a restaurant seating 100 on the main deck and a spacious entrance saloon combining the staircases to the main and promenade decks into which was built a chief steward's office for the reception of passengers. She even had a card room on her lower main deck and a timbered smoke room on her boat deck. With her hull painted buff, the same shade as that used in the prewar **Munster** and **Leinster**, a funnel of the same colour, white upperworks and green boot topping she left Belfast for Liverpool under the command appropriately, of Captain Peter Mullan. Without his courage and seamanship, she would simply have been just another wartime wreck awaiting clearance in the Mersey approaches. She was renamed **Lady Killarney**, perhaps a little awkwardly combining her own and her predecessor's name.

The cruising yacht **Lady Killarney** (1911) lying alongside Princes Landing Stage at Liverpool – a new role for a well-travelled ship.

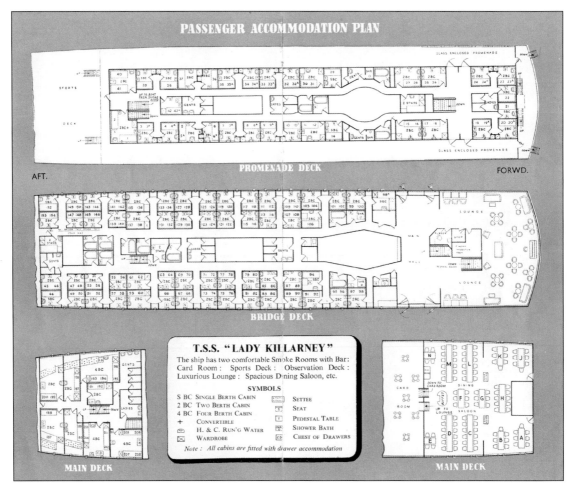

Accommodation plan for **Lady Killarney**.

The cargo traffic from Belfast to Liverpool and Manchester continued to expand and on 1 July 1948 the elderly **Lancashire Coast** was transferred at a book price of £1,000 to become Belfast Steamship's **Ulster Hero**.

The Dutch-built **Suffolk Coast** had her German oil engine replaced during 1948. She was equipped with a British Auxiliaries engine which increased her speed from a nominal 9 knots to a secure 10 knots. The **Denbigh Coast**, on the Liverpool to Bristol Channel and Penzance route, was dealt with similarly the following year, and the **Dorset Coast** in 1950.

The last of the Falmouth tenders was disposed of in 1949 when the **Cornish Coast** was sold to M H Bland & Company for similar duties at Gibraltar. From then on local contractors were used for transhipment of goods. A unique ship in the entire group was commissioned in 1949, the **Adriatic Coast**. She was ordered from Hall Russell & Company Limited at Aberdeen and equipped with the now standard British Auxiliaries 8-cylinder oil engine. Engines, of course were aft, but so too were the bridge and accommodation. She had three hatches, No 1 in the forward well deck served by a single derrick, and numbers 2 and 3 each served by cranes.

A one-off new build was the **Adriatic Coast** (1949) with engines and accommodation aft and three hatches forward, Nos 2 and 3 served by electric cranes.

Also in 1949, an important purchase, that of the Zillah Shipping and Carrying Company, managed by William A Savage Limited, was completed for a sum of £450,000. The company had fifteen steam coasters mostly employed in the coastal bulk cargo tramp trades. The tramp trades took the ships far and wide and most of the masters had foreign going certificates. All the ships names finished with the suffix **-field**.

Following the acquisition, the **Orkney Coast**, formerly the **Fire Queen** in the Gilchrist fleet, was transferred to Zillah as **Dransfield**. Under Coast Lines' ownership the company was rebranded as Zillah Shipping Company Limited and the steamers were all replaced by neat engines-aft motor ships by 1958, many bought on the second-hand market from Dutch shipowners.

Two ships were transferred to the Belfast Steamship Company in 1949, at a concession of £1,000 each. On 27 August 1949 the **Avon Coast** was renamed **Ulster Star** and on 3 September the **Medway Coast** was given

the Belfast name **Ulster Duchess**. The ships had been acquired before the war from the remnants of Fisher-Renwick, Manchester London Steamers Limited.

For some time, Coast Lines had been interested in the South African coastal trades centred on Cape Town, and in particular in Thesen's Steamship Company which owned and managed ships under the trading banner Union Steamship Company, South Africa. The original company had been established in the late 1860s by two Norwegian brothers. In 1926 the Houston Line of London purchased the assets and goodwill of the company after it had been facing losses due to competitive road and rail freights. The Houston Line, which later sold the company to Mitchell Cotts who also owned the Saint Line from 1937, increased the earnings of the Thesen's company by expanding the geographical coverage of the coastal service to both Indian Ocean ports and the Atlantic coast. Purchase of shares by Coast Lines led to its majority interest in Thesen's by 1949.

Coast Lines' holdings in South Africa were then rebranded Coast Lines (Africa) Pty although the Thesen's and Union Shipping banners were retained as trading names. However, the ships had the suffix 'Coast' added to their names in due course.

The move into South African waters reflected the recognition that the Coast Lines group had pretty much saturated the domestic coastal, Irish cross-channel and near Continental trades. Coast Lines was aware that it needed to raise its sights if it were to expand further. It is notable that the General Steam Navigation Company did exactly the same thing when it invested in a Canadian enterprise in 1955, and tried to emulate Coast Lines efforts in South Africa two years later - GSN also recognising that it had saturated its core trades and could expand no more. However, the risks involved in stepping out into the unknown were considerable and GSN barely turned a profit on its foreign ventures. Coast Lines did have a handle on the South African coastal market through its longstanding transhipment agreement with the Union-Castle Line at Southampton and London; Thesen's provided the same service principally between Cape Town and Natal, sometimes beyond. Investment in Thesen's was, nevertheless, a bold move.

Two United States wartime standard freighters, *William Bursley* and *Gurden Gates*, were bought in 1949. Glen & Company of Glasgow also successfully bid for ships, while many others went to overseas owners. They were N3-S-A1 type ships, the so called 'Yankee Jeep', of 1,791 tons gross, equipped with a single triple expansion steam engine and had a service speed of 10 knots. Nearly all of the class were built at yards in Superior on the Great Lakes. Thirty-one ships of the class were delivered, most of them in 1943, each coal-fired rather than oil-fired at the request of the British, for charter to the Ministry of War Transport. They were full scantling ships with a length of 260 feet and a deadweight capacity of 2,900 tons. Engines and accommodation were amidships and there were two hatches in the forward well deck and two in the aft well deck. They required a crew complement of 23 men. They were single deck ships and had an attractive cruiser stern and were known collectively with their oil-fired counterparts as the Baltic Type Coaster.

The *William Bursley* was ceded to Coast Lines new venture in South Africa, Coast Lines (Africa) Pty Limited, and registered at London under the name *Damara*. The *Gurden Gates* was placed in the ownership of A Coker & Company Limited and given the name *Baltic Queen*; ownership of the *Baltic Queen* reverted to Coast Lines Limited within the year when Coker was sold by Coast Lines for just £12,000. Both ships were sold to the same Italian shipowner in 1950 having in the meantime provided useful tonnage until new ships could be commissioned.

Coast Lines' elderly steamer *Somerset Coast* transferred to the Belfast, Mersey & Manchester Steamship Company in 1950 and was given the new name *Mountstewart*. Sir Alfred retired as Chairman on 31 March 1950 at the end of a remarkable career. He was succeeded by Captain A R S Nutting OBE, who for some time had been Vice Chairman of Coast Lines. Captain Nutting had served on the Board for many years. His first contact with Coast Lines was when Alfred Read approached the Bank of Ireland for loans to build the *Ulster Monarch* and her sisters in the 1920s; at that time Captain Nutting was Governor of the Bank of Ireland.

The new Chairman's first task was to authorise the refinancing of Coast Lines Limited in order to consolidate debts owing from the post-war rebuilding programme. The post-war years had cost the company dearly while it strove to recover from its wartime losses and rebuild its business. The total debt at this time was about £2 million. Nevertheless, reassurance was gained from both the Belfast Steamship Company and Burns & Laird Lines which had enjoyed buoyant freight demand, while Irish cattle continued to bring year-round income to both companies.

Much of Coast Lines' core trade, however, was in competition with both rail and road and since both had been nationalised in 1948 the rules of combat had become blurred and Coast Lines increasingly lost trade to the two government-owned mega- groups. Coast Lines also needed to do some clear-headed thinking about roll-on roll-off traffic; it also needed to look at the unit load trade which was beginning to appear on the Irish Sea.

Baltic Queen (1943) laid up at Liverpool alongside the redundant British & Irish passenger steamer *Longford* during 1950.

CHAPTER 9

'MINI LINERS' – THE EARLY 1950s

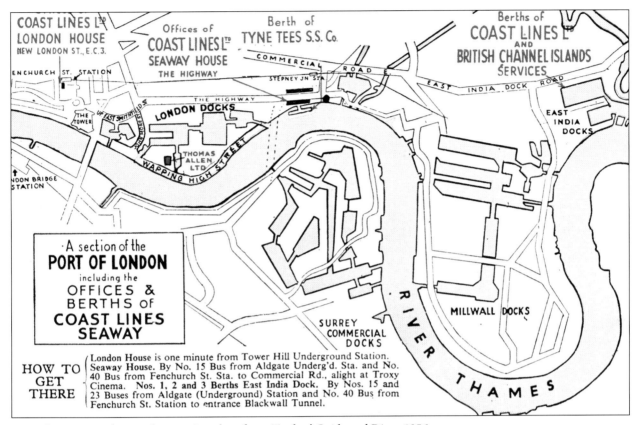

Map of Coast Lines' power bases at London, from *Traders' Guide and Diary 1956.*

With the retirement of Alfred Read, management of the group moved from London to Liverpool.

The new board of Coast Lines Limited neither focused its energies on roll-on roll-off traffic nor unit load systems. Bearing in mind that a roll-on roll-off ferry had been introduced on the railway-operated Stranraer to Larne service in 1939 by the first ***Princess Victoria***, and reintroduced in 1947 by the second ship of the same name, that the railways had operated an American-built tank landing craft, the ***Mowbray Road***, for wheeled freight between Belfast and Barrow in 1949, and that the Atlantic Steam Navigation Company Limited was busy carrying lorries between Preston and Larne, it is extraordinary that the Coast Lines' board made little effort to emulate these services. The unit load concept was also being applied by a number of carriers, not least British Railways, with the standard railway container, and even Coast Lines' own subsidiary David MacBrayne Limited had used large boxes to ease loading and unloading of small mixed consignments of goods for many years.

The vehicle deck aboard the ***Princess Victoria*** (1939), which operated briefly between Stranraer and Larne, and was mined and sunk in May 1940.

[University of Glasgow Business Records Archive]

What the board did focus on was a new 'mini-liner' to act as relief on all the group's cross-channel services and to serve between Glasgow and Dublin in summer. The estimated cost of the ship was just over £800,000 and to help cover this a loan of £400,000 was secured from the Ship Mortgage Finance Corporation with annual interest charges fixed at 4¾%. Specifications and design details were discussed with Harland & Wolff and within a short time Coast Lines committed to the construction of the new vessel.

The design of the ship was a monument to the 1920s successful design of the **Ulster Monarch** and all her consorts. But the world had moved on and a totally new specification was needed, in particular one that allowed for roll-on roll-off traffic, both accompanied private cars and lorry traffic. The design should also have allowed for unit load cargo handling rather than just for traditional break bulk goods. A further fundamental flaw was that the specification allowed for passenger berths on three decks providing facilities that would never be fully utilised on winter relief work, and rarely required on the Glasgow to Dublin seasonal summer service. The specification provided for 246 first class berths and 142 third class and a total passenger certificate for 750 in winter and 1,200 in summer. In addition, the specification included for permanent fittings for 138 head of live cattle and eight horses to be provided in the 'tween decks, while No 2 hold was to have restraining hooks set in the tween decks for 50 cars, every vehicle to be loaded and unloaded by crane. The board had acted extremely conservatively, but its members were very proud of their part in placing the order for their 'mini-liner'.

The board of Coast Lines at this time was clearly content with the favourable trading conditions of the early 1950s and with the consequent buoyant financial receipts. The complacency this generated throughout the whole group was extremely dangerous and would inevitably allow others to steal the march. Group policy stated that all vessels be maintained to high standards such that refit periods tended to be extensive; a policy that certainly contributed to the longevity of many of the ships. Crew quarters were always to be better than their competitors provided, and all ships were to be equipped with every safety and navigational device that was available. Laudable though this policy was, it said nothing about keeping up with new cargo handling techniques to provide greater efficiency and economic benefit to the shipper. This complacent attitude was prevalent for a number of years until, too late, the board slowly realised that their business was being overtaken by competitors.

The only company in the group that did successfully buy into the ro-ro concept was Tyne-Tees Steam Shipping Company (see Chapter 11). Belfast Steamship and Burns & Laird flirted with the new technology but it was at too late a stage in the development and adoption of the system elsewhere in the Irish Sea. Fortunately, the unit load system was taken up more earnestly and this did provide a lifeline for the Coast Lines' group. In the meantime, the directors placed more weight on their historical achievements than they did on the need for change.

Nevertheless, the returns for the year 1951 for the entire group showed that it had carried over 4 million tons of general cargo and 500,000 head of cattle. It also carried over 1 million passengers mainly on its overnight services to the north and south of Ireland. The business of the group was described as 'passenger and cargo lines operating to schedules; coastwise tramps available for charter as and when required; holiday cruises and voyages; wharves and stevedoring; and shiprepairing'. There were 109 vessels in the group in service at the end of 1951.

The 1950s were years of strong growth in a number of the coastal and Irish Sea sectors. The easterly flow of live cattle from Ireland was a major source of income within the group, with a variety of finished products and engineering goods returning back to Ireland. The cross-channel passenger trade thrived despite the arrival of the airplane, although passenger traffic was always seasonal with a winter decline in passenger numbers save for the Christmas and New Year period. The same was the case on the Liverpool to London passenger service which was now advertised as a summer cruise, with four ships operating throughout the year with calls either at Cork or Dublin on most northerly passages as well as the obligatory calls at Falmouth and Southampton. Passengers were no longer carried on the Belfast to Newcastle and Middlesbrough run which was reduced to a weekly service, while the Manchester to Leith service had been withdrawn after the war although cargo could still be transhipped at Belfast for eastern Scotland and north-east England.

The last of the engines aft, bridge and accommodation amidships cargo motor ships was commissioned in 1951, the **Western Coast**. She had been ordered from the Goole Shipbuilding & Repairing Company Limited, that company having tendered the lowest price and having considerably undercut the Ardrossan yard. The **Western Coast** was equipped with a 7-cylinder oil engine built by British Polar Engines Limited at Glasgow, and her design service speed of 12 knots was adequately achieved on trials. She was essentially similar to the earlier motor cargo ships built at Ardrossan.

The Coast Lines' fleet undertook a 20% downsizing in number during 1951. Three ships were chartered to the new African subsidiary. The **Baltic Coast** had been returned from A Coker and sailed for Cape Town early in 1951 and was renamed **Cape Coast** later in the year. The **Carrick Coast**, which with **Fife Coast** were the first motor cargo ships to be built for Coast Lines, was also chartered to Coast Lines (Africa) Pty Limited and given the name **Zulu Coast**. In addition, the **Dorset Coast** was chartered to Coast Lines (Africa) Pty Limited through the Union Steamship Company of South Africa Limited and renamed **Matabele Coast**; all three ships retained Liverpool as their port of registry. The existing ships managed by Thesen's Steamship Company of

Cape Town for the Union Steamship Company South Africa, and now owned by Coast Lines – the Dutch-built motor ships **Basuto** and **Namaqua** dating from 1937 and 1938 respectively, the steamship **Swazi** built in 1922 by W J Yarwood & Sons, Northwich, and the **Mashona** – were all given the suffix 'Coast' to their names in the period between 1951 and 1953. They were all small, engines aft, vessels of 246/247 tons gross.

The **Dorset Coast** (1938), built as **Saxon Queen** for the British Channel Islands company, went to Thesen's on charter and was renamed **Matabele Coast**.

Thesen's **Mashona** (1944) was renamed **Mashona Coast** in 1953. She was originally the standard 'Channel Tanker' **Chant 44**.

[T Rayner]

Also, during 1951, the **Denbigh Coast** went to Burns & Laird as **Lairdsfern**, the **Kentish Coast** to the British Channel Islands Shipping Company Limited without change of name, and the **Suffolk Coast** went to Tyne-Tees also without change of name. The chartering of six ships in total to other companies in the group represented a significant reduction in the Coast Lines' fleet. Lloyd's Register 1951/1952 shows a fleet of 23 ships of which just four were steamships (s), one of which was the seasonal cruise ship **Lady Killarney**, the remainder single and twin-screw (ts) motor ships (m), of which the **Sark Coast** was laid up awaiting sale:

	Year	Gross tons
m. **Adriatic Coast**	'49	1,050
m. **Anglian Coast** (ts)	'35	594
m. **Antrim Coast**	'37	646
m. **Atlantic Coast** (ts)	'34	890
m. **British Coast** (ts)	'34	889
m. **Caledonian Coast** (ts)	'48	1,265
m. **Cape Coast** (ts)	'48	1,722
m. **Clyde Coast**	'38	511
m. **Devon Coast**	'37	972
s. **Eastern Coast**	'22	1,223
s. **Hampshire Coast**	'41	1,224
m. **Hibernian Coast** (ts)	'47	1,258
s. **Lady Killarney** (ts)	'12	3,222
m. **Matabele Coast**	'38	500
m. **Mersey Coast**	'38	509
m. **Moray Coast**	'40	687
s. **Northern Coast**	'21	1,211
m. **Ocean Coast** (ts)	'35	1,173
m. **Pacific Coast** (ts)	'47	1,188
m. **Sark Coast** (ts)	'45	318
m. **Southern Coast**	'43	869
m. **Welsh Coast**	'38	646
m. **Zulu Coast**	'34	380

The Register states also that the Aberdeen Steam Navigation Company Limited owned one motor ship; the Belfast Steamship Company Limited two passenger motor ships and six steamships; British Channel Islands Shipping Company Limited three motor ships; the British & Irish Steam Packet Company Limited six motor ships, including three passenger ships, and five steamships; Burns & Laird Lines Limited ten motorships, including three passenger ships, and seven steamships; the Tyne-Tees Steam Shipping Company Limited owned eight motor ships and five steamships; and Zillah Shipping Company Limited sixteen steamships.

On 13 March 1952 the **Cape Coast**, on charter from Coast Lines to Coast Lines (Africa) Pty. Limited, was badly damaged by fire 8 miles from Boma in the River Congo on passage from Matadi, 92 miles up the River Congo, to Boma which is still 62 miles from the sea. She was on an extended voyage along the Atlantic coast as part of the new sailing schedule for the Union Steamship Company. The ship was beached in the river three days later, was declared a constructive total loss and left to the underwriters. She was later repaired and sold by the underwriters to give a further nine years commercial service before she was lost in a typhoon on passage from Kuching to Hong Kong.

The *Baltic Coast* (1947) seen in Table Bay wearing a Thesen's funnel but before adopting the new South African name *Cape Coast*.

[Andrew Duncan]

The **Hampshire Coast** transferred to the Tyne-Tees Steam Shipping Company in 1952 without change of name. But the big event of the year was the delivery of the 'mini liner' **Irish Coast** resplendent in full Coast Lines' livery – the pride and joy of the company directors. She was launched by the Chairman's wife, Mrs Nutting, as sponsor for the new ship which she proudly named **Irish Coast**. The ship was delivered to Coast Lines Limited on 16 October. Her maiden commercial voyage commenced at Liverpool on the evening of 1 November under Captain J Wilson, relieving the **Ulster Prince** on the overnight run to Belfast. The **Longford**, relief ship for some years, was decommissioned, laid up in Morpeth Dock and put up for sale.

The 'mini liner' *Irish Coast* (1952) seen on an evening departure from Glasgow for Dublin in July 1967.

[author]

Sea Breezes, April 1953 ran an article on the *Irish Coast*, which included a description of her public rooms:

On 'B' deck, in the entrance hall, panelled in white African mahogany, is the purser's bureau. Opposite this there is a smart little shop, with its bright window display. Opening from the entrance hall, the doors to the dining room have panels of ornamental glass, the design of which echoes the pattern in the damask curtains that are the key to the colour scheme of the dining room – crimson, white and gold. Crimson in the curtains and the deep leather upholstery of the dining chairs, white in the sycamore of the furniture and doors, and gold in the satinwood with which the walls are panelled. The unobtrusive electric lighting is assisted by small individual lamps on each table.

The lounge on 'A' deck is furnished in shades of soft rose and pastel blue, with full length curtains in a charming print material. The walls are panelled in tinted willow wood, which, owing to the way it catches the light, has a 'quilted' look. There is a fireplace containing a realistic log fire, with a surrounding hearth of 'peach blossom' marble. The furniture consists of easy chairs, and settees, all upholstered, card tables and writing tables. Specially woven rugs cover the deck and ample mirrors are provided.

On the promenade deck, the main smoking room, which has a fully equipped bar, is panelled in chestnut wood, and the window curtains have a pattern of chestnut leaves. Around the sides of the room is continuous seating upholstered in coral leather. The seats are divided by wide arms, so that each person sits in easy chair comfort. The armchairs and settees are also covered in hide, some coral coloured, and some blue, and there are two niches formed in the curved panelling, illuminated by concealed lights and embellished with hand-wrought ironwork.

Separate from the main suite of rooms is an intimate cocktail bar on the sun deck, recessed into the funnel. It is semi-circular in shape, with the bar at the focal point. Comfortable settees are fitted around the sides, and above them hangs a set of early 19th century sporting prints – Henry Aitkin's 'Casualties of the Hunting Field' – displayed to advantage on the limed oak panelling.

As was the custom in the early 1950s the cocktail bar was exclusively men only, woe betide any lady that should step over the threshold! The efficacy of this male haven was questioned right from the start when it was invaded by a bevy of ladies each night during a brief shakedown cruise with invited guests. The cruise called at Glasgow, Liverpool and Dublin and at each port the ship was open to the press for inspection.

Third class accommodation was aft and included a smoking room and cafeteria, adorned with neither panelling nor patterned curtains! Two- and four-berth cabins were available to hire and there were large male and female 'sleeping rooms'. There was also a large general room and a ladies' room. As with the other ships of this class, the third class passengers were remote from the life-saving equipment stowed in the central island which, of course, housed the first class passengers. Nevertheless, some life rafts were stowed aft and life jackets were available in numerous locations about the passenger accommodation.

The annual routine of the *Irish Coast* involved relieving the *Ulster Prince* and then the *Ulster Monarch* on the Liverpool and Belfast service from October to December after which she went onto the Fishguard and Cork roster to relieve the *Innisfallen* for her annual refit. In January and February the *Irish Coast* stood in for the *Munster* and *Leinster* on the Dublin and Liverpool service, and in March and April she was relief for both the *Royal Ulsterman* and *Royal Scotsman* on the Glasgow to Belfast route. In May and early June the *Irish Coast* stood down for her annual refit in time for her to commence her own service between Glasgow and Dublin towards the end of June. The Glasgow and Dublin service closed each year at the end of September.

On 7 April 1953 another Coast Lines' ship was lost while serving Thesen's operations when the *Zulu Coast*, built as *Carrick Coast*, was wrecked. She stranded in fog 2 miles north of the Groene River on a voyage from Cape Town to Port Nolloth with oil in drums and general cargo. Port Nolloth is at the mouth of the Orange River. The ship suffered badly in the heavy swell pounding the shore and was abandoned to the underwriters as a constructive total loss.

The *Carrick Coast* (1934), second of the new generation of motor ships built in the 1930s, was transferred to Thesen's in 1951 and renamed *Zulu Coast*.

The *Zulu Coast* was replaced by the *Herero Coast*. She had been completed in the Netherlands in 1950 for Dutch shipowners Kunst & Pekelder as *Poseidon*. She was purchased by Coast Lines Limited, renamed *Herero Coast* and chartered directly to the Union Steamship Company of South Africa Limited. Her Dutch-built 6-cylinder oil engine sustained a service speed of 9½ knots.

Flagship of the fleet, the *Irish Coast*, was proudly dispatched to Spithead in May 1953 for the Coronation Naval Review. She was commanded by Captain J Wilson as senior master of the Coast Lines group. The ship was home to a select gathering of invited guests for what was effectively a short cruise from Liverpool and back.

The *Lady Killarney* attracted quite a following with passengers rebooking aboard ship for their next cruise the following year. In 1953 she ran 13 cruises, starting on 15 May and finishing on 1 October. All the high season cruises between 5 June and 10 September were of 13 days duration, those outside this season were of six days duration all to a diverse programme of West Highland venues.

The 1953 brochure states:

> All cruises commence on Fridays. Passengers embark between 5 pm and 5.45 pm at Princes Landing Stage, Liverpool. The TSS *Lady Killarney* sails at 6 pm prompt and on return arrives at approximately 11 am.

The 1953 brochure for cruises operated by TSS *Lady Killarney*, now in full Coast Lines colours, her former pastel coloured hull being difficult to maintain.

A new style of shelter deck cargo ship was launched from the yard of Charles Hill & Sons Limited at Bristol on 18 November 1953. Named **Lancashire Coast** she was the first of two near-identical sisters with engines and accommodation aft and of just over 1,400 tons deadweight. She was fitted with a 5-cylinder Clark-Sulzer oil engine which provided a service speed of 12 knots. Her near sister, **Cheshire Coast**, was launched from the Birkenhead yard of Cammell Laird & Company on 6 January 1954. The pair had three hatches served by derricks capable of lifting ten tons. They were placed on the Belfast to Newcastle cargo service with intermediate calls at various Scottish ports as required, a service on which they quickly acquired a reputation for reliability.

The **Cheshire Coast** (1954) off the Waterloo Dock entrance at Liverpool wearing the red and black funnel of the Belfast Steamship Company.

[author]

On 20 September 1954, the new cargo ship **Fife Coast** was launched at George Brown (Marine) & Company at Greenock. She was a smaller version of the **Lancashire Coast** and **Cheshire Coast** with only two hatches but had an equally impressive array of cargo handling gear.

She was handed over to Coast Lines on 3 December. A near sister to the **Fife Coast**, the **Essex Coast** was delivered in 1955 having been launched at Ardrossan on 24 March. She was placed on the 'northabout' cargo service between Liverpool and Leith.

Launch of the **Fife Coast** (1954) at Greenock on 20 September 1954.

[George Brown & Company (Marine) Limited]

Coast Lines' management was clearly very pleased with its new ships and reported in the Coast Lines Seaway Traders Guide and Diary for 1956:

The advent of these vessels has enabled a number of our shippers and consignees and others interested in the coasting trade to visit the ships at their various ports of call and to see for themselves the vast improvements that have been made in the design and equipment of the modern coasting motor ship, and to meet officers, engineers and some of the crew responsible for navigating their valuable cargoes round the coasts of our islands. There is ample evidence to show that our visitors have invariably been pleased with their inspections, not only of the ships themselves, the mysteries of the navigating aids controlled from the bridge, and the modern and greatly improved officers' and men' quarters, but a number of the more energetic and perhaps more technically minded have been edified and impressed by a visit to the engine room.

The **Mersey Coast** was fitted with a new German made engine during 1953 providing her again with her prewar speed of 10½ knots. All in all, Coast Lines Limited appeared prosperous and returned a dividend of 7½% to its shareholders. The company was aware that it should be investing more in keeping abreast with the unit load and roll-on roll-off developments but for the moment it was content to pay its shareholders well, rather than cut the dividend and introduce new cargo handling techniques.

A number of the old steamers were disposed of in 1954. The old **Lancashire Coast**, **Ulster Hero** since 1948, **Cambrian Coast**, **Ulster Merchant** since 1947 and the **Northern Coast** were sold for demolition. Sister to **Northern Coast**, the **Eastern Coast** went for further service with a Bermudan owner. The **Northern Coast** and **Eastern Coast** were the last of the cargo steamships in the Coast Lines fleet, although the Belfast Steamship Company still had some. Also, during the year, the motor ship **Moray Coast** transferred to British Channel Island Shipping and became their **Jersey Coast**.

The *Jersey Coast* (1940) was built as the *Moray Coast* and was a product of the Ardrossan Dockyard.

The **Anglian Coast** was placed on charter to Thesen's Shipping Company in 1955 and renamed **Griqua Coast**. Her consort, the **Welsh Coast**, went that year to British Channel Islands Shipping and became their **Guernsey Coast**.

During 1954 two new initiatives posed threats to Coast Lines' business. The London-based Anglo-Continental Container Services chartered a vessel specifically for the carriage of containers between Preston and Larne. Until then it had sent the containers via the roll-on roll-off former landing craft operated by Atlantic Steam

Navigation Company as deck cargo. Within the year there were three ships on charter maintaining eight sailings per week through Preston. The second threat came from Northern Ireland Trailers, formed in 1953 to facilitate the carriage of open-topped boxes on existing services across the Irish Sea. In due course specially designed containers were introduced, and then the cargo ships **Stella Mary** and **Noach** were taken on charter followed by the steamship **Loch Linnhe** to operate regular services between Preston and Larne and Ardrossan and Larne. In addition, Atlantic Steam Navigation now had a twice daily service from Preston to Larne and one service a day to Belfast operated by four of its 'Empire' ships, each carrying lorries and trailers from far and wide along with available unit load cargoes. Plans were also in hand to build two purpose-built ships for wheeled and unit load traffic complete with luxury first class accommodation.

So just how did Coast Lines respond to this competition? The Coast Lines' board prepared a grossly flawed business plan to justify ordering, in 1955, a consort for the *Irish Coast*. The plan ignored all changing patterns of trade on the Irish Sea, again allowing for passengers' cars to be craned aboard, again disregarding the preference of many shippers for unit load transport and ignoring declining passenger numbers on the ferries due to increasing competition from air traffic. But worse, the plan was that the new ship was to be a direct replacement for the elderly *Lairdshill* on the year-round Glasgow to Dublin service, a service that carried few passengers in the winter months and relied on year-round income from Irish cattle shipments to Glasgow.

Neither the passenger traffic nor the live cattle trade was assured for anything approaching the 25 year design life of the proposed ship. The decision to place a firm order for another 'mini-liner' with Harland & Wolff at a cost of £1.13 million would tax not only Coast Lines Limited dearly, but place a financial burden on all component companies within the Coast Lines Group. This extraordinary head-in-the-sand decision on the part of the directors was a complete contrast to the conservative and steady years the company enjoyed under Sir Alfred Read; there is no plausible reason why they should need to order an obsolescent unit, virtually a repeat order of the *Irish Coast*, at great expense and for no justifiable reason, other than to satisfy their own personal pride.

Robert Sinclair wrote:

> The Ship Mortgage Finance Corporation was applied to for assistance but the board found it necessary to raise a further half million by way of a rights issue to finance this and other items of capital expenditure. There were arguments for building the *Irish Coast* and arguments against, but this ship was 'a luxury that Coast Lines could not afford'.

For better or worse, the new ship was launched on 21 August 1956, by Lady Glentoran, wife of the Northern Ireland Minister of Commerce… She was named *Scottish Coast* and was the last in a line of thirteen motor ships commencing with the *Ulster Monarch* in 1929 which had been built to the same general design for the Coast Lines Group. At her launch Captain Nutting observed ruefully that she had cost more than the combined cost of the *Ulster Monarch* and her two sisters twenty seven years before.

Throughout much of 1955 discussions took place with the Irish Government regarding the sale of the British & Irish Steam Packet Company. This company was suffering at the hands of the Irish trade unions that were established when the Irish Free State became the Republic of Ireland in 1949. As a consequence, the sharing of catering and engineering facilities at Liverpool was no longer possible and separate superintendents had now been established at Dublin.

This placed a significant cost on the company which Coast Lines did not wish to carry. Although the Irish Government was keen to buy the company, neither a realistic price could be agreed nor terms set in the interests of both parties. The British & Irish company remained in the group – and did so for the next ten years when the sale was, finally, agreed.

On 8 March 1955, Sir Alfred Read, at the age of 83, died peacefully at his retirement home in Lisbon. Royal Mail Lines brought his body home to England. After a short service at the Missions to Seamen at Southampton, his coffin was placed aboard the *Adriatic Coast* and he was buried, as he had wished, at sea. He was survived by his third wife, Lady Elsa Read. He had four children by his first marriage and a son by his third marriage. That year his former company returned a profit of just over £1.5 million and paid a handsome dividend of 10% to its shareholders, a signal that all was well. However, times were changing and Coast Lines was not yet party to that change.

The second 'mini liner' was intended as a replacement for Burns & Laird Lines' *Lairdshill* (1921) on the Glasgow and Dublin route, a ship with accommodation for just 80 first class passengers.

CHAPTER 10

MISSED OPPORTUNITIES 1956-1960

Coast Lines still had a diverse set of departures based at Liverpool via the West Waterloo river lock. The Falmouth, Plymouth, Southampton and London service, also calling at Penzance on return, was based at Bramley Moore Dock, West Side and Nelson Dock, West Side.

Sailings to and from Glasgow, Greenock and Ardrossan were handled at Trafalgar Dock, West Side, and to Aberdeen, Dundee, Leith, Inverness and Moray Firth Ports, Kirkcaldy, Stornoway, Newcastle and Middlesbrough from Trafalgar Dock East Side. Nelson Dock, North Side dealt with sailings to and from Bristol, Avonmouth, Cardiff, Swansea, Newport, Milford Haven and south coast ports. Princes Dock North Side was still home to the British & Irish Steam Packet overnight

passenger service and South Side to the Belfast Steamship Company passenger service.

Coast Lines' second mini liner, the **Scottish Coast**, was launched in August 1956. She was destined to become an expensive burden on the resources of the company built to a design that made her obsolete before she was even delivered.

The 1938 Dutch-built motor ship **Clyde Coast** had her black funnel and white chevron painted over in the crimson and red of the Belfast Steamship Company when she was transferred in 1956. She was renamed **Ulster Senator** and placed on the Liverpool and Londonderry service.

The *Clyde Coast* (1938), seen here in the River Avon, transferred to the Belfast Steamship Company in 1956 and was renamed *Ulster Senator*.

[Richard Parsons collection]

The cruise ship **Lady Killarney** carried out her final cruise season in 1956. The ship had been losing money over the previous two years, not because she was under patronised but because her money-making season was short and her year-round upkeep increasingly expensive. The ship had even been given new boilers only two years previously and was fit for a few more seasons work.

The **Lady Killarney** had evolved since she was first introduced by Coast Lines as a seasonal cruise vessel in 1947. Her yellow hull had been painted over in a more practical dark green in time for the 1950 season and in 1952 she appeared in full Coast Lines' livery save

that she had red boot topping instead of the customary black. She was originally equipped with 172 cabins but this was increased to 200 in the 1947/48 winter refit. Her final cruise left Liverpool on Friday 21 September and she retuned back to Princes Landing Stage the following Thursday, moving across the river to lay up in Wallasey Dock. She was sold to the British Iron & Steel Corporation and left Liverpool under tow for Port Glasgow just before Christmas 1956. It was widely believed that the **Irish Coast** would operate some cruises in 1957, but this was not the case as the **Irish Coast** was committed to ferry duties throughout the cruising season.

Advertisement for the final summer of yachting cruises to
the Western Isles by *Lady Killarney* in 1956.

Passenger list and menu TSS *Lady Killarney*.

Cruises were resumed in 1958 by British Railways using the Heysham to Belfast steam turbine ferry **Duke of Lancaster**. Not as well appointed as the Coast Lines' ferries, she nevertheless took on the role of cruise ship in spring and autumn, and roamed as far south as Portugal and as far north as Norway. Captain J B Wright from the Belfast Steamship Company, and former master of the **Lady Killarney**, usually accompanied the **Duke of Lancaster** as pilot, whenever she visited the Western Isles. The **Duke of Lancaster** completed her last cruise to the Western Isles in 1963.

Ominously Coast Lines Limited returned a profit of just £1.1 million in 1956 – a 26% fall against the previous year's profit. This reflected the increased wheeled freight on the Preston to Larne and Belfast service of the Atlantic Steamship Company Limited, now trading under the banner The Transport Ferry Service, and of the unit load services operated by Anglo-Continental Container Services. There was also a drop in passenger numbers as the business community increasingly looked to the new air services operating between a variety of centres in England and Scotland to Belfast and Dublin. Coast Lines had been confident that this would not happen as people preferred the comfort and hospitality of the ships rather than the process of flying. What had been overlooked, of course, was the time saving in travelling by air, which in business terms was money saved.

A brief respite to the roll-on roll-off onslaught from the Atlantic Steamship Company was given from an unexpected quarter at the end of July 1956. Until then services at Preston were maintained by the **Empire Cedric**, **Empire Cymric**, **Empire Doric**, **Empire Gaelic** and **Empire Nordic**. The Suez Crisis, caused by the Egyptian Government seizing the Suez Canal, required all the Empire ships under management of the Atlantic Steamship Company, including those on commercial service, to be made ready by mid-August to sail for the Mediterranean. After a period of inactivity several of the ships left with troops and their equipment for Port Said after a call at Malta. Ferry duties in the eastern Mediterranean followed before the Preston-based ships returned in January 1957. Seven coasters had been chartered to maintain the unit load traffic but no trailers or lorries had been shipped out of Preston or Larne in the interim.

The respite was short lived and had a sting in the tale. On 2 September 1957 the new vehicle and unit load ship **Bardic Ferry** entered service between Preston and Larne, followed in October the following year by sister ship **Ionic Ferry**. The **Bardic Ferry** was state-of-the-art and should have been the final wake-up call for the Coast Lines' board. She could accommodate about 60 lorries and trailers on the main deck which was accessed by a stern ramp. The headroom on this deck was enough for even the highest vehicles then allowed on the roads, and the deck was strengthened should the military ever require the ships to transport heavy vehicles and tanks. On the upper deck aft, 20 containers could be stowed with the ships' own 20 ton deck crane. Passenger accommodation comprised berths for 55 passengers in two classes with separate dining rooms and lounges. Wake-up call or not, the directors of Coast Lines appeared to take little heed of the blossoming of Frank Bustard's original vision, a vision that had come to reality with funding subsequent to the purchase of the company by the British Transport Commission in April 1954.

The **Ionic Ferry** (1958) arriving from Larne below Preston Dock in the River Ribble. Note the crane aft to handle unit loads and the large access to the vehicle deck.

[author]

On New Year's Day 1957 Coast Lines forsook its offices in the Royal Liver Building as the lease had expired, and moved to premises at Water Street. The company chose newly-completed offices owned by the Reliance Marine Insurance Company; Managing Director, Arnet Robinson was also a Director of the Insurance Company and a favourable lease for the third and fourth floors of the building was obtained along with space for a large passenger booking office on the lower ground floor.

The new *Scottish Coast* took her maiden voyage on 4 March 1957. Unlike the *Irish Coast*, the *Scottish Coast* initially wore the funnel colours of the Belfast Steamship Company and shortly afterwards adopted the colours of Burns & Laird Lines Limited. Although the

outline of the Coast Lines' chevron was picked out by rivet heads on the funnel, the new ship was destined never to wear her owners colours. Her lifeboats did carry an embossed Coast Lines' ensign in full colour alongside the ship's name throughout the career of the ship under the Red Ensign.

But despite the error of ordering the ship in the first place, the *Scottish Coast* was a most attractive looking vessel, very much the pinnacle of conventional ferry design on the Irish Sea. Her saloon restaurant was decorated in a Highland theme, no doubt thought appropriate for a ship intended to spend her career sailing between the Clyde and the Liffey.

The traditional ferry design of the *Scottish Coast* (1957) was obsolete before she was commissioned, but she was an attractive and well-proportioned ship. She is seen here at Dublin.

Technically, like her earlier sister, the ship was built to a high standard. She was propelled by two trunk type 10-cylinder airless injection Harland-B&W oil engines working on the two-stroke cycle. There were two continuous steel decks and a lower deck forward and aft of the machinery space, together with poop, bridge, forecastle, sun and navigating bridge decks. The hull was divided into twelve watertight compartments and the double bottom was divided for fresh water, water ballast and oil fuel with the forward and after peaks arranged for water ballast along with a large trimming tank for water ballast forward. The ship was equipped with a fire detection system and a CO_2 fire extinguishing system. Like the *Irish Coast*, she had stabilizers, a bow rudder

and electro-hydraulically operated steering gear. This was the very last cross-channel ship on the Irish Sea to be equipped with an 80-seater restaurant offering full silver service and all the comforts that a passenger travelling to New York would expect aboard one of Cunard's prestigious liners.

The *Scottish Coast* completed her first job in July 1957, standing in for the *Ulster Monarch* which was on extended refit in Belfast. She then commenced on the Glasgow and Dublin service for which she was intended, making three round trips per week. Her funnel was repainted in Burns & Laird Line colours with a pale blue band between the black and red parts of the funnel.

The former incumbent, *Lairdshill*, was withdrawn and put on the sale list. At the end of November, the *Scottish Coast* was registered in the name of Burns & Laird although she was not officially transferred to them until the following year.

The elderly turbine steamer *Lairds Isle* completed her final summer season on the Burns & Laird daylight service between Ardrossan and Belfast at the end of August 1957. Facing an expensive special survey, she was disposed of. Her role on the seasonal daylight service was taken up in 1958 by the *Irish Coast*, still in full Coast Lines' ownership and Coast Lines' livery. She was not quite as fast as the old turbine steamer and required over five hours for the crossing. It is extraordinary that an overnight ferry with berths for over 300 passengers should be placed on a day service in which the doors to a high proportion of her gross tonnage were kept locked and the holds were almost empty, there being no time for cargo handling at Belfast before the return sailing! That being said, the ship was successful on the route in that, generally, she had good passenger loadings. Between the autumn and spring she maintained her relief programme working on the other passenger routes operated by the group.

The recently completed *Essex Coast* left the Coast Lines' fleet in 1957 when she passed to the Belfast, Mersey and Manchester Steamship Company to become their *Mountstewart*. It is interesting that the new units delivered in the 1950s differed from their predecessors in that they were bridge and accommodation aft but more specifically in that they had greater deadweight. The *Essex Coast* was typical of this trend. The need for larger ships was simply economy of scale, but it overlooked the greater time required for cargo handling at each port and the consequent loss of sea time available to the larger ships. In reality they provided no tangible economic benefit to the company, only a complete rethink of cargo handling methodology could do this for Coast Lines Limited and its associate companies.

In the face of the economy of scale the small motor ship *Cambrian Coast* was purchased. She had been built by N.V. IJsselwerf, Rotterdam for Rederij Holland N.V. as *Jan T*. She was a small ship of just 524 tons gross, but of useful capacity for some of the lesser capacity routes served within the Coast Lines group. She was mainly employed on the Ardrossan to Larne cargo route which also handled some unit load traffic.

The *Cambrian Coast* (1957) passing the Crosby Light. She was bought as an almost new ship from her Dutch owners.

[FotoFlite]

The directors of Coast Lines had one more trick up their sleeves on how to lose money. Until now Coast Lines had acquired other companies in order to expand its business and to quell competition. For some inexplicable reason, in 1958, they opted to buy William Sloan & Company Limited. This company operated cargo-liner services with ancient steamships weekly between Glasgow and Bristol Channel ports, including Swansea, Cardiff and Bristol, and twice-weekly between Belfast and Bristol. The services were losing money, the assets were antiquated, the company was grossly undercapitalised and the future looked gloomy in the face of containerisation and more efficient road haulage.

Graham Langmuir and Graeme Somner describe what happened in their history of William Sloan:

Great changes occurred in June 1958 when the issued share capital of William Sloan & Company Limited was bought by Coast Lines Limited of Liverpool. The company name was retained but its significance became eroded as sailings were modified and finally integrated into those of the Coast Lines group of companies. Within a very short time of this change in control, Coast Lines transferred two of their motor vessels to the Clyde-Bristol Channel sailings. These were the **Fife Coast** (1954) and **Western Coast** (1951), which took the names **Fruin** and **Tay** respectively in 1958. Soon afterwards **Annan** (1907), the faithful coal burner, was sent to breakers in Holland, having served the company for 51 years.

William Sloan & Company in its day had been a highly successful coastal liner company. It dated from 1825 when schooners were used in the chemical trade from Glasgow via the Forth & Clyde Canal to Newcastle, Hull and London. From 1858 the company focussed on the Glasgow and Bristol Channel trades, with calls at Belfast and ports along the South Wales coast terminating at Bristol. In 1891 the company bought the Silloth to Dublin service of Robert Henderson and later ordered the new passenger and cargo ship **Yarrow** for this service. The Bristol ships carried up to 70 passengers, until in 1932 it was deemed best to remove the passenger accommodation, demand having seriously declined with the Recession, reduce the gross tonnage and focus on general cargo only.

The **Western Coast** (1951) transferred to newly acquired William Sloan & Company Limited in 1958 and was renamed **Tay**.

The **Lairdsfern** came back into Coast Lines' ownership in 1958 taking up her former name of **Denbigh Coast**. The **Kentish Coast** was returned from British Channel Island Shipping while the status quo was retained when the **Mersey Coast** passed to that company without change of name.

The single deck motor ship **Somerset Coast** was purchased from Clelands (Successors) Ltd, Wallsend-on-Tyne, early in 1958. She had a large deadweight of 1,734 tons and was equipped with a 7-cylinder oil engine built by British Polar Engines at Glasgow which provided a service speed of 11 knots. She had been ordered by Williamstown Shipping Company Limited, Comben, Longstaff & Company Limited, as **Somersetbrook** and the order was taken over by Coast Lines shortly before the ship was launched on 20 March 1958. Coast Lines took delivery of the ship in August. She had three hatches each served by a single 10 ton derrick. She was used on a variety of services including the Dagenham to Cork cargo service which was operated for the Ford Motor Company.

The **Somerset Coast** (1958) was ordered as **Somersetbrook** for Comben Longstaff & Company Limited and completed for Coast Lines.

[T Rayner]

More importantly in 1958 Coast Lines finally recognised the need to encompass the unit load system. Until now it had dealt with containers, including the standard railway containers, on an ad hoc basis accommodating them as deck cargo or on the passenger ships in the 'tween decks. However, the Directors were not willing to fund new ships and looked around their empire for vessels suitable for conversion. To this end the Zillah single deck general cargo ships **Brentfield** and **Birchfield**, built in 1956 and 1957 by George Brown & Company (Marine) Limited at Greenock and the Ardrossan Dockyard Company respectively, were transferred and placed under direct Coast Lines' ownership on 4 December. The ships had a 7-cylinder Clark-Sulzer oil engine that provided a service speed slightly in excess of 11 knots, and had been designed for the general coastal tramping trades where prospects had weakened since the ships were commissioned. As built, they had three hatches and three holds, the hatches were served by one 3-ton and two 6-ton derricks operated by hydraulic winches.

The *Brentfield* (1955) seen on trials before delivery to Zillah Shipping Company for use in the charter market.

[George Brown & Company (Marine) Limited]

The ships were dispatched to Ardrossan for conversion to unit load carriers. They had Nos 2 and 3 hatches plated over to give a flush deck for the carriage of containers, and all the deck cargo handling gear was removed. The deep tank amidships and the coffer dam abaft No 3 hold were removed to provide a single 130 feet long unobstructed hold space. In addition, the mainmast was removed and replaced with a lighter structure on the monkey island above the bridge. The **Brentfield** was given the traditional J & G Burns name **Spaniel** and the **Birchfield** became **Pointer**. Their funnels were painted in the colours of the newly-created Link Line Limited, black with a coloured chevron: green, with a red inner band. The ships required a crew of 14 who enjoyed comfortably appointed accommodation.

The *Spaniel* (1955), ex-*Brentfield*, after conversion to unit load carrier; note the mixed nature of the unit loads on deck.

[author]

The *Spaniel* and *Pointer* carried 36 trailers and containers, the trailers stowed below deck along with the majority of the containers, while twelve containers three abreast could be carried on the flush deck aft of the single hatch. Each ship was scheduled to arrive alongside ready to start discharging at Liverpool and at Belfast by 8 am, the *Pointer* under command of Captain Peter Miller and the *Spaniel* under Captain N Blundell.

Coast Lines registered the Link Line Limited as a new company in December 1958 at Belfast; the original name, Coasters Limited, was quickly dropped. Although managed by the Belfast Steamship Company, Link Line remained under Coast Lines' ownership. This was an important distinction as Belfast Steamship, being Conference signatories, could not operate a service for road hauliers; however, there was no such reason why Coast Lines could not do so.

The new unit load service commenced on 21 January 1959. The service required a nightly crossing from Liverpool and Belfast, the ships using the Waterloo entrance at Liverpool and berthing at East Victoria Dock and at Spencer 'A' Quay at Belfast. At each terminal there was a 15-ton crane to load and unload the containers and trailers. The containers were made of aluminium alloy specially for the service. Existing road hauliers within the group now came to the fore, particularly the Liverpool Cartage Company. At Belfast the Ulster Ferry Transport Company was also key to the success of the new service. Formed in 1956, as successor to Northern Ireland Eggs Limited, for the carriage of eggs in specially designed boxes via the Atlantic Steam Navigation Company's Empire ships, the company agreed to change to the new service preferring Liverpool, with its favourable road and rail connections as the distribution point, rather than Preston. This one contract alone provided for 30% of the capacity of the ships on eastbound voyages. Coast Lines had finally arrived in the new era!

In March, Coast Lines acquired Northern Ireland Trailers Limited. At the time of the takeover the company was operating a daily service between Ardrossan and Larne and between Preston and Larne using chartered ships which were able to carry containers, trailers and flats all loaded and unloaded by crane. The company retained its own identity and its operational headquarters at Preston Docks.

British Railways had already introduced purpose-built unit load ships on the Heysham to Belfast route during 1958. The *Container Enterprise* commenced in April and the *Container Venturer* in October 1958 after which they operated an overnight service connecting with rail services at both ends. The ships carried between 50 and 60 railway-type containers depending on their size and type. They were loaded and unloaded by crane attached to the four corners of the container roof. The ship had two very wide hatches which ran almost the full length of the hold with steel pontoon, watertight, hatch covers on the upper deck and flush steel hatch covers on the main

deck. There was a third small hold forward which allowed two containers to be stowed side by side. The steel hatch covers were specially strengthened for containers to be carried as deck cargo.

A new cargo ship was launched in January 1959 at Ardrossan and named *Dorset Coast*. She had been designed specifically for the Ford Motor Company Dagenham and Cork service and took up duty in February displacing the *Somerset Coast*. The *Somerset Coast* was inspected for possible conversion for unit load work but structural complications made this difficult. As a consequence, she was transferred later in the year to Queenship Navigation Limited as *Richmond Queen* and applied to the charter market. In return, the big steamer *Tudor Queen* came from Queenship to Coast Lines' ownership but was sold for demolition at Troon eight months later. The *Herero Coast*, which for the previous six years had been on charter from Coast Lines to Thesen's at Cape Town was finally transferred to that company and registered at Cape Town.

On 31 December 1959 the Belfast, Mersey and Manchester Steamship Company merged with the Belfast Steamship Company. The merged cargo and cattle services were branded 'Belfast and Liverpool Joint Service' while the Mersey fleet was neither renamed nor were the buff and black topped funnels repainted in red and black.

The Link Line Belfast unit load service acquired a third ship to act as relief and to supplement the daily departures as demand required. This was the *Saxon Queen*, a motor ship, which was transferred from Queenship Navigation Limited in 1959, and had originally been commissioned in 1938 as the *Yewmount* for John Stewart & Company Shipping Limited, Glasgow. She was painted in full Link Line colours and given the name *Lurcher*. She was an unusual choice, but the *Lurcher* was never fully converted for unit load operation; as a low-cost stop-gap she was eminently suitable for a role that left her with plenty of opportunity in the charter market which took her as far as the Baltic on at least one occasion.

On 18 July 1960, the *Denbigh Coast* sank after colliding with Irish Shipping's freighter *Irish Maple* in the Crosby Channel, off Liverpool. The *Denbigh Coast* was on passage from Manchester to Belfast. The ten members of the crew were all taken off safely by the dredger *Hilbre Island* and by one of the port pilot cutters, both of which had been nearby. The ship sank in just ten minutes.

Lloyd's reported, morning of 18 July:
> The motorship *Irish Maple* (6,128 tons) - New Orleans for Liverpool and Glasgow - registered at Limerick – in collision with the motor ship *Denbigh Coast* (479 tons) – owned by Coast Lines Ltd. – registered at Liverpool – bound Manchester for Belfast – in the Mersey. *Denbigh Coast* sank, but the crew were saved.

Ironically, the crew of the **Denbigh Coast** had only just returned to work after a two week long seamen's strike for a 44-hour week and a £4 per week pay increase. The ship was on relief duty while one of the two Belfast Steamship company cargo ships, **Ulster Spinner** or **Ulster Weaver**, was away on refit. The strike had played havoc with holiday makers booked for Belfast during the Glasgow Fair week while the **Royal Ulsterman** and **Royal Scotsman** lay idle, bow to bow, alongside the Broomielaw.

Belfast Steamship Company's **Ulster Weaver** (1946), and later to become **Kentish Coast**, on her way down the Manchester Ship Canal from Pomona Docks to Belfast.   *[author]*

The traditional trades were suffering. Declining passenger numbers on the trunk cross-channel services impacted on revenue, particularly on the Glasgow and Dublin route operated by the almost brand-new **Scottish Coast**. Coast Lines' **Irish Coast** still maintained the summer only day service between Ardrossan and Belfast. Increasing demand for accompanied cars on the route was catered for with each vehicle painstakingly craned on and off ship while its owner looked on in a state of shock. Loading and unloading at Belfast often delayed the afternoon departure; this caused a late arrival at Ardrossan and delayed train connections to Glasgow. For the remainder of the year the **Irish Coast** managed her relief programme which took her first to Belfast, then to Cork and finally to Dublin. Passengers cars could be loaded and unloaded at Princes Landing Stage, Liverpool, by a tortuous arched roadway that gave access via the cattle ramp to the 'tween deck.

The traditional cargo services remained reasonably buoyant and all of the routes now offered a unit load provision although much of the cargo remained break bulk, particularly on coastal liner services such as Liverpool to London. Passenger carrying on the London service was limited to summer only and offered as a cruise holiday, booked single or return. The route was essentially the province of the sisters **Hibernian Coast** and **Caledonian Coast**, although the **Pacific Coast** and **Ocean Coast** were also used for part of the summer season. The **Pacific Coast** was used for some charter work in the off seasons on the London route in the late 1950s; she was running to Finland for United Baltic Corporation on more than one occasion, while the **Adriatic Coast** was also similarly employed at other times.

The 1950s had been a decade of missed opportunities, inappropriate capital investments and a deep hankering on the part of the directors for company tradition. It was not the only company in Britain to act in this way; the General Steam Navigation Company of London had conducted its affairs in exactly the same way, both companies believing they would ride out the 'storm of innovation'. As the decade closed, orders were placed by Coast Lines for two purpose-built unit load ships, one from Ardrossan and one from Charles Hill & Sons Limited at Bristol, to expand the remit of Link Line Limited. The company directors still showed no interest in developing roll-on roll-off traffic, either for commercial vehicles or for use by ferry passengers, their private cars and commercial traffic.

The **Caledonian Coast** (1948), having just locked out of the Waterloo Dock entrance, and looking slightly the worse for wear.

[author]

CHAPTER 11

THE UNIT LOAD ERA AT LAST

Another collision off Liverpool, another sinking. Robert Forsyth reports:

At 5.15 pm on 21 January 1961 the *Lurcher*, outward bound for Glasgow with generals, including two heavy machinery lifts of 140 tons each for Colville's new steel works at Glasgow, was in collision in fog off New Brighton with the Greek motor ship *Stamatios G Embiricos*. The *Lurcher* sank in 7 minutes in 60 feet of water, fortunately without loss of life. Captain M B Leask and his crew of eleven were rescued due to the prompt action of a tug. The *Lurcher* herself was raised on 24 February and beached but her career was over and she was abandoned as a constructive total loss.

The ship was lost off the North Tower Buoy. The big Greek motorship had been built in 1956 and was well equipped. Despite both vessels navigating slowly with the aid of radar, the strong tidal currents of the channel put them onto a collision course that was realised too late. The Greek freighter struck the *Lurcher* on the starboard side at the after end of No 2 hold, cutting a large gash in the hull above and below the water line. As always, the greater momentum of the larger ship meant that the smaller vessel came off worst. The *Lurcher* was later beached and patched up ready to lock-in at Birkenhead to lay-up in the Wallasey Dock where she was surveyed and later condemned.

The *Lurcher* (1938) lying in Wallasey Dock, Birkenhead, after she was sunk on 21 January 1961. Note the survey marks on the hull and the temporary patch towards the stern.

The two new unit load ships destined for Link Line were launched and christened *Buffalo* on 2 May at Ardrossan and *Bison* at Bristol on 11 July 1961. The *Buffalo* was launched by Mrs W McCoubrey, wife of the general manager of the British & Irish company, and the *Bison* at Charles Hill & Sons' yard in Bristol by Mrs F R Hooker, wife of Coast Lines Company Secretary. Containers were to be carried in the 'tween decks and vehicles in the hold. The 'tween decks did not extend throughout the length of the hold so that space was available to stow high loads including vehicles. The ships each had two hatches with MacGregor folding hatch covers that were operated electrically. Crew accommodation was second to none with single cabins available to all and separate accommodation reserved for relief crew members.

The launch of the *Bison* on 11 July 1961 showing how little room there was available at Bristol to accommodate the launch.

[Robin Craig collection]

The new ships were substantially bigger than the *Pointer* and *Spaniel* and offered 50% more cargo capacity. In anticipation of their entering service a new berth at North Side Trafalgar Dock had a 25-ton crane installed and similar equipment was provided at Belfast. The *Bison* and *Buffalo* entered service in January 1962, the *Buffalo* under the command of Captain Peter Miller, and the *Bison*, Captain Stanley Newton. The displaced *Pointer* and *Spaniel* moved to Ardrossan to start a new daily unit load departure from both Ardrossan and Belfast.

The *Buffalo* (1961) in Link Line colours at her North Side berth in Trafalgar Dock overshadowed by the power station and its 'Three Ugly Sisters'.

[Richard Parsons courtesy of John D Hill]

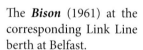

The *Bison* (1961) at the corresponding Link Line berth at Belfast.

[Norman Hesketh]

An interesting departure from normal routine took the *Antrim Coast*, under Captain E Maddrell, to Londonderry to load two articulated railcars made redundant with the closure of County Donegal Railways. The railcars were destined for the Isle of Man Railway. The *Antrim Coast* was almost the only ship in the fleet that could load such a cargo and cope with the shallow berth available at Douglas.

A rival twice weekly unit load service between Londonderry and Preston was started by Anglo-Irish Transport Limited in 1961. The elderly steamer *Loch Linnhe* was chartered for the service; she had the capacity to load up to 31 containers. This was eventually countered by Coast Lines with a service between Portrush and Preston, Portrush Harbour then being still owned by Coast Lines, whereas Londonderry could offer no suitable facilities for the service.

In November 1961, Coast Lines bought out the North of Scotland Orkney & Shetland Shipping Company Limited of Aberdeen. This company was in financial difficulties caused by its commitment to building the new passenger ship *St Clair*. It welcomed Coast Lines bid of £1.1 million, and the sale, a veritable fire sale, was agreed. This was a company with a long and proud history which had served the North Isles well over the years. Its revenue derived from export of livestock and chilled fish to the mainland, import to the islands of essential goods and commodities and, of course, the passenger and summer tourist trade. During the 1950s the passenger trade had ebbed away and with it a considerable source of revenue.

Coast Line's management of the Scottish company was of the 'hands off' style and the North Company was left to develop its own trade in the manner that its managers knew best from long experience. The Coast Line's Directors clearly expected a return on this investment; they little realised that the conventional shipping and cargo handling methods of the North Company would need complete replacement in the next few years if the service was to survive without state funding. Interestingly all the ships in the fleet were motor ships, the eldest being the Shetland inter-island 'steamer' *Earl of Zetland*.

The North of Scotland Orkney & Shetland Shipping Company Limited inter-island ferry *Earl of Zetland* (1939) alongside at Lerwick.

[author]

The *Griqua Coast*, former *Anglian Coast*, and chartered to Thesen's since 1955 was finally bought outright and raised the South African flag over her stern. The *Anglian Coast* was one of the first batch of motor cargo ships and had been built at Sunderland in 1935. Her consort, the *Matabele Coast*, had been on charter even longer, and she too finally had Liverpool painted out on her stern in favour of Cape Town. The *Matabele Coast* was originally sent to Cape Town in 1951. She had been built in the Netherlands in 1938 and became *Dorset Coast* in 1947.

The Clyde Shipping Company, sold the rights and goodwill of its Glasgow and Belfast to London service to Coast Lines Limited in 1961. No ships were transferred in the deal. The Clyde Shipping Company, long established in the coastal liner trades from Glasgow to Irish Sea Ports and to London, was keen to focus on its towage business based at Glasgow. Coast Lines put the *Lancashire Coast* on the weekly Irish service. In April 1962 Coast Lines acquired a majority holding in Ulster Ferry Transport Limited, a company that started as Northern Ireland Eggs Limited, and which was now heavily committed to Link Line services across the Irish Sea. The company was responsible for groupage of small consignments in single containers from centres in Ireland to similar centres in England and Scotland.

An old favourite, the *Atlantic Coast*, was sold to the Union Steamship Company of South Africa Limited and renamed *Pondo Coast* in 1962. As *Atlantic Coast*, working alongside *British Coast*, she had inaugurated the revamped Liverpool to London service via Dublin, Falmouth and Southampton, with berths for a few passengers. The pair were the direct successors on the route to the big passenger steamer *Southern Coast* and her smaller capacity consort *Western Coast* which they replaced in the mid-1930s. Also sold during the year was Coast Lines' interest in the Ardrossan Dockyard (see Chapter 4).

In 1962 the *Mersey Coast* returned from her spell of duty with the Channel Island company and was again resplendent in Coast Lines' colours. She was replaced by the *Forth* which had been serving the Sloan Bristol Channel services – she became the *Southern Coast* under British Channel Island Shipping Company's ownership.

The *Mersey Coast* now tended to work on a variety of services as required, particularly to the Bristol Channel. The *Mersey Coast* displaced the *Kentish Coast*, which was sold for further service under the Italian flag.

The various road haulage interests were brought together to report to a new Liverpool Road Haulage Board which in turn reported directly to the Coast Lines' board. The new group was diverse and covered all types of road haulage and delivery interests. It comprised Thomas Allan Limited at London and the Liverpool Cartage Company Limited, both of which had long served within the Coast Lines group, John Foreman Limited, A S Jones & Company Limited, and the recently acquired Northern Ireland Trailers Limited and James Hemphill Limited.

Cammell Laird at Birkenhead launched a new ship for Coast Lines on 17 July 1962. She was given the name **Wirral Coast** by her sponsor, Mrs Hill, the wife of the Secretary of the Liverpool Steamship Owners' Association. The ship was a smaller version of the **Bison** and **Buffalo** and intended for the new service between Portrush and Preston to compete with that from Londonderry operated by Anglo-Irish Transport Limited. However, until shore facilities including a groupage facility at Londonderry became available, the new ship commenced a new twice-weekly service between Liverpool and Dublin.

A Westminster committee investigation of ferry services to Northern Ireland reported in October 1962. The Coast Lines group was described as operating ships of pre-war design which compared unfavourably against the three Dukes based at Heysham and the recently introduced car ferry **Caledonian Princess** at Stranraer. The report omitted to state that the British Transport Commission had earlier confessed that its Irish Sea services were run at a loss, implying that tax payers' money was used to make up the difference. No such funding from the public purse was ever forthcoming to the Coast Lines' services. The report also omitted to state that the first class accommodation on both the Burns & Laird and the Belfast Steamship Company overnight ships was of a far higher standard than that offered on the overnight railway service between Heysham and Belfast.

During 1962 the General Steam Navigation Company started exploring the possibilities of a containerised unit load corridor across the North Sea. GSN recognised that this could not sensibly be done in isolation and called a seminar in Amsterdam to explore likely routes, types of vessels and potential partners. Various companies, including Coast Lines and others from Holland and Germany attended, and a variety of companies showed considerable interest in forming a consortium. The main discussion centred on the difficult issue of how best to cope both with containers and roll-on, roll-off traffic.

In 1963, Ian Churcher, the GSN General Manager in Holland, held another meeting with those parties that had shown interest the previous year. Mr Churcher had committed himself to the idea of going down the roll-on, roll-off route with provision for unit load containers on trailers. Churcher was also convinced that the optimum route should be Hull to Rotterdam and he even identified suitable wharves for conversion to fit his plan.

Coast Lines recognised that the potential for the route could be massive if the plan was right for the trade on offer. Coast Lines said to Churcher, yes we want in, and nominated its subsidiary company the Tyne-Tees Steam Shipping Company as its stakeholder. This achieved two objectives, first the directors at Newcastle knew and understood the North Sea trades better than the Coast Lines' staff at Liverpool and second, should the venture fail then Tyne-Tees would take the sting, not Coast Lines. Within the year the proposed nightly roll-on roll-off ferry service between Hull and Rotterdam, to be known as North Sea Ferries, had an agreed funding consortium. This comprised the Dutch companies Hollandsche Stoomboot Maatschappij and Phs. Van Ommeren collectively with a 40% stake, GSN with a 35% stake, the German owned Argo Line joining with A Kirsten a 20% stake and the Tyne-Tees Steam Shipping Company a 5% stake. The new service would be carried out by two purpose-built ferries to be built to an innovative design with a drive-through vehicle deck extending the length of the ships, passenger berths and reclining seats for about 250 and a capacity of about 1,900 tons deadweight. Orders were placed for two identical ships with A G Weser, Seebeckwerft at Bremerhaven.

The **Devon Coast** transferred to Queenship Navigation Limited as **Windsor Queen** in 1963. The **Dorset Coast** was sent on demise charter to the railways for service between Folkestone and Boulogne that year returning to her owners two years later. This was a valuable charter that brought much needed income to Coast Lines.

A German ship was purchased in March 1963; she was given the name **Terrier**. She had been built in the Netherlands and launched in May 1957 as **Ebba** for Det Dansk-Norse Dampskibsselskab (R A Robbert) of Copenhagen. As the **Terrier**, her cargo spaces were stripped out ready for unit load traffic. She could carry up to 31 units, but this was increased two years later to 37 after the hold had been further modified. She took up the Dublin service allowing the **Wirral Coast** to transfer to the new Portrush route. The container and vehicle service between Portrush and Preston commenced on 16 September 1963; a 25-ton crane had been installed during the summer. Early in 1964 Coast Lines acquired a controlling interest in Anglo-Irish Transport Limited.

W Paul Clegg explains how the services evolved in an article in *Sea Breezes*, August 1968:
> In the event the Link Line sailings were withdrawn altogether after the last ex-Liverpool departure on October 30 1964, and from November 2 Anglo-Irish Transport Limited became responsible for sailings from Preston to both Portrush and Londonderry. Generally, there have been three or four sailings weekly between Preston and Londonderry and two per week between Preston and Portrush.
>
> Throughout it has been necessary to use three ships, one of which served 'Derry only, and the other two calling at both ports, but this pattern is not consistent, as it has been known for one ship to serve Portrush only for lengthy periods.

So where did the ships come from? They were brought in from W A Savage Limited formerly the Zillah Shipping Company Limited.

Paul Clegg again:

> The Savage vessel *Fallowfield* was the first to berth at Portrush, under the new arrangement, on November 3. She has been very closely associated with the Portrush station ever since. She was built in Holland in 1953 as *Medusa*, but was taken into the Savage fleet the following year, with a gross tonnage of 556, though she looks larger. Near the end of the year [1964] the *Fernfield* also took up the Preston-Ulster services for Anglo-Irish, operating throughout mainly to Londonderry, frequently calling at Portrush on her return voyage.
>
> Built at Waterhuizen (as was the *Fallowfield*) she did not become a member of the Savage fleet until 1958... The third member of the trio, the *Earlsfield*, joined the company service towards the end of 1965. Again Dutch-built (1952) she was originally named *Coquetdyke*, and joined the Savage fleet in 1956.

Relief ship for the chartered Savage boats was generally the *Cambrian Coast*.

The *Fernfield* (1954), below Preston Dock on the River Ribble, on her way to Londonderry in September 1968.

[author]

The British & Irish cargo ship *Inniscarra* was converted for unit load and wheeled traffic in 1964 to serve between Newry and Liverpool, replacing the longstanding break bulk and cattle service between those ports.

At Coast Lines' Annual General Meeting in 1964, it was announced that the trading profit of Coast Lines in 1963 was slightly up on the previous year at just over £1 million, a reflection of the new unit load services. Nevertheless, the interests of the group remained diverse with a total of 88 ships registered in December 1963.

The huge success of the various unit load and trailer services had one unfortunate side effect. The directors of Coast Lines were now lulled into a sense of false security that diverted them from the urgent need to develop their own roll-on roll-off freight services as the logical and sensible way forward for their various Irish trades.

Chairman Nutting died in service in March 1964 at his home in Surrey. Sir (Montague) Arnet Robinson was elected his successor while retaining his previous executive role. Arnet Robinson had been made a Knight Bachelor on 16 July 1963 for his services as Chairman of the Mersey Docks & Harbour Board and to industry. Sir Arnet Robinson is on record as saying that he was still committed to maintaining the high standards of his cross-channel fleet. In reality he had his eye sensibly set on roll-on roll-off tonnage. In the 14 years Captain Nutting had led the company several misjudged decisions had been made and money had been lost. Opportunity to develop new cargo handling methods already proved successful by others had been tardy. The Coast Lines group was in a much less robust state in 1964 than it had been in 1950 when Captain Nutting took over; Arnet Robinson and his directors had their work cut out for them.

Arnet Robinson, Chairman of Coast Lines Limited 1964, Chairman of the Mersey Docks & Harbour Board 1954-1962, President Dock & Harbour Authorities Association 1961-1962, Director Martins Bank Limited, Director Cammell Laird & Company Limited.

[The Newspaper Service Limited, 1968]

In 1958 Arnet Robinson, like Alfred Read before him, had a Liverpool pilot cutter named after him. Sadly, the **Sir Alfred Read** was sunk by a mine on 28 December 1917 off Anglesey, 29 men aboard the ship were lost, there were only two survivors. The **Arnet Robinson**, however, remained in service until 1982.

The two remaining pre-war passenger cargo ships were disposed of in 1964. The **British Coast**, converted to cargo-only in 1948, was sold to owners in Newfoundland who renamed her **Newfoundland Coast**, and in March the **Ocean Coast** was sold to Greek owners adopting the name **Effy**. In addition, the **Antrim Coast** passed to the British Channel Island Company as **Sark Coast**. The **Pacific Coast**, built as a replacement for her

pre-war namesake lost in the war, was used as relief on the London service. More poignantly she was deployed alongside the overnight Dublin ferry, operated by the **Leinster** and **Munster**, from 1962 onwards to carry passengers' cars, a service that allowed a select number of passengers to sleep on board. The **Antrim Coast** had served this role in 1961 with capacity for 50 cars but no passengers. This hugely inefficient system persisted until 1966, with **Pacific Coast** and **Adriatic Coast** offering a nightly service in summer 1964, and **Pacific Coast** and **Mersey Coast** the following year. The **Pacific Coast** generally spent the winter months on charter, travelling to the Baltic for the United Baltic Corporation, or to the Mediterranean for Ellermans.

The **Munster** (1947) preparing for her evening departure to Dublin at her berth in Princes Dock, Liverpool, in July 1964.

[author]

The Belfast overnight service was also supported in summer by supplementary cargo services for crane-loaded cars. The Belfast Steamship Company provided its own cargo ships for this duplication.

For the moment the **Hibernian Coast** and **Caledonian Coast** continued to ply between Liverpool and London departing from the East India Dock in London and East Trafalgar Dock at Liverpool every Friday afternoon or Saturday morning depending on cargo working. The

passenger accommodation remained in great demand during the summer months, not surprising at a return fare of just £50 all inclusive.

The Belfast Steamship Company service between Manchester and Belfast closed in 1963 in favour of a road connection to Liverpool. The **Ulster Weaver** transferred back to Coast Lines as **Kentish Coast** at the end of June 1964 while the **Ulster Spinner** then traded between Belfast and Liverpool.

The **Kentish Coast** (1946), formerly **Ulster Weaver**, again wearing the white chevron of Coast Lines Limited.

The viability of the Aberdeen Steam Navigation Company had been lost early in 1962 when the linoleum trade finished. The **Hadrian Coast**, which had maintained the London service for much of the time since 1948, made the last sailing to London on 4 July 1962. Before that she had been working between Liverpool and Cork for several weeks, until on 9 March 1962 she ran aground off Monkstown Bay in thick fog with a local pilot aboard. The vessel was refloated on 20 March, undamaged. **Hadrian Coast** was sent on charter to the British Channel Islands Shipping Company in July and eventually returned to Coast Lines' ownership in February 1964. The Aberdeen company then ceased to trade.

View looking aft from the bridge aboard **Hadrian Coast** (1941) in Aberdeen Steam Navigation Company colours.

[E J Charman]

In 1964 the British Channel Island company's **Guernsey Coast** was sunk in collision on 6 August at about 0245 hours. The ship was under the command of Acting Master Captain Healy, and was carrying 46,800 trays of tomatoes from St Peter Port to Shoreham. The ship was struck almost at right angles by the Liberian steamship **Catcher**, of 7,238 tons gross, which was on passage from Antwerp to San Juan in Puerto Rico. The **Guernsey Coast** had been proceeding at full speed in thick fog and was monitoring the radar target of the **Catcher** as she approached. The collision occurred in a position some 26 miles north east of Cap de la Hague. The stem of the **Catcher** caught the **Guernsey Coast** on the port side at the after part of No 2 hold and heeled the ship over to starboard. The ship was cut almost to the centre line and sank in 7 minutes. Eight of the crew of ten were able to scramble aboard the Liberian ship via rope ladders but the Chief Engineer, who was attempting to close down the engine, was lost when the ship sank. The master, who was with the Chief Engineer, was later picked up from the sea.

It was reported at the subsequent Inquiry that:

> This collision is but another example of the imperative necessity of navigators appreciating that the provision of radar does not excuse a breach of the collision regulations... In the opinion of the Court, this collision was contributed to by the wrongful act and default of Captain Healy in navigating his vessel at excessive speed in fog and not stopping the engines on hearing a fog signal forward of the beam.

The owners of the **Catcher** declined to appear at the Inquiry but it is believed that she too was travelling at excessive speed.

A similar incident had occurred in the Crosby Channel on 10 November 1961 when the Guinness boat **The Lady Gwendolen** ran down and sank Zillah's **Freshfield**. The **Freshfield** had anchored in poor visibility just inside the buoyed channel to the Mersey. The dredger **Wirral** followed her and also anchored just upstream. At all times both ships sounded their bell. The **Freshfield** was carrying a full load of china clay from Par to Runcorn. **The Lady Gwendolen**, inbound from Dublin with 640 tons of stout, hit the **Freshfield** below the bridge on the starboard side rolling her over to such an extent that she rapidly started to take on water. The nine crew members safely took to a life raft and were picked up by the **Wirral**. At the subsequent Inquiry the master of the Guinness boat was severely reprimanded, the key to the master's evidence being 'that if I had not had radar, I would not have travelled at that speed'. The earlier loss of the **Lurcher** in the Mersey, also in 1961, was not, however, attributable to excessive speed in fog.

In 1965 the **Lancashire Coast** and **Cheshire Coast** were transferred to the Belfast Steamship Company without change of name. The **Stormont**, ex-**Fife Coast**, and **Mountstewart**, ex-**Essex Coast**, left Belfast ownership and came into Coast Lines' ownership. The container ships **Spaniel** and **Pointer** left Coast Lines for Burns & Laird Lines to continue on the Ardrossan to Belfast service, and later between Preston and Belfast or Larne. The **Dorset Coast** returned from her charter to British Rail and was sent to Ardrossan for modifications so that she could enter the container trade.

The **Pointer** (1956) was transferred to Burns & Laird ownership in 1965 without change of name and continued to work between Ardrossan and Belfast alongside her sister **Spaniel**.

[author]

The **Dorset Coast** (1959) arriving at Preston Dock during 1972 when her registered owner had become Belfast Steamship Limited (P&O Short Sea Shipping Limited).

[Jim McFaul]

The coastal charter trades had become specialised and the general charter market had declined rapidly. As a consequence, the last ships of the fleet of Queenship Navigation Limited were sold, the **Osborne Queen**, **Richmond Queen** and **Windsor Queen**, and the company ceased trading at the end of 1965. The Zillah fleet, again largely working in the charter market, had also been sold apart from the three ships on charter to Anglo-Irish Transport working the Preston to Portrush and Londonderry unit load services.

The Dublin and Glasgow passenger service was poorly patronised during the early 1960s, especially in the off-season. On some winter nights there were only a handful of first class passengers and a few third class wanting a night out on the Irish Sea aboard the **Scottish Coast**. It was no surprise when it was announced that

the thrice weekly winter service was to be reduced to two sailings a week. This left the **Scottish Coast** tied up alongside at Glasgow for three days out of seven. On the other main cross-channel passenger routes there was a noticeable drop in first class passengers as more business travellers were attracted by the time saving offered by air travel. Early in 1965 the **Scottish Coast** stood down from Dublin sailings to be prepared for a new role replacing the **Irish Coast** on the seasonal Ardrossan to Belfast day service. For this she was given an ugly car lift on her foredeck which allowed 'rapid' loading and unloading of up to 25 passengers' cars. The **Irish Coast** now served on the Glasgow and Dublin route in summer until the **Scottish Coast** finished her summer season at Ardrossan, when the **Scottish Coast** resumed her duties between Glasgow and Dublin, and the **Irish Coast** was once again the relief ship.

The *Scottish Coast* (1957), with her car loading gantry on the foredeck, seen in Princes Half Tide Dock on arrival from Belfast on 20 May 1967.

[author]

Negotiations had been going on once again to sell the British & Irish interests to the Irish Government. Discussion had been ongoing throughout 1964 with the Irish Government favourably inclined towards safeguarding its major sea routes to Great Britain, and onwards to Europe, with Irish ships manned by Irish seamen. First mooted 30 years previously, this time the deal was finally struck, as Craig J M Carter announced in *Sea Breezes*, April 1965:

> After being a member of the Coast Lines group for nearly 50 years, the 129 year old British & Irish Steam Packet Co. Ltd., more commonly known as the B & I Line, has been sold to the Irish Government...

The deal involves the whole of the issued share capital of B & I which was a wholly owned subsidiary of Coast Lines, less certain assets not directly related to the company's shipping services...

The sale took place in February 1965 with formal handover of the business throughout February and into March. The deal realised just over £3.6 million pounds. The main outward change to the Dublin and Cork services was the new marketing brand, B+I Line, which the new owners quickly adopted. They also settled on a new logo comprising a broken orange circle with a horizontal arrow.

The Liverpool and Dublin overnight ferry *Leinster* (1947) passing through the Princes Half Tide Dock on arrival at Liverpool in May 1967, sporting the new B+I livery.

[author]

The cargo ship *Kilkenny* (1937) was one of the smaller ships included in the sale of British & Irish to the Irish government. She is seen her off the Waterloo Dock entrance at Liverpool on 21 July 1966.

[author]

As it turned out the purchase was a bold move on the part of the Irish Government. The Dublin service had long competed with the railway ships operating from nearby Dun Laoghaire to Holyhead with its fast rail connection to London. The Liverpool passenger service, therefore, held only a small hinterland with travellers heading for the north Midlands, the north east and north west of England. Besides, the Dublin company had become the most expensive of the subsidiary companies to maintain in post war years; Coast Lines had done well in shedding its responsibility for Dublin and Cork.

The new owners had to invest heavily in the company to provide roll-on roll-off ships both for the Dublin to Liverpool service and a new service between Cork and Swansea. One tangible benefit, however, was immunity from the British National Union of Seamen's strike which

commenced in May 1966 – although the stevedores still had problems with unit load and containers which they recognised as a threat to their livelihoods.

But the icing on Coast Lines' cake that year was not necessarily the windfall £3.6 million but the start of North Sea Ferries operations on 17 December 1965 with the maiden voyage of the Hull-registered *Norwave* departing from Hull. Her sister *Norwind* was registered at Rotterdam and arrived in service three months later with a maiden departure from Rotterdam on 21 March 1966. The ships proved the right capacity to develop the new trade and it was quickly demonstrated that unit load containers could easily be accommodated on trailers. Tyne-Tees received a most satisfactory dividend on its investment at the end of the year.

North Sea Ferries *Norwave* (1965) in the King George Dock at Hull. She is approaching the lock to enter the Humber on her overnight sailing to Rotterdam.

[author]

CHAPTER 12

ROLL-ON ROLL-OFF AND P&O

With money in the bank the directors sat back and mulled over how they wished to develop their business. Early in 1966 they agreed that they needed to replace the *Ulster Monarch* and *Ulster Prince* on the Liverpool and Belfast service and the *Royal Scotsman* and *Royal Ulsterman* on the Glasgow and Belfast route. The Liverpool overnight service was the easier decision to make, it was obvious that two roll-on roll-off car and vehicle passenger ferries were needed to maintain the overnight service with departures six nights per week. The question was the precise specification for the ships. Experience from North Sea Ferries clearly dictated a ferry dedicated to wheeled traffic with a garage deck headroom sufficient for the highest of road vehicles and a garage the whole length of the ship. The North Sea Ferries' design allowed the carriage of unit loads on flats that could be towed on and off ship by a tractor. Passenger accommodation should be targeted at the overnight routine with berths available and comfortable seating for those that did not want to hire a berth.

The directors made their last bad decision: they opted for a vehicle deck extending half the length of the ship, most of which had low headroom that excluded most commercial traffic and was accessed by a stern door. They then said we will carry unit loads in a hold forward of the machinery space. This was the outline specification that they took to Cammell Laird who then worked it up into a full design. Coast Lines was not alone in going for this design and

Ellerman's Wilson Line ordered the bigger ferry *Spero* on the same lines as well; both companies learning the error of their ways in due course.

By way of compensation a specification was later also drawn up for one more vehicle ferry to replace the Glasgow twins and to replace the Ardrossan to Belfast ferry, be it *Scottish Coast* or *Irish Coast*. This ship was to operate between Ardrossan and Belfast on a daylight return schedule at a fast design speed of 20 to 21 knots. The specification also allowed for a drive-through garage deck, as had the *Norwave*, and headroom enough for all but the tallest of road vehicles. Northern Ireland Trailers agreed to use the new ship for unit loads stowed on trailers. The passenger accommodation was to be fitted out as a day boat with restaurants, cafes and lounges designed for passengers to spend their money in. This outline specification also went to Cammell Laird to work into shape, but at a later date.

In the autumn of 1966, the *Ulster Monarch* and *Ulster Prince* stood down and were put on the for sale list. Their place was taken by the *Scottish Coast* and the *Irish Coast* as an interim measure pending the commissioning of the new car ferries. The *Lairds Loch* which had earlier closed the Glasgow and Londonderry passenger service for Burns & Laird, now took on the Glasgow and Dublin service.

Belfast Steamship Company's *Ulster Prince I* (1937) laid up in Morpeth Branch Dock, Birkenhead, in February 1967. The suffix 'I' released her old name for the new car ferry; she was sold in April.

[author]

One of the new Belfast car ferries had been ordered from Cammell Laird and the other from Harland & Wolff at Belfast, while the new Ardrossan ferry was ordered from Cammell Laird at Birkenhead. The new **Ulster Prince** was launched at Belfast by Lady Erskine of Rerrick on 13 October 1966, and the **Ulster Queen** by Lady Robinson, the Chairman's wife, on 1 December at Birkenhead. During 1966 the **Fife Coast** transferred to Tyne-Tees in exchange for their **Novian Coast** and **Frisian Coast**.

The **Dorset Coast** was converted for container carrying at Smith's Dock, North Shields. She was equipped with Ermine type steel sliding 'tween decks fitted to her hold to allow a total of 44 containers to be carried. She took up duty in her new role between Liverpool and Belfast in December. The **Kentish Coast** visited Lisbon and the Mediterranean for two round trips under charter to Ellerman & Papyanni Lines Limited; her master was Captain Fullerton.

Tyne-Tees Steam Shipping Company's *Frisian Coast* (1937) came under Coast Lines' direct ownership without change of name in 1966 and was sold the following year.

A considerable expense to the Coast Lines' group, indeed to the nation, was the strike called by the National Union of Seamen on 15 May which lasted until 21 June. Virtually all the company's ships were affected by the action during which expenses were accrued while no income was gained. The loss in profit calculated for this period was a massive £800,000. A number of assets were sold in order to make up the shortfall, bearing in mind that the company was now committed to building three new vehicle ferries. In quick succession 25% of the holding in Anglo-Irish Transport Limited was sold to the Atlantic Steam Navigation Company, and Thesen's Steamship Company, Cape Town, and other South African interests were sold to Grindrod, Gersigny & Company (Pty), Limited, then merged with African Coasters to form Unicorn Lines. One addition was the Liverpool haulage company Jarvis Robinson Transport which became wholly owned by Coast Lines adding a further 80 or so lorries to the road haulage portfolio.

The **Mersey Coast** was sold, last of the pre-war vessels save for the **Frisian Coast**, but seeing further service under the Greek flag. Her role in supporting the Dublin ferries as a car transporter was now over and so there was no need to charter her out in winter. Three of the four remaining ships in the British Channel Islands Shipping Company were sold while the **Mountstewart**, one time **Essex Coast**, transferred to the Channel Islands company. The elderly **Hadrian Coast** was disposed of for further service with Greek owners.

W A Savage sold its four remaining ships to Coast Lines in 1967 and 1968. The ships were the **Grangefield** dating from 1954, and the three small ships, **Earlsfield**, **Fernfield** and **Fallowfield** operating the Preston to Portrush and Londonderry unit load service for Anglo-Irish Transport Limited, now partly owned by the Transport Holding Company. W A Savage then ceased to trade.

The *Grangefield* (1954) was one of four ships to transfer from W A Savage to Coast Lines before Savage ceased trading in 1968.

[Fotoflite]

Employment for some of the bigger ships was found on the charter market. With the Suez Canal closed after the Five Days War in June 1967, special services had to be run into the Mediterranean to connect at Liverpool for ports east of Suez. The **Caledonian Coast** and **Cheshire Coast** were chartered to Thos. & Jno. Brocklebank Limited for several voyages to the Mediterranean. They were given the names **Makalla** and **Malabar** respectively. The **Malabar** was returned to her owners in October 1967

and was then chartered to the Prince Line as **Spartan Prince** before returning to her owners in 1971. The **Lancashire Coast** was also chartered to Prince Line, in April 1968, as **Trojan Prince** and, returned to Coast Lines in mid-1969. The **Pacific Coast** found service with the Mossgiel Shipping Company until summer 1967 when she reverted to her old duties on the London to Liverpool service.

The *Makalla* (1948) on charter to Thos. & Jno. Brocklebank Limited; a ship better known as the *Caledonian Coast*.

[Mike Lennon]

The Prince Line funnel colours with the Coast Lines chevron clearly embossed on the plating of *Trojan Prince* (1954), again better known as *Lancashire Coast*, outward bound in the Manchester Ship Canal above Barton Lock on 7 April 1968.

[author]

Sadly, on one of the voyages south aboard **Pacific Coast**, a carbon monoxide discharge from a faulty domestic boiler killed two passengers while they were asleep in their cabin. The incident occurred on the first night out from Liverpool. When the **Caledonian Coast** was available after her Mediterranean holiday at the end of the year, the **Pacific Coast** was laid up at Liverpool, and following a brief charter to Ellerman's was sold in July 1968. The **Lancashire Coast** was also chartered to Ellerman's after her Prince Line work. The ships wore an Ellerman funnel but retained their own names. The **Adriatic Coast** did one round trip for Prince Line also early in 1968 before taking up service between Liverpool and Belfast.

The big event during 1967, was, of course, the introduction of the new **Ulster Prince** and **Ulster Queen** on the Liverpool and Belfast overnight service. During their

construction the management of the Belfast Steamship Company had increasingly been guided by the directors at Liverpool in a soft merging of interests, presumably as a watch over Coast Lines' investment in the new ships. The **Ulster Prince** took her maiden voyage on 19 April and the **Ulster Queen** on 6 June, replacing the **Scottish Coast** and **Irish Coast** respectively. The service was later stepped up from six nights a week to seven with the introduction of a Sunday night sailing. They were a compromise, with not enough headroom on the vehicle deck to stow commercial vehicles and a hold wastefully designed for unit loads. They were comfortable though, as far as passengers were concerned. They had accommodation for 288 first class passengers who enjoyed a restaurant, cafeteria, smoke room and a lounge with aircraft type seating for unberthed passengers. Second class offered berths for 140 passengers in two, three and four berth cabins.

The new Belfast car ferry **Ulster Queen** (1966) negotiating the Princes Half Tide Dock on arrival at Liverpool.

[author]

The **Scottish Coast** took up her summer duties between Ardrossan and Belfast for the last time in May 1967. In the autumn she transferred to the Glasgow and Belfast service replacing the **Royal Scotsman** at the end of September. That ship was sold in anticipation of the new Burns & Laird car ferry building at Birkenhead. The **Royal Ulsterman** was withdrawn at the end of December, and she too was sold, becoming a support ship for the nuclear submarine trials programme for Cammell Laird, Birkenhead. This left the **Scottish Coast** to maintain three departures per week from either port. The **Irish Coast** went back to the Glasgow and Dublin route replacing the **Lairds Loch**.

It was finally realised that the new Belfast ships were neither vehicle ferry nor unit load carrier. Being unable to carry commercial vehicles meant that their income depended largely on passenger receipts and accompanied cars. The ships could carry 120 cars which were turned on a turntable at the forward end of the garage ready to be driven off at the destination. Even the

two class passenger system was outdated and wasteful of space. Once again, it would seem, Coast Lines had missed the boat.

Not so the new ferry nearing completion at Cammell Laird's yard for the Burns & Laird Ardrossan service. She was everything the Belfast sisters were not, the ship being designed around the vehicle deck and not the passenger accommodation. Launched on 8 August 1967, she was christened **Lion** by Mrs Norman Knight, wife of Burns & Laird Lines' general manager. She was designed as a one class ship with accommodation for up to 1,200 day passengers and 170 cars. The vehicle deck included a retractable mezzanine deck for cars. The garage had a height of 14 feet 6 inches sufficient for most commercial vehicles, of which about 40 could be taken each trip. She took her maiden voyage on 3 January 1968 after being open to the public at Glasgow after Christmas. Meanwhile the **Scottish Coast** continued the overnight service from Glasgow to Belfast until she was replaced by the **Irish Coast** in spring 1968.

The new vehicle ferry **Lion** (1967) setting out from Ardrossan to Belfast on a calm morning in July 1969.

[author]

The *Irish Coast* closed the Glasgow and Dublin passenger and cargo service on 11 February 1968 when she berthed at Glasgow. 'Ever rising costs leading to increasing deficits' were blamed. It was obviously an on-the-spot decision as the service was already advertised in the 1968 Guide and Diary. As a consequence, the *Scottish Coast* was rostered to run alongside the *Lion* between Ardrossan and Belfast, providing additional one-class passenger accommodation on peak summer Saturdays later in the year. In the event she was usually lightly loaded. The *Irish Coast* took her last sailing from Glasgow to Belfast on 10 April 1968 and then retired to Morpeth Dock, Birkenhead, her place again taken by the *Scottish Coast*. In August the *Irish Coast* was sold to become the Epirotiki cruise ship *Orpheus*. The *Scottish Coast* was transferred from Burns & Laird ownership to Coast Lines during the year as were the container ships *Spaniel* and *Pointer*.

The *Hibernian Coast* and the *Caledonian Coast* were both sold in 1968, the London passenger service having ceased. The *Adriatic Coast* was sold and the *Kentish Coast*, displaced from Belfast to Bristol duties, was also sold. The *Tay* returned briefly to Coast Lines' ownership before she too was sold in June following closure of the Sloan service between Belfast and Bristol (the link between Belfast and Glasgow had ceased in 1965). William Sloan's *Talisker* and *Kelvin*, built in 1955 as *Ulster Pioneer* and *Ulster Premier*, briefly came under Coast Lines' ownership prior to their being sold, the *Talisker* in June and the *Kelvin* later in the year. William Sloan & Company now ceased to trade.

The *Kelvin* (1955) departing from Bristol City Docks.

[Malcolm Cranfield collection]

The *Talisker* (1955) on the approach to the River Avon off Battery Point, Portishead on 22 August 1965. She is accompanied by C J King & Sons tug *Sea Gem*.

[Malcolm Cranfield]

The **Essex Coast** came back into the fleet from her spell on the Channel Islands service. This was due to the closure of the British Channel Islands Company and its services between London, St Peter Port and St Helier. The company stated that it 'found it impossible to continue in the face of modern developments in cargo handling'. The **Mountstewart** and **Cyprian Coast**, also on Channel island duties, were returned to their owners.

Difficulties in getting into and out of Portrush Harbour were the reason stated for withdrawing the Preston to Portrush service at the end of June 1968. The **Fallowfield**, which was also sailing to Newry, was then withdrawn and chartered to the B + I line at Dublin. Anglo-Irish continued to run **Wirral Coast** between Preston and Newry, occasionally Preston to Belfast, its former managers Link Line having ceased to operate ships in 1967.

In December 1968 Sir Arnet Robinson stood down as Chairman of Coast Lines and his other board duties in the group and was succeeded by Mr K W C Grand, a board member since 1962. On his retirement, Sir Arnet was elected Honorary President of Coast Lines; this was the only appointment of President ever made by the company.

On New Year's Day 1969 John Turner was appointed Managing Director. Messrs Grand and Turner created two new companies called Coast Lines (Management) Limited and Coast Lines (Services) Limited, with the objective of overseeing the operational management of the group which they divided into separate functions the shipping, divided regionally, and vessels chartered out. The Irish Sea Division included all Belfast Steamship and Burns & Laird responsibilities plus Coast Lines' unit load services to Northern Ireland.

The North of Scotland, Orkney & Shetland Shipping Company had survived the rationalisation programme unscathed; not so the Tyne-Tees Steam Shipping Company. It had withdrawn from the bulk trades in 1963 with the sale of three of its ships. In 1966 it had begun to offer a unit load service to the Continent and with it came the unit load carrier **Stormont** from the Irish Sea. Further ships were sold such that by January 1968 there were only eight vessels left in the fleet. During the year one of the larger ships was replaced by the **Grangefield**. At the end of the year there was just the **Stormont**, **Grangefield** and **Yorkshire Coast** and all that was left of the services was Newcastle and Middlesbrough to Antwerp and Rotterdam and Newcastle to Hamburg and Bremen. In 1969 the **Grangefield** was sold and the **Stormont** then became the dedicated Dutch ship and the **Yorkshire Coast** worked the German service with weekly departures.

The **Lancashire Coast** was converted by Harland & Wolff into a car and cattle carrier in 1969. Her masts and cargo handling derricks were removed, the three original hatches were plated over and two new hatches were created on both the upper and main decks. Cargo doors were fitted in the shell plating in way of the shelter deck and by means of a shore ramp, cars could be driven on and off the ship and cattle walked on and off on the hoof. Cars for stowing in the lower hold could be shore craned on and off through the two newly-fitted hatches. On completion she took up service between Liverpool and Belfast.

The **Lancashire Coast** (1953) after her conversion to car and cattle carrier in 1969. She is seen laid up at Fleetwood with a P&O pale blue funnel.

[World Ship Photo Library]

The various conversions that had taken place did lead to stability problems. The **Pointer** put into Douglas with a shifted cargo and a 17° list to starboard in September 1968 on passage from Larne to Preston. A heavy lift crane was used to correct the situation. That being said the purpose-built **Wirral Coast** lost two containers overboard in fierce weather on 11 November 1969. She was escorted to a berth at Birkenhead to correct her list before she could dock at Liverpool.

In October 1968 the **Mountstewart** was chartered to Cunard-Brocklebank for a single trip to the Mediterranean and this was followed by a charter to Moss Hutchison returning from the Mediterranean in January. She was returned to her owners in March 1969 and sold. The **Scottish Coast** too went to new owners in the autumn as Hellenic Cruises' **Galaxias**. The **Earlsfield** was also sold as surplus to the Preston unit load service.

The *Wirral Coast* (1962) arriving at Birkenhead having lost two containers in severe weather in November 1969.

[Gerald Drought]

The *Mountstewart* (1955), originally the *Essex Coast*, seen on one of her Mediterranean trips under charter prior to her sale from Coast Lines in March 1969.

[Mike Lennon]

The Irish government owned B+I Line invested a large amount of cash in updating its services. The new drive-through ferry **Munster** started on the Dublin and Liverpool route on 6 May 1968, followed by sister **Leinster** on 1 June 1969. The new ships could cater for 1,000 passengers on both day and night crossings. The **Munster** was bought on the stocks from her German shipbuilder, Werft Nobiskrug GmbH at Rendsburg, but was of modern Swedish design. Her sister was built to the same design by Verolme Cork Dockyards Limited. The

two former namesakes, traditional overnight ferries built in 1948, were then sold. The old **Innisfallen** closed the Fishguard to Cork service at the beginning of November 1969 and was put up for sale. A new service started between Cork and Swansea when the new drive-through ferry, also named **Innisfallen**, commenced in May 1970 after a short initial period relieving at Dublin. She was a smaller version of the Dublin ships and was built by Werft Nobriskrug GmbH. Second and third generation ships were introduced in due course.

The drive-through ferry **Innisfallen** (1969) arriving at Swansea. She was delivered to B+I ready to start her new service between Cork and Swansea in May 1970.

[author]

Chairman Grand retired in 1970 and John Turner was elected the sixth and last Chairman of Coast Lines Limited, retaining his executive duties. During the year the board divided the Coast Lines assets between Coast Lines (Management) Limited and Coast Lines (Services) Limited, all the ships being registered under the latter except the **Fernfield** and **Cheshire Coast**, both of which were chartered out, the **Cheshire Coast** still working with Prince Line as **Spartan Prince**. The chartered ships became the property of Coast Lines (Management) Limited. This did not affect the Belfast Steamship Company, Burns & Laird and Tyne-Tees. Ulster Ferry Transport Services was amalgamated with Link Line.

The **Lion** started overnight commercial runs between Ardrossan and Belfast in January 1971, displacing

the **Fallowfield** and **Dorset Coast** from the service. The **Dorset Coast** was then used at Preston and later transferred to the Belfast Steamship Company.

The **Cambrian Coast** was sold early in 1971 and the **Cheshire Coast** later in the year. The **Fallowfield** and **Fernfield** were also sold, their places taken by chartered tonnage through Transport Holdings interests in the Atlantic Steamship Company. In addition, the **Owenglas** was taken on charter from Greenore Ferry Services at Dublin to support the Preston and Northern Ireland container services and given the temporary name **Irish Coast**, the only time a chartered ship was given a corporate name and painted in the company livery. She had been built in Holland in 1970 and remained on charter until 1975.

The **Fallowfield** (1953) in Princes Dock, Liverpool, in May 1971, complete with Coast Lines funnel but still wearing the red boot topping of her former owners W A Savage Limited.

[P H Boot]

In February 1971 the group lost a ship in circumstances that should not have occurred. The Burns & Laird cargo ship **Lairdsfield** sailed from Middlesbrough with steel plate and steel columns destined for Cork and Passage West. She turned over just at the mouth of the Tees with the loss of ten lives. The subsequent Inquiry decided that the loss of the ship was due to the improper loading and stowage of the cargo leading to inadequate stability, in particular, the loading of 250 tons of steel plate as deck cargo at the request of the charterers to facilitate ease of unloading.

In August 1971, following a meeting between John Turner and Donald Anderson of P&O, Coast Lines agreed to a cash buy-out by P&O valued at £5.6 million. In their agreement to the deal, the Coast Lines' directors were then confident that P&O would allow Coast Lines to continue to trade independently, much as it had allowed the General Stream Navigation Company to retain its own vision and identity since it was purchased by P&O in 1920. How wrong they were, as there followed an almost immediate merger of Coast Lines' staff and assets with those of GSN to form P&O European and Air Transport Division in October 1971.

Britain was on the verge of entering the European Economic Community and P&O recognised the increased trade this would create and wanted just two things from Coast Lines. First, P&O wanted the share in North Sea Ferries held by the Tyne-Tees Steam Shipping Company and second, it wanted the vast network of road haulage companies that had been acquired and developed by Coast Lines over the years. The remaining assets it saw little future for. Tyne-Tees Steam Shipping Company retained ownership of its share in North Sea Ferries, as did General Steam Navigation retain its share, until in October 1972 they were both taken over by P&O.

This situation obviously begs the question whether Coast Lines should have sold out to P&O in the first place, the original tantalising invitation being 'Would Coast Lines like to join the P&O family?'.

Robert Forsyth, a careful and measured commentator wrote:

It was probably not necessary. Coast Lines could have continued and could have financed the expansion

and development that would have been necessary in the future.

Carry on they might have done, but a rights issue would have been necessary. Then a bid might have been made on terms that the shareholders would not have been able to refuse. Indeed, even while the talks with P&O were under way an approach was made and withdrawn when the situation was explained to the bidder.

In the event it was not long before Coast Lines disappeared into the corporate machinery of P&O. This was compounded by the divisional structure created when Coast Lines and GSN were brought together to form P&O Ferries under the Chairmanship of John Turner; P&O had its own financial problems and needed to simplify the reporting of its hundred or so companies to a mere five divisions.

P&O Short Sea Shipping Limited was formed at the close of 1971 and comprised 34 ships. It included a diverse collection of companies: the Coast Lines' group – Belfast Steamships Company, Burns & Laird Lines, Coast Lines Services, North of Scotland company and Tyne-Tees; Bennett Steam Shipping; European Unit Routes; General Steam Navigation Company; Southern Ferries; and a 50% share in North Sea Ferries.

Coast Lines' **Bison** was renamed **Norbank** when Coast Lines had her 'removed' to North Sea Ferries. She was used to commence running a container service between Hull and Rotterdam in late October 1971. Sistership **Buffalo** was later renamed **Norbrae** and joined the **Norbank** on the service in February 1972. The two ships each had a capacity for 91 standard 20 feet containers. The two new North Sea Ferries container ships were intended to provide a supplementary cargo service to the already hard-pressed drive-through vehicle and passenger ferries **Norwave** and **Norwind**. However, the two container ships were dogged by labour problems at Hull and in March 1973 the **Norbank** stood down and was sub-chartered to MacAndrews Shipping Company (MacAndrews & Company) for its Liverpool to Bilbao container service. Things did not improve at Hull and in December 1973 the **Norbrae** was also withdrawn.

Norbank (1962), formerly the Link Line unit load vessel *Bison*, wearing the North Sea Ferries orange funnel.

Second generation passenger and vehicle ferries, the British-registered *Norland* and Dutch *Norstar*, were commissioned by North Sea Ferries during 1974. The new ships displaced the *Norwave* and *Norwind* to a new Hull and Zeebrugge service. The *Norland* (1973) is seen in the Humber at the start of her overnight passage to Rotterdam. *[author]*

Meanwhile the *Lancashire Coast*, *Terrier* and *Wirral Coast* were sold in 1972, and the *Dorset Coast* chartered out. The *Spaniel* and *Pointer* transferred to Belfast Steamship Company for the container service between Liverpool and Belfast. Tyne-Tees sold the *Yorkshire Coast*, leaving just the *Stormont* alone on alternate departures for the Netherlands and Germany.

The *Spaniel* was sold in 1973 to the Isle of Man Steam Packet Company Limited and renamed *Conister*, and the *Dorset Coast* was transferred to the General Steam Navigation Company. The *Dorset Coast* spent the whole of 1974, and parts of 1975 and 1976 on charter to Greenore Ferries working from Sharpness. Meanwhile, the *Buffalo* (as *Norbrae*) became *Roe Deer*

for European Unit Routes operating out of Tilbury. The attrition was relentless.

In December 1974, P&O established Pandoro (P and O RO) to operate a commercial roll-on roll-off service between Fleetwood and Larne and Fleetwood and Dublin, the latter in conjunction with B+I. Pandoro was an amalgamation of P&O's Ferrymasters, established in 1972, with Northern Ireland Trailers and Ulster Ferry Transport. It was a logical development given the availability of the former Coast Lines' road haulage network. The new ships were *Bison* which entered service in February 1975 and *Buffalo* which commenced four weeks later. They had been built by J J Sietas at Hamburg.

The evolution of P&O on the Irish Sea continued with Pandoro and the roll-on roll-off sisters *Buffalo* (1975), seen here leaving Fleetwood for Larne, and *Bison*.

[author]

John Turner retired in December 1974 and Ian Churcher took over the mantle of Chairman of P&O Ferries – Coast Lines lost a dear ally. Inevitably the old company titles were now replaced by 'P&O Ferries' and all ships were repainted in a new corporate livery, blue hull adorned with the script 'P&O Ferries' in white and plain blue funnel.

During 1975 the closure of the Ardrossan to Belfast service, operated by the all-blue *Lion*, was announced. She finished duty on 12 February 1976. The reason given was that shippers had transferred to the more convenient route between Stranraer and Belfast operated by the railways; in truth the ship was earmarked for a new service across the Channel from Dover. The Liverpool to Belfast ferries, unsuitable though they were, lasted until the service was closed in 1981. Towards the end, labour

difficulties dogged the operation of the *Ulster Queen* and *Ulster Prince*, and in its final year the service lost a massive £1 million. There had even been talk of new tonnage for the route but this was killed when P&O's bankers insisting that they withdraw from all loss-making enterprise.

Former Chairman Sir Arnet Robinson died at the age of 77 in May 1975.

The *Stormont* had continued on her North Sea unit load work until 1976, when her services were terminated. She served from Newcastle to Germany and the Netherlands, occasionally with supplementary voyages by one of GSN's small cargo ships, usually *Ortolan*.

The *Stormont* (1954), originally *Fife Coast*, wore the colours of Tyne-Tees until 1976 when she adopted the pale blue corporate funnel of P&O.

One company in the former Coast Lines' portfolio that did benefit from P&O ownership was the North of Scotland Orkney and Shetland Shipping Company. As P&O Scottish Ferries a new ship named *St Ola* replaced her former namesake on the Pentland Firth crossing between Scrabster and Stromness in 1975. She was a drive through ferry with part of the vehicle deck reserved for livestock. A new freight ferry running to Leith was commissioned in 1975 and given the unlikely name *ROF Beaver*. She visited a variety of island jetties for the burgeoning North Sea oil industry. In April 1977 a 'new' vehicle ferry was

commissioned for the passenger service from Lerwick and Kirkwall to Aberdeen and given the traditional name *St Clair*. The previous incumbent, now renamed *St Clair II*, continued on relief work until June and was sold. P&O continued to develop the company while enjoying the profits derived from the oil boom. P&O ultimately lost control of the services in 2000 when the Scottish Executive appointed a consortium led by Caledonian MacBrayne and the Royal Bank of Scotland which, under the banner 'Northlink', promised to build three brand new ferries for the services. And this it did.

The *ROF Beaver* (1971) about to enter the lock on departure from Leith on 27 February 1985 on one of the final cargo services from Leith to Orkney and Shetland.

[author]

Today, there are a number of tangible vestiges of the former Coast Lines' empire. North Sea Ferries, now rebranded P&O Ferries, is one, Coast Lines' subsidiary Tyne-Tees Steam Shipping Company having been a founder member. Nevertheless, the link to Coast Lines was always covert; the difference between the Tyne-Tees operations to the Continent and today's massive ferries working out of Hull is so extreme that a link of any kind is now hard to recollect. The Irish government sold its interests in cross-channel shipping in 1995 when the private company Irish Ferries took on the Dublin route, now serving Holyhead rather than more distant Liverpool, and the former Cork route now running on the shorter limb from Rosslare to Pembroke Dock. This company also, therefore, holds its antecedents within the Coast Lines' story. Finally, the P&O Irish Sea commercial and passenger routes, also derive from this story.

The *St Ola* (1974) in her original livery with a plain blue funnel and black hull, seen arriving at Stromness in June 1976.

[author]

North of Scotland Orkney and Shetland Shipping Company received new tonnage through P&O, including the passenger and vehicle ferry *St Clair* (1965) seen arriving at Lerwick in P&O Ferries livery.

[author]

REFERENCES

Campbell, Colin & Fenton, Roy 1999 *Burns and Laird*. Ships in Focus Publications, Longton

Chandler, George 1960 *Liverpool Shipping Short History*. Phoenix House Limited, London

Cowsill, Miles 1990 *By Road Across the Sea: The History of the Atlantic Steam Navigation Company Ltd*. Ferry Publications, Pentlepoir, Dyfed

Langmuir, Graham & Somner, Graeme 1987. *William Sloan & Co Ltd, Glasgow 1825 – 1968*. World Ship Society, Kendal

McRonald, Malcolm 2005. *The Irish Boats, Volume 1, Liverpool to Dublin*. Tempus Publishing Ltd, Stroud

Robins, Nick & Meek, Donald 2008. *The Kingdom of MacBrayne*. 2nd edition. Birlinn Ltd, Edinburgh

Robins, Nick 2014. *The Tyne-Tees Steam Shipping Company and Its Associates*. Bernard McCall, Portishead

Robins, Nick & Tucker, Colin 2015 *Coast Lines Key Ancestors: M Langlands & Sons*. Bernard McCall, Portishead

Robins, Nick & McRonald, Malcolm 2017 *Powell, Bacon and Hough, Formation of Coast Lines Limited*. Bernard McCall, Portishead

Robins, Nick & McRonald, Malcolm 2018 *The Burns and Laird Family Interests in the Formation of Coast Lines*. Coastal Shipping Publications, Portishead

Saunders, Andy 2010 *Convoy Peewit: Blitzkrieg from the Air and Sea 8 August 1940*. Grub Street, London

Sinclair, Robert 1990 *Across the Irish Sea, Belfast Liverpool Shipping Since 1819*. Conway Maritime Press Ltd., London

Smyth, Hazel 1984 *The B&I Line, a Brief History of the British & Irish Steam Packet Company*. Gill and Macmillan Ltd., Dublin

Somner, Graeme 2000 *The Aberdeen Steam Navigation Company Ltd*. The World Ship Society, Gravesend

Talbot-Booth E C 1938 *The British Merchant Navy 1937-8*. Sampson Low, Marston & Co. Ltd., London

FLEET LIST

1) Powell, Bacon & Hough Lines Limited

Name	P, B & H Service	Gross tons	Comments
Powell, Bacon & Hough Lines Limited from F H Powell & Company			
Western Coast	1913-1915	1,166	Built by W Harkess & Son Ltd., Middlesbrough, 1913 as *Hopeful* for F H Powell & Co., to Powell, Bacon & Hough Lines Ltd., renamed *Western Coast*; 24 February 1915 sunk by torpedo off Beachy Head on passage London to Liverpool.
Wirral Coast	1913-1916	640	Built by W Harkess & Son Ltd., Middlesbrough, 1907 as *Sussex Coast* for F H Powell & Co., to Samuel Hough, to F H Powell & Co.; 1908 renamed *Truthful*, later transferred to Watchful Steamship Company; 1913 to Powell, Bacon & Hough Lines Ltd., renamed *Wirral Coast*; 1916 sold to Limerick Steamship Co., Limerick, renamed *Claddagh*; 1918 sold to City of Cork Steam Packet Co. Ltd.; 1924 sold to Ellerman's Wilson Line Ltd., renamed *Nero*; 1927 sold to General Steam Navigation Co. Ltd., London, sold to Ellerman's Wilson Line Ltd., sold to Ada Cristina Piazza in D'Arrigo, Catania, Italy, renamed *Cristina*; 1929 sold to E Patanè, Trieste, renamed *Gagliardo*; 1931 sold to Ivo Vacchi Suzzi, Trieste, renamed *Imola*; 1933 sold to Dante Pompei, Antona, renamed *Marchigiano*; 1935 sold to Societa Italiana ATIL, Genoa; 13 March 1936 sank in Red Sea following explosion on passage Genoa to Assab.
Graceful/Somerset Coast	1913-1917	1,149	Built by Sir Raylton Dixon & Co., Middlesbrough, 1911 as *Graceful* for F H Powell & Co.; 1913 to Powell, Bacon & Hough Lines Ltd., renamed *Somerset Coast*; 21 April 1917 sank in collision off Bardsey Island on passage Bristol to Liverpool.
Eastern Coast	1913-1919	1,612	Built by Swan Hunter & Wigham Richardson Ltd., Newcastle, 1903 as *Powerful* for F H Powell & Co.; 1913 to Powell, Bacon & Hough Lines Ltd., renamed *Eastern Coast*; 1917 owner renamed Coast Lines Ltd.; 1919 sold to British Hispano Line, Cardiff, renamed *Perez*; 1920 sold to Harken Steamship Co., Swansea, renamed *Eaton Grove*; 1923 sold to John Alan MacDonald, Glasgow, resold to Vaccaro Bros & Co., La Ceiba, Honduras, renamed *Alegria*; 1924 sold to Standard Fruit & Steamship Corporation, La Ceiba, Honduras; 1936 sold to J S Webster & Sons, Kingston, Jamaica, renamed *Allister*; 29 May 1942 sunk by torpedo off Grand Cayman Island on passage Kingston to Tampa.

Monmouth Coast	1913-1919	874	Built by W Harkess & Son Ltd., Middlesbrough, 1906 as *Faithful* for F H Powell & Co.; 1913 to Powell, Bacon & Hough Lines Ltd., renamed *Monmouth Coast*; 1917 owner renamed Coast Lines Ltd.; 1919 sold to Richard P Care, Cardiff, resold to Camber Shipping Co., Cardiff, resold to Miller Steamship Co. Ltd., Hull; 1922 sold to Sociedade Geral de Commercio e Transportes Ltda., Lisbon, renamed *Silva-Gouveia*; 23 December 1927 wrecked at Paya Rostro Peton Pardas, Spain, 5 miles from Cape Torinaña on passage from Hamburg to Oporto.
Powell, Bacon & Hough Lines Limited from F H Powell & Company and Samuel Hough Limited			
Cornish Coast	1913-1915	676	Built by W Harkess & Son Ltd., Middlesbrough, 1904 for F H Powell & Co., then to F H Powell & Co. and Samuel Hough Ltd.; 1913 to Powell, Bacon & Hough Lines Ltd.; 3 March 1915 sunk in Mersey in collision on passage Rochester to Birkenhead.
Dorset Coast	1913-1915	672	Built by W Harkess & Son Ltd., Middlesbrough for F H Powell & Co.; sold 1908 to F H Powell & Co. and Samuel Hough Ltd.; 1913 to Powell, Bacon & Hough Lines Ltd.; 1915 sold to Thomas Steven & Co., Edinburgh, renamed *Arbonne*; 26 February 1916 sunk by torpedo near the Kentish Knock lightship, Lower Thames on passage Le Havre to Newcastle.
Norfolk Coast	1913-1918	782	Built by W Harkess & Son Ltd., Middlesbrough, 1910 launched as *Hopeful*, completed as *Norfolk Coast*; for F H Powell & Co. and Samuel Hough Ltd.; 1913 to Powell, Bacon & Hough Lines Ltd.; 1917 owner renamed Coast Lines Ltd.; 18 June 1918 sunk by torpedo south east of Flamborough Head on passage Rouen to Newcastle.
Devon Coast	1913-1934	782	Built by W Harkess & Son Ltd., Middlesbrough, 1909 as *Graceful* for British & Continental Steamship Co. (Alfred H Read, Manager); 1910 to F H Powell & Co., to F H Powell & Co. and Samuel Hough Ltd., renamed *Devon Coast*; 1913 to Powell, Bacon & Hough Lines Ltd.; 1917 owner renamed Coast Lines Ltd; 1934 sold to Brook Shipping Co., London, renamed *Devonbrook*; 1937 sold to Companhia de Navegação Norte Sul, Rio de Janeiro, renamed *Sao Pedro*; 1943 sold to Companhia Commercio e Navegação, Rio de Janeiro; 1952 scrapped at Rio de Janeiro.
Hampshire Coast	1913-1915 1915-1936	787	Built by W Harkess & Son Ltd., Middlesbrough, 1911 for F H Powell & Co., to F H Powell & Co. and Samuel Hough Ltd.; 1913 to Powell, Bacon & Hough Lines Ltd.; 8 February 1915 wrecked at Shoreham on passage Liverpool to London, register closed; 1915 wreck sold to J Esplen, Liverpool, refloated, repaired and sold to Powell, Bacon & Hough Lines Ltd.; 1917 owner renamed Coast Lines Ltd.; 1936 sold to Monroe Brothers, Liverpool, renamed *Kylebay*; 1937 sold to Walton Steamship Co., Newcastle; 1950 scrapped at Dunston-on-Tyne

Powell, Bacon & Hough Lines Limited from John Bacon Limited			
Sir Edward Bacon	1913-1914	483	Built by Irvine Shipbuilding & Engineering Co. Ltd., Irvine, 1899 as *Birker Force* for W S Kennaugh & Co., Whitehaven; 1912 sold to John Bacon Ltd., renamed *Sir Edward Bacon*; 1913 to Powell, Bacon & Hough Lines Ltd.; 1914 sold to J Bennetts & Co., Penzance, renamed *Pivoc*; 1919 sold to Holman Coal & Shipping Co. Ltd., Penzance; 22 January 1922 beached and abandoned near Rouen on passage Rouen to Swansea; declared constructive total loss.
Edith	1913-1916	116	Built by John Thompson, Northwich, Cheshire, 1880 for Cheshire Amalgamated Salt Works Ltd., Winsford; 1889 sold to Salt Union Ltd., London; 1893 sold to John Bacon Ltd.; 1913 to Powell, Bacon & Hough Lines Ltd.; 1916 sold to H & C Grayson Ltd., Liverpool, resold to Kymo Shipping Co. Ltd., Liverpool; 1921 sold to Wadsworth Lighterage & Coaling Co. Ltd., Liverpool; 1930 scrapped.
Enniscorthy	1913-1916	42	Built by W J Yarwood & Sons Ltd., Northwich, Cheshire, 1908 for John Bacon Ltd.; 1913 to Powell, Bacon & Hough Lines Ltd.; 1916 sold to United Grain Elevators Ltd., Liverpool; 1935 scrapped.
Sir George Bacon/Gower Coast	1913-1917	804	Built by Dundee Shipbuilders Co. Ltd., Dundee, 1899 as *Prestonian* for Henry Tyrer & Co., Preston; 1900 sold to John Bacon Ltd.; 1913 renamed *Sir George Bacon*, to Powell, Bacon & Hough Lines Ltd., renamed *Gower Coast*; 1917 sold to Ford Shipping Co. Ltd., Glasgow; 4 April 1917 sunk by mine off Tréport on passage Newcastle to Tréport.
Pembroke Coast	1913-1930	809	Built by J Fullerton & Co., Paisley, 1912 as *Clydeholm* for J B Couper, Glasgow, completed as *Sir Roger Bacon* for John Bacon Ltd.; 1913 to Powell, Bacon & Hough Lines Ltd., renamed *Pembroke Coast*; 1917 owner renamed Coast Lines Ltd.; 1930 to City of Cork Steam Packet Co. Ltd.; 1931 renamed *Blarney*; 1933 sold to Wexford Steamships Co, Wexford, renamed *Wexfordian*; 29 February 1936 wrecked on Dogger Bank, off Wexford.
Gloucester Coast	1913-1936	919	Built by George Brown & Co., Greenock, 1913 as *Sir Walter Bacon* for John Bacon Ltd., to Powell, Bacon & Hough Lines, renamed *Gloucester Coast*; 1917 owner renamed Coast Lines Ltd.; 1936 sold to Bristol Steam Navigation Co. Ltd., renamed *Alecto*; 2 May 1937 sank in collision off North Hinder Lightship, Ostend, on passage Swansea to Rotterdam.
Harfat	1913-1939	128	Built by W J Yarwood & Sons Ltd., Northwich, Cheshire, 1911 for John Bacon Ltd.; 1913 to Powell, Bacon & Hough Lines Ltd.; 1917 owner renamed Coast Lines Ltd.; 1939 sold to Tay Sand Co. Ltd., Dundee; 15 January 1952 foundered off Dundee on passage River Tay to Dundee.

Pennar	1913-1948	130	Built by W J Yarwood & Sons, Northwich, Cheshire, 1907 for John Bacon Ltd.; 1913 to Powell, Bacon & Hough Lines Ltd.; 1917 owner renamed Coast Lines Ltd.; 1948 sold to J Wilson & James Robert Wilson; sold to James Massey, London; 1950 sold to S J Hadlow, Sittingbourne, stripped and used as a lighter; c1969 believed broken up.

Powell, Bacon & Hough Lines Limited from Samuel Hough Limited

Annie Hough/ Lancashire Coast	1913-1919	1,110	Built by John Scott & Co., Kinghorn, Fife, 1900 as *Delta* for Bailey & Leetham, Hull; 1903 acquired by Thos. Wilson Sons & Co. Ltd., Hull; 1904 sold to Samuel Hough Ltd., renamed *Annie Hough*; 1912 transferred to Annie Hough Steamship Co. Ltd.; 1913 to Powell, Bacon & Hough Lines Ltd.; 1914 renamed *Lancashire Coast*; 1917 owner renamed Coast Lines Ltd.; 1919 sold to The Steamship Arwyco Ltd, Liverpool (Roberts, Brining et al., Liverpool), renamed *Arwyco*; 1927 sold to Trafford Steamship Co. Ltd., London; 1929 sold to General Navigation Co. (of Canada) Ltd., Vancouver; 1935 sold to Lisardo Garcia, Puerto Cortés, Honduras, resold to Alfredo Garcia, renamed *Corisco*; 1941 sold to A Garcia & Compania Ltda., Havana, Cuba, renamed *Corinto*; 1950 scrapped at Fieldsbro, New Jersey.
Southern Coast	1913-1936	1,872	Built by Grangemouth & Greenock Dockyard Co. Ltd., Grangemouth, 1911 as *Dorothy Hough* for Samuel Hough Ltd.; 1913 to Powell, Bacon & Hough Lines Ltd., renamed *Southern Coast*; 1917 owner renamed Coast Lines Ltd.; 1936 sold to Falkland Islands Co. Ltd., London, renamed *Lafonia*; 26 March 1943 sunk in collision near Coquet Island, Northumberland on passage London to Greenock.

Powell, Bacon & Hough Lines Limited

Stonehenge	1913-1916	732	Built by S P Austin & Hunter, Sunderland, 1876 as *Fenton* for Milnes & Chaytor, London; 1891 sold to Earl of Durham; 1896 sold to Lambton Collieries Ltd.; 1902 sold to Isaac W Laing then to Isaac W Laing and Francis D Laing; 1904 ownership reverted to Isaac W Laing on death of partner; 1911 sold to Kempock Steamship Co. Ltd., Glasgow, resold to Henry W Page, Liverpool; 1913 renamed *Stonehenge*, sold to Powell, Bacon & Hough Lines Ltd.; 1916 sold to Harold Harrison & Edward T Lindley, London, resold to Stonehenge Steamship Co. Ltd., London; 1917 sold to John Harrison Ltd., London; 1921 sold to Antwerp Steamship Co. Ltd., London (H Harrison Shipping Ltd.); 1922 sold to John Harrison Ltd., London, resold to MacNab, Rougier & Co. (Italy) Ltd., London; 1923 sold to Ganlobis Ltd., London, resold to A Giuffrida di C. Catania, Italy, renamed *Adone*; 6 March 1932 wrecked near Pozzallo on passage Cotrone to Licata.
Suffolk Coast	1913-1916	780	Built by W Harkess & Son Ltd., Middlesbrough, 1913; 7 November 1916 captured and scuttled by German U Boat off Cap Barfleur on passage Glasgow to Fécamp.

West Flandria	1913-1916	97	Built at Willehoeck, Netherlands, 1904 as Belgian-owned *West Flandria*; 1913 sold to Powell, Bacon & Hough Lines Ltd.; 1916 sold to the Board of Trade, later Ministry of Shipping.
Northern Coast	1914-1920	1,189	Built by Sir Raylton Dixon & Co. Ltd., Middlesbrough, 1914; 1917 owner renamed Coast Lines Ltd.; 1920 to British & Irish Steam Packet Co. Ltd., renamed *Lady Martin*; 1936 to British & Irish Steam Packet Co. (1936) Ltd.; 1938 sold to A/S Eestis Laevandus, Tallinn, Estonia, renamed *Pearu*; 1940 seized by Russia, renamed *Vodnik*; 14 August 1941 sunk by German aircraft near Prangli Island on passage Kronstadt to Tallinn.
Irish Coast	1915-1916	603	Built by Murdoch & Murray, Port Glasgow, 1904 as *Rosslyn* for Rosslyn Steamship Co. Ltd., Glasgow; 1915 sold to Powell, Bacon & Hough Lines Ltd., renamed *Irish Coast*; 1916 sold to Associated Portland Cement Manufacturers (1900) Ltd., London, renamed *Landport*; 1917 sold to Albert Chester, Middlesbrough; 1923 sold to Iona Shipping Co., Ltd., Newcastle; 9 December 1925 sank in collision off Flamborough Head on passage Newcastle to Portsmouth.
Kentish Coast	1915-1928	758	Built by Dundee Shipbuilding Co. Ltd 1908 as *La Flandre* for Cie. D'Armament des Flandres, Bruges; 1915 sold to Mann, MacNeill & Steeves, renamed *Hinderton*; 1915 sold to Powell, Bacon & Hough Lines Ltd., renamed *Kentish Coast*; 1917 owner renamed Coast Lines Ltd.; 18 November 1928 aground off Plymouth, salvaged and scrapped at Lelant.
Wexford Coast/Pentland Coast	1915-1920 1930-1934	423	Built by J Fullerton & Co., Paisley, 1915; 1917 owner renamed Coast Lines Ltd.; 1920 to City of Cork Steam Packet Co. Ltd., renamed *Blarney*; 1930 to Coast Lines Ltd., renamed *Pentland Coast*; 1934 sold to John S Monks Ltd., Liverpool, renamed *Coastville*; 21 November 1940 on passage Liverpool to Bangor (Co Down), dragged and fetched up on rocks at Ballymacormick Point; 26 December 1940 refloated, towed to Belfast and broken up.
Welsh Coast	1915-1920 1922-1936	1,070	Built by Charles Hill & Sons, Bristol, 1915; 1917 owner renamed Coast Lines Ltd.; 1920 to City of Cork Steam Packet Co. Ltd., renamed *Macroom*; 1922 to Coast Lines Ltd., name reverted to *Welsh Coast*; 1936 sold to Monroe Brothers Ltd., Liverpool, renamed *Kyleglen*, later transferred to Kyle Shipping Co. Ltd., Liverpool; 1937 sold to Bristol Steam Navigation Co. Ltd., Bristol, renamed *Melito*; 1950 sold to Fairwood Shipping & Trading Co. Ltd., Swansea, renamed *Fairwood Oak*; 1955 sold to Holderness Steamship Co. Ltd., Hull, renamed *Holdervale*; 1957 scrapped at Charlestown, Fife.
Western Coast	1916-1917	1,394	Built by Dublin Dockyard Co., Dublin, 1916; 1917 owner renamed Coast Lines Ltd.; 17 November 1917 sunk by torpedo off Eddystone Light on passage Portsmouth to Barry Roads.

Suffolk Coast	1917-1938	870	Built by W Harkess & Son Ltd., Middlesbrough, 1917, owner renamed Coast Lines Ltd.; 1938 sold to Kyle Shipping Co. Ltd (Monroe Brothers Ltd) Liverpool; 1939 renamed *Kylebank*, later sold to Consolidated Fisheries Ltd., Grimsby, renamed *East Anglian*; 1940 sold to George W Grace & Co. Ltd., London, renamed *Sussex Oak*; 1951 to Grace and Chancellor Ltd., Lowestoft; 1954 sold to Holderness Steamship Co., Ltd., Hull, scrapped at Redhaugh-on-Tyne.

2) Coast Lines Limited

See above for: *Eastern Coast*, *Gloucester Coast*, *Kentish Coast*, *Lancashire Coast*, *Monmouth Coast*, *Devon Coast*, *Norfolk Coast*, *Northern Coast*, *Pembroke Coast*, *Somerset Coast*, *Southern Coast*, *Suffolk Coast*, *Welsh Coast*, *Western Coast*, *Wexford Coast*, and the Bristol Channel lighters *Harfat* and *Pennar*.

Ships that came into Coast Lines direct ownership following takeovers between 1917 and 1943 – note that some other companies retained their original identity, although they were wholly owned by Coast Lines Limited.

Name	Coast Lines Service	Gross tons	Comments
Acquired with Rogers & Bright, Volana Shipping Company Limited, Liverpool, 1917			
Volpone	1919	531	Built by R Williamson & Son, Workington, 1907 as *Volpone* for Volana Shipping Co. Ltd. (Rogers & Bright); 1917 Volana Shipping Co. Ltd. acquired by Coast Lines Ltd.; 1919 to Coast Lines Ltd; sold to Regis Shipping Co. Ltd., Cardiff; 1920 renamed *Lyme Regis*; 1925 sold to British Lines Ltd. (Stuart H Biscoe); 1925 sold to Continental Lines Ltd., renamed *Continental Coaster*; 1928 sold to William A Wilson, Southampton; 1936 sold to James S Hooper; 1936 sold to Don David Coastal Shipping Co. Ltd., Hove; 1939 sold to British Isles Coasters Ltd.; 24 September 1940 sunk by torpedo off Great Yarmouth by E-Boat *S 30* on passage from London to Tyne.
Volturnus	1919	615	Built by R Williamson & Son, Workington, 1912 as *Volturnus* for Volana Shipping Co. Ltd. (Rogers & Bright Ltd.); 1917 Volana Shipping Co. Ltd. acquired by Coast Lines Ltd.; 1919 to Coast Lines Ltd.; 1 November 1919 mined and sunk 5 miles south east of Skaw light vessel, on passage Deptford to Copenhagen.
Volhynia/Gower Coast	1919-1932	617	Built by R Williamson & Son, Workington, 1911 as *Volhynia* for Volana Shipping Co. Ltd. (Rogers & Bright Ltd.); 1917 Volana Shipping Co. Ltd. acquired by Coast Lines Ltd.; 1919 to Coast Lines Ltd; 1920 renamed *Gower Coast*; 1932 sold to John Kelly Ltd., renamed *Millisle*; 21 March 1941 sunk by German aircraft 2 miles east of Helwick light vessel on passage Cardiff to Cork.

Volana/Cornish Coast	1919-1935	616	Built by R Williamson & Son, Workington, 1913 as *Volana* for Volana Shipping Co. Ltd. (Rogers & Bright Ltd.); 1917 Volana Shipping Co. Ltd. acquired by Coast Lines Ltd.; 1919 to Coast Lines Ltd.; 1920 renamed *Cornish Coast*; 1935 sold to Monroe Brothers Ltd., Liverpool, renamed *Kyle Queen*; 1936 to Kyle Shipping Co. Ltd. (Monroe Brothers); 1937 sold to Walton Steamship Co. Ltd., Newcastle-on-Tyne; 1951 sold to Sultan Muhanli ve Kardesleri Bayrum ve Makrut, Istanbul, Turkey, renamed *Kardesler*; 1955 sold to 'Meso' Vapur Isletmesi, Istanbul, renamed *Meso*; 1956 sold to Zeki ve Ziya Somnez Izzet Kirtil, Istanbul, renamed *Emel*; 1956 sold to Zeki ve Ziya Somnez, Istanbul; 1982 sold to Somnez Denizcilik ve Tikaret AS, Istanbul, renamed *Aksel I*; 1985 sold to Gazanfer Akar, Istanbul; 1997 renamed *Sile I*; 2005 reported scrapped.
Acquired with H L Stocks & Company Limited (Furness Withy & Company Limited), Kirkcaldy, 1918			
Kirkcaldy	1919	525	Built by Gourlay Brothers & Co., Dundee, 1902 as *Kirkcaldy* for Kirkcaldy & London Steamship Co. Ltd. (Stocks, Turnbull & Co.); 1910 Kirkcaldy & London Steamship Co. Ltd. acquired by Furness Withy & Co. Ltd. and retitled Kirkcaldy, Fife & London Steamship Co. Ltd.; 1916 to H L Stocks & Co. Ltd.; 1918 H L Stocks & Co. Ltd. acquired by Coast Lines Ltd.; 1919 to Coast Lines Ltd, then to Sligo Steam Navigation Co. Ltd.; 1935 scrapped at Ardrossan.
New Abbotshall/Durham Coast	1919-1946	783	Built by Goole Shipbuilding and Repairing Co. Ltd., Goole 1911 as *New Abbotshall* for Kirkcaldy, Fife & London Steamship Co. Ltd.; 1916 to H L Stocks & Co. Ltd. (Furness Withy & Co. Ltd.); 1918 H L Stocks & Co. Ltd. acquired by Coast Lines Ltd.; 1919 to Coast Lines Ltd.; 1920 renamed *Durham Coast*; 1946 sold to Chandbali Steamer Service Co. Ltd., Calcutta, India; 1948 renamed *Rama-Raja*; 1957 scrapped at Calcutta.
Acquired with M Langlands & Sons, Glasgow and Liverpool, 1919			
Princess Beatrice	1919-1920	1,015	Built by D & W Henderson & Co. Ltd., Meadowside, Glasgow, 1893 as *Princess Beatrice* for M Langlands & Sons; 1919 M Langlands & Sons acquired by Coast Lines Ltd.; 1920 sold to Carron Company, Falkirk, renamed *Avon*; 1928 scrapped at Bo'ness.
Silver City	1919-1920	313	Built by Ardrossan Drydock & Shipbuilding Co. Ltd., Ardrossan, 1901 as *Silver City* for Aberdeen, Leith & Moray Firth Steam Shipping Co. Ltd., Aberdeen; 1914 Aberdeen, Leith & Moray Firth Steam Shipping Co. Ltd. acquired by M Langlands & Sons.; 1919 M Langlands & Sons acquired by Coast Lines Ltd.; 1920 sold to Cullen, Allen & Co. Ltd. (T S Wilson), Belfast; 1924 sold to Wilson & Reid Ltd., Belfast; 1926 sold to W A Munn, St John's, Newfoundland; 1938 sold to Job Bros & Co.; 1947 sold to Venezuelan owners — out of register by 1951.

Princess Louise/Clyde Coast	1919-1923 1925	868	Built by D & W Henderson & Co., Partick, Glasgow, 1888 as *Princess Louise* for M Langlands & Sons; 1919 M Langlands & Sons acquired by Coast Lines Ltd.; 1920 renamed *Clyde Coast*; 1923 to Burns & Laird Ltd., renamed *Setter*; 1925 to Coast Lines Ltd., renamed *Clyde Coast*; 1925 to City of Cork Steam Packet Co. Ltd.; 1926 renamed *Macroom*; 1929 scrapped at Port Glasgow.
Lady Tennant/Elgin Coast	1919-1920 1923-1930	452	Built by Napier & Miller Ltd., Yoker, Glasgow, 1904 as *Lady Tennant* for Nobel's Explosives Co. Ltd., Glasgow; 1914 sold to Stornoway Shipping Co. Ltd., Stornoway; 1916 to M Langlands & Sons; 1919 M Langlands & Sons acquired by Coast Lines Ltd.; 1920 to British & Irish Steam Packet Co. Ltd.; 1923 to Coast Lines Ltd.; 1924 renamed *Elgin Coast*; 1930 to British & Irish Steam Packet Co. Ltd., renamed *Kilkenny*; 1936 sold to Capt. H W B Ohlmeyer, Hamburg, Germany, renamed *Lisa*; 1962 sold to T O & H T Vavatsioulas, Salonica, Greece, renamed *Orestis*; 1969 sold to A Pastrikos & G & D Papageorgiou, Thessaloniki, Greece, renamed *Margio*; 1974 scrapped in Greece.
Princess Ena/Fife Coast	1919-1932	665	Built by MacIlwaine & MacColl Ltd., Belfast, 1892 as *Glenariff* for Antrim Iron Ore Co. Ltd., Belfast; 1908 sold to M Langlands & Sons, renamed *Princess Ena*; 1919 M Langlands & Sons acquired by Coast Lines Ltd.; 1920 renamed *Fife Coast*; 1932 sold to Giovanni Rizzo fu Giacomo, Genoa, Italy, renamed *Siciliano*; 1934 sold to Francesco Buccafusca, Messina, Italy; 1936 sold to Societa Anonima Gestione Armamento Navi, Genoa, Italy; 1937 sold to Leonardo Mangiarotti, Genoa, renamed *Mino*; 1939 sold to Marcello Messina, Genoa, renamed *Amalia Messina*; 1940 taken over by Italian Navy; 1947 scrapped.
Princess Helena/Moray Coast	1919-1935	677	Built by Caledon Shipbuilding & Engineering Co. Ltd., Dundee, 1905 as *Princess Helena* for M Langlands & Sons; 1919 M Langlands & Sons acquired by Coast Lines Ltd.; 1920 renamed *Moray Coast*; 1935 sold to J N Vlassopoulo, Ithaca, Greece, renamed *Olga*; 1936 sold to Danube Steamship Trading Co. Ltd., London, renamed *Olga S*; 1937 sold to Cape Lines Ltd., London, renamed *Caper*; 1938 sold to Alcyone Shipping Finance Co. Ltd. London, renamed *Pacifico*; 4 June 1940 sunk at Dunkirk as a blockship.
Princess Thyra/Orkney Coast	1919-1937	781	Built by Russell & Co., Port Glasgow, 1909 as *Princess Thyra* for M Langlands & Sons; 1919 M Langlands & Sons acquired by Coast Lines Ltd.; 1920 renamed *Orkney Coast*; 1937 sold to O/Y Wirma (A Wihuri), Kulosaari, Finland, renamed *Wilpas*; 29 December 1939 sunk off Vasa by gunfire from Russian submarine *SC 311*.

Princess Melita/ *Highland Coast*	1919-1938	1,094	Built by Ramage & Ferguson Ltd., Leith, 1912 as *Princess Melita* for M Langlands & Sons; 1919 M Langlands & Sons acquired by Coast Lines Ltd.; 1920 renamed *Highland Coast*; 1938 sold to Soc. Anon. di Nav. Rimorchi e Salvataggi (D Tripovitch & Ci.), Trieste, Italy, renamed *Tripolino*; 1 November 1942 sunk by torpedo fired by British aircraft in Gulf of Bomba on passage Benghazi to Tobruk.
Princess Irma/Cheshire Coast	1919-1946	1,122	Built by Sir W G Raylton Dixon & Co. Ltd., Middlesbrough, 1915 as *Princess Irma* for M Langlands & Sons; 1919 M Langlands & Sons acquired by Coast Lines Ltd.; 1920 renamed *Cheshire Coast*; 1946 sold to Union d' Enterprises Marocaines, Casablanca, Morocco, renamed *Caid Allal*; 1951 sold to Simon D Attar (Cie. Orano-Marocaine), Casablanca, renamed *Rab*; 1955 scrapped at Savona, Italy.
Acquired with Tedcastle & McCormick & Company Limited, Dublin, 1919			
Blackwater	1919-1920	678	Built by Ailsa Shipbuilding Co. Ltd., Troon, 1907 as *Blackwater* for Tedcastle, McCormick & Co. Ltd., Dublin; 1919 Tedcastle, McCormick & Co. Ltd. acquired by British & Irish Steam Packet Co. Ltd.; to Coast Lines Ltd.; 1920 sold to Samuel Kelly, Belfast; 1937 to Lady Mary Kelly as executor on the death of Samuel Kelly; 1937 to John Kelly Ltd.; 1952 renamed *Ballygowan*; 1954 scrapped at Rainham, Kent.
Dublin/Cardigan Coast	1919-1920 1922-1928	711	Built by John Fullerton & Co., Paisley, 1904 as *Dublin* for Tedcastle, McCormick & Co. Ltd., Dublin; 1919 Tedcastle, McCormick & Co. Ltd. acquired by British & Irish Steam Packet Co. Ltd.; to Coast Lines Ltd,; 1920 to British & Irish Steam Packet Co. Ltd.; 1922 to Coast Lines Ltd., renamed *Cardigan Coast*; 1928 sold to R & D A Duncan (William Clint), Belfast, renamed *Themston*; 1950 sold to Tyson, Edgar Shipping Ltd.; 1952 scrapped at Rosyth.
Acquired with Little Western Steamship Company, Penzance, 1920			
Cloch	1920	745	Built by Dobie & Co., Govan, 1883 as *Cloch* for Clyde Shipping Co., Glasgow; 1893 sold to George P Bazeley & Sons (Little Western Steamship Co.), Penzance; 1920 George Bazeley & Sons Ltd. acquired by Coast Lines Ltd., sold to Carron Company, Falkirk, renamed *Grange*; 1925 scrapped at Bo'ness.
Mercutio	1920-1925	872	Built by J & G Thomson, Clydebank, 1879 as *Mercutio* for Gledhill & Dishart, Leith; 1884 sold to Marshall, Dodson & Co.; 1888 sold to Dodson & Craig; 1889 to William H Dodson & Co.; 1891 sold to George P Bazeley & Sons (Little Western Steamship Co.), Penzance; 1905 to George P Bazeley & Sons Ltd., Penzance; 1920 George Bazeley & Sons Ltd. acquired by Coast Lines Ltd.; 1925 scrapped at Preston.

Norfolk Coast	1920-1932	981	Built by Archibald McMillan & Son Ltd., Dumbarton, 1894 as **Valencia** for James H Goodyear, Liverpool; 1894 to 'Valencia' Steamship Co. Ltd. (Goodyear & Co.), Liverpool; 1910 sold to George P Bazeley & Sons (Little Western Steamship Co.), Penzance, renamed **Cadoc**; 1910 to George Bazeley & Sons Ltd., Penzance; 1920 George Bazeley & Sons Ltd. acquired by Coast Lines Ltd., renamed **Norfolk Coast**; 1932 sold to Vincenzo Mirabella, Catania, Italy, renamed **Resurrectio**; 1948 sold to Mauritzio Rossi, Catania, renamed **Daniela** – out of register by 1959.
Acquired with London Welsh Steamship Company Limited (Furness Withy), West Hartlepool, 1923			
Glamorgan Coast	1923-1932	684	Built by Smith's Dock Co. Ltd., Middlesbrough, 1912 as **Channel Trader** for Furness, Withy & Co. Ltd., West Hartlepool; 1913 to London Welsh Steamship Co. Ltd. (Furness, Withy & Co. Ltd.), West Hartlepool; 1923 London Welsh Steamship Co. Ltd. acquired by Coast Lines Ltd., renamed **Glamorgan Coast**; 13 September 1932 wrecked on North Point, Cape Cornwall, on passage Bristol to Penzance.
Yorkshire Coast	1923-1938	702	Built by Dundee Shipbuilding Co. Ltd., Dundee, 1913 as **Llanelly Trader** for Furness, Withy & Co. Ltd., West Hartlepool; 1913 to London Welsh Steamship Co. Ltd. (Furness, Withy & Co. Ltd.), West Hartlepool; 1923 London Welsh Steamship Co. Ltd. acquired by Coast Lines Ltd., renamed **Yorkshire Coast**; 1938 sold to Ivan L Bulic, Split, Yugoslavia, renamed **Solin**; 1941 seized by Italian Government, renamed **Marino**; 1946 acquired by Jadranska Slobodna Plovidba, Vranjic, Yugoslavia; 1949 taken over by State Enterprise Jugoslavenska Linijska Plovidba, Vranjic; 1957 to Kvarnerska Plovidba, Rijeka, Yugoslavia; 1963 scrapped at Split.
Acquired with Grahamstown Shipping Company Limited, Glasgow, 1923			
Denbigh Coast	1924-1929	411	Built by Caird & Co. Ltd., Greenock, 1891 as **Grouse** for G & J Burns, Glasgow; 1904 to G & J Burns Ltd.; 1920 G & J Burns Ltd. acquired by Coast Lines Ltd.; 1922 owner renamed Burns & Laird Lines Ltd.; 1922 sold to Grahamston Shipping Co. Ltd. (T L Duff & Co.), Glasgow, renamed **Kelvindale**; 1923 Grahamston Shipping Co. Ltd. acquired by Burns & Laird Lines Ltd.; 1924 to Coast Lines Ltd., renamed **Denbigh Coast**; 1929 to David MacBrayne (1928) Ltd., Glasgow, renamed **Lochdunvegan**; 1934 owner name reverted to David MacBrayne Ltd.; 1948 scrapped at Faslane.
Acquired with Michael Murphy Limited, Dublin, 1926			
Anglesey Coast	1929-1937	863	Built by Dublin Dockyard Co. Ltd., Dublin, 1911 as **Enda** for Michael Murphy Ltd., Dublin; 1926 Michael Murphy Ltd. acquired by British & Irish Steam Packet Co. Ltd.; 1929 to Coast Lines Ltd., renamed **Anglesey Coast**; 1937 to London & Channel Islands Steamship Co. Ltd. (Cheeswright & Ford), London, renamed **Norman Queen**; 1937 sold to Kyle Shipping Co. Ltd. (Monroe Brothers), Liverpool, renamed **Kylecroft**; 1955 scrapped at Llanelli.

Cardigan Coast	1929-1937	781	Built by Dublin Dockyard Co. Ltd., Dublin, 1913 as *Patricia* for Michael Murphy Ltd., Dublin; 1926 Michael Murphy Ltd. acquired by British & Irish Steam Packet Co. Ltd.; 1929 to Coast Lines Ltd., renamed *Cardigan Coast*; 1937 sold to William Thomas & Sons, Anglesey, renamed *Eilian Hill*; 1955 scrapped at Hendrik-ido-Ambacht, Netherlands.
Monmouth Coast	1933-1945	878	Built by Ayrshire Dockyard Co. Ltd., Irvine, 1924 as *Grania* for Michael Murphy Ltd., Dublin; 1926 Michael Murphy Ltd. acquired by British & Irish Steam Packet Co. Ltd.; 1933 to Coast Lines Ltd., renamed *Monmouth Coast*; 24 April 1945 sunk by torpedo fired by submarine *U-1305*, 7 miles north east of Tory Island, on passage Sligo to Liverpool.
Acquired with Antrim Iron Ore Company, Belfast, 1929			
Antrim Coast	1929-1933	1,001	Built by Ramage & Ferguson Ltd., Leith 1905 as *Ploussa* for Thomas Cowan, Leith; 1916 Sold to Antrim Iron Ore Co. Ltd., Belfast, renamed *Glentaise*; 1929 Antrim Iron Ore Co. Ltd. acquired by Coast Lines Ltd., renamed *Antrim Coast*; 1933 sold to Soc. Algéro-Marocaine de Nav., Oran, France, renamed *Regina Pacis*; 1934 sold to Scotto, Ambrosino, Pugliese Fils & Cie., Oran; 1936 sold to P Cottaropoulos & G Theophylactos (Soc. Franco-Tunisienne d'Armement), Marseilles, France, renamed *Prado*; 1939 French Navy Auxiliary Minesweeper *AD 372*; 10 December 1942 seized by German Government; 1943 to Kriegsmarine, renamed *Netzleger XI*; 29 August 1944 scuttled at Marseilles; 1947 raised and scrapped.
Aberdeen Coast	1929-1934	1,013	Built by Londonderry Shipbuilding & Engineering Co. Ltd., Londonderry, 1903 as *Glendun* for Antrim Iron Ore Co. Ltd., Belfast; 1929 Antrim Iron Ore Co. Ltd. acquired by Coast Lines Ltd., renamed *Aberdeen Coast*; 1934 sold to Efesar Ltd., Manchester, renamed *Efesar*; 1935 sold to E Jakobson, Pärnu, Estonia, renamed *Ray*; 1935 scrapped.
Acquired with Henry Burden Jr., & Company Limited, Poole, 1937			
Palmston	1937	430	Built by J Fullerton & Co., Paisley, 1907 as *La Plata* for La Fluvial (a Carbone), Argentina; 1917 sold to Instone Transport & Trading Co. (S Instone & Co., Ltd.), London, renamed *Palmston*; 1922 to S Instone & Co., Ltd., London; 1923 sold to Invicta Coal & Shipping Co., Ltd., Sandwich, Kent (C E Hallett); 1926 sold to Henry Burden, Jr., & Co. Ltd. (London & Poole Steamship Co.), Poole; 1937 Henry Burden, Jr., & Co. Ltd. acquired by Coast Lines Ltd., sold to James Mitchell & Co. Ltd., Leith; 1940 sold to Risdon, Beazley Ltd., Southampton; 1946 sold to T & W Colasei Ltd., London; 1947 sold to A/S Rederiet 'Anholt' (R L Albertsen), Copenhagen, Denmark, renamed *Amos*; 1962 scrapped at Randers.

Burdenna IV	1937-1938	146	Built by King's Lynn Slipway Co. Ltd., King's Lynn, 1920 as ***Anglomex No 1*** for Anglo-Mexican Petroleum Co. Ltd., London; 1930 to Eagle Oil & Shipping Co. Ltd., London; 1933 sold to Henry Burden, Jr., & Co. Ltd. (London & Poole Steamship Co.), Poole, renamed ***Burdenna IV***; 1937 Henry Burden, Jr., & Co. Ltd. acquired by Coast Lines Ltd.; 1938 sold to Thomas W Dawson; 1939 sold to Stevinson, Hardy & Co. Ltd., London; 1940 sold to Enidtown Shipping Co. Ltd. (Comben, Longstaff & Co. Ltd.); 1946 sold to Ministry of Transport (Ross & Marshall Ltd. managers); 1947 sold to John Harker Ltd., Knottingley; 1948 renamed ***Bardale H***; 1969 scrapped.
Acquired goodwill and remaining assets of Fisher, Renwick Manchester-London Steamers Limited, Manchester, 1939			
Thames Coast	1939-1946	1,045	Built by William Dobson & Co. Ltd., Newcastle, 1914 as ***Cuirassier*** for Fisher, Renwick Manchester-London Steamers Ltd., Manchester; 1939 Fisher, Renwick Manchester-London Steamers Ltd. acquired by Coast Lines Ltd., renamed ***Thames Coast***; 1946 sold to New Dhobra Steamships Ltd., Bombay, India; 1947 sold to Malabar Steamship Co. Ltd., Bombay, renamed ***Jagdamba***; 30 December 1948 ashore 30 miles south of Tuticorin, refloated and declared constructive total loss; 1951 scrapped at Madras.
Avon Coast	1939-1949	1,036	Built by William Dobson & Co. Ltd., Low Walker-on-Tyne, 1922 as ***Sapper*** for Fisher, Renwick Manchester-London Steamers Ltd., Manchester; 1939 Fisher, Renwick Manchester-London Steamers Ltd. acquired by Coast Lines Ltd., renamed ***Avon Coast***; 1949 to Belfast Steamship Co. Ltd., renamed ***Ulster Star***; 1954 scrapped at Briton Ferry.
Medway Coast	1939-1949	1,014	Built by Tyne Iron Shipbuilding Co. Ltd., Newcastle, 1924 as ***Sentry*** for Fisher, Renwick Manchester-London Steamers Ltd., Manchester; 1939 Fisher, Renwick Manchester-London Steamers Ltd. acquired by Coast Lines Ltd., renamed ***Medway Coast***; 1949 to Belfast Steamship Co. Ltd., renamed ***Ulster Duchess***; 1955 scrapped at Port Glasgow.
Acquired with South Wales & Liverpool Steamship Company Limited (Robert Gilchrist & Company), Liverpool, 1943			
Victor	1943	437	Built by Hutson & Sons Ltd., Glasgow, 1907 as ***Victor*** for Glasgow Steam Coasters Co. Ltd. (John M Paton & Peter D Hendry, Glasgow; 1914 sold to North Eastern Steam Shipping Co. Ltd. (G Elsmie & Son), Aberdeen; 1917 sold to South Wales & Liverpool Steamship Co. Ltd., Liverpool (Robert Gilchrist & Co.); 1943 South Wales & Liverpool Steamship Co. Ltd. acquired by Coast Lines Ltd.; 1943 sold to Ribble Shipping Co. Ltd., Liverpool (William J Ireland); 1947 to H Harrison (Shipping) Co. Ltd. (William J Ireland); 1948 sold to Glynwood Navigation Co. Ltd. (William G Thomas), renamed ***Lady Wood***; 1953 scrapped at Llanelli.

Perdita	1943-1945	543	Built by Mackay Brothers, Alloa, 1910 as **Perdita** for South Wales & Liverpool Steam Ship Co. Ltd. (Robert Gilchrist & Co.); 1943 South Wales & Liverpool Steamship Co. Ltd. acquired by Coast Lines Ltd.; 1945 sold to Mersey Ports Stevedoring Co. Ltd.; 1951 sold to Giovanni Fornara, Genoa, Italy; 1952 renamed **Sedula**; 1953 renamed **Susanna**; 10 February 1953 stranded and later sank over reef 30 miles north of Jeddah, on passage Naples to Jeddah.
Portia/Shetland Coast	1943-1946	801	Built by John Duthie Torry Shipbuilding Co., Aberdeen, 1925 as **Portia** for South Wales & Liverpool Steamship Co. Ltd. (Robert Gilchrist & Co.); 1943 South Wales & Liverpool Steamship Co. Ltd. acquired by Coast Lines Ltd.; 1945 renamed **Shetland Coast**; 1946 to Michael Murphy (1937) Ltd., Dublin, renamed **Portia**; 1950 to Zillah Shipping Co. Ltd. (W A Savage Ltd.), renamed **Fairfield**; 1955 scrapped at Troon.
Fire Queen/Orkney Coast	1943-1949	652	Built by Ailsa Shipbuilding Co. Ltd., Troon, 1921 as **Arclight** for 'Light' Shipping Co. Ltd. (Ross & Marshall Ltd.), Greenock; 1933 sold to Gilchrists Traders (Steamships) Ltd. (F B Johnson), Liverpool, renamed **Fire Queen**; 1936 owners renamed Robert Gilchrist & Co.; 1943 Robert Gilchrist & Co. acquired by Coast Lines Ltd.; 1945 renamed **Orkney Coast**; 1949 to Zillah Shipping & Carrying Co. Ltd. (W A Savage Ltd.), Liverpool, renamed **Dransfield**; 1949 owner renamed Zillah Shipping Co. Ltd.; 1955 scrapped at Troon.

Vessels built for or purchased by Coast Lines Limited

Name	Coast Lines Service	Gross tons	Comments
British Coast	1919-1922	1,940	Built by Swan Hunter & Wigham Richardson Ltd., Sunderland, 1919 as **War Shannon** for Shipping Controller; completed for Coast Lines Ltd. as **British Coast**; 1922 sold to Moss Steamship Co. Ltd. (James Moss & Co. Ltd.), Liverpool (Royal Mail Group), renamed **Etrib**; 1930 to James Moss & Co. (Moss Line) Ltd., Liverpool; 1934 to Moss Hutchison Line Ltd., Liverpool; 1935 Moss Hutchison Line Ltd acquired by General Steam Navigation Company; 14 June 1942 sunk by torpedo fired by German submarine **U-522**, 400 miles west of Portugal on passage Carthagena to Liverpool.

Western Coast	1919-1922	1,928	Built by Swan Hunter & Wigham Richardson Ltd., Sunderland, 1919 for Shipping Controller (launched without name); completed for Coast Lines Ltd. as *Western Coast*; 1922 sold to Moss Steamship Co. Ltd. (James Moss & Co. Ltd.), Liverpool (Royal Mail Group), renamed *Esneh*; 1930 to James Moss & Co. (Moss Line) Ltd., Liverpool; 1934 to Moss Hutchison Line Ltd., Liverpool; 1935 Moss Hutchison Line Ltd acquired by General Steam Navigation Company, London; 1948 sold to Olympus Navigation Co. Ltd. (N P Lanitis), Famagusta, renamed *Tefkros*; 1951 sold to Winly Navigation Co. Ltd., Hong Kong; 1954 sold to Choon Kee Navigation Co. Ltd., Hong Kong; 1958 renamed *Shun On*; 1959 scrapped at Hong Kong.
Somerset Coast	1919-1950	1,353	Built by Harland & Wolff Ltd., Govan, 1919; 1950 to Belfast, Mersey & Manchester Steamship Co. Ltd., renamed *Mountstewart*; 1955 scrapped at Troon.
Princess Olga/ Lancashire Coast	1920-1948	1,104	Built by Sir Raylton Dixon & Co. Ltd., Middlesbrough, 1920 as *Princess Olga* for M Langlands & Sons but completed for Coast Lines Ltd., renamed *Lancashire Coast*; 1948 to Belfast Steamship Co. Ltd., renamed *Ulster Hero*; 1954 scrapped at Barrow.
Northern Coast	1920 1922-1954	1,211	Built by A & J Inglis Ltd., Pointhouse, 1920 as *Ayrshire Coast* but launched as *Northern Coast*; 1921 completed for British & Irish Steam Packet Co. Ltd., Dublin as *Lady Valentia*; 1922 to Coast Lines Ltd., renamed *Northern Coast*; 1954 scrapped Passage West, Cork.
Lydia	1922-1923	1,133	Built by J & G Thomson Ltd., Clydebank, 1890 as *Lydia* for London & South Western Railway, Southampton; 1919 sold to Thomas Sales, through agency of James Dredging, Towing & Transport Co. Ltd.; 1920 to James Dredging, Towing & Transport Co. Ltd., Southampton; 1921 sold to Capt. Montagu Yates and later repossessed by James Dredging, Towing & Transport Co. Ltd.; 1922 sold to British & Irish Steam Packet Co. Ltd. and then to Coast Lines Ltd.; 1923 sold to Nav. à Vaplonienne G Yannoulato Frères, Greece, renamed *Ierac*; 1924 to S A Ionienne de Nav. à Vap. 'Yannoulatos'; 1927 renamed *Ierax*; 1929 sold to Hellenic Coast Lines Co. Ltd., Greece; 1933 scrapped at Savona, Italy.

Irish Coast	1922-1938	240	Built by Larne Shipbuilding Co., Larne, 1900 as *Mayflower* for Mayflower Steamship Co. Ltd. (Hugh Foster), Belfast; 1902 sold to Coast Transit Co. Ltd., Falkirk (James Boyle), resold to Cardigan Commercial Steam Packet Co. Ltd. (David I Evans), Cardigan; 1904 sold to R & D Jones Ltd., Liverpool, resold to Mayflower Steamship Co. Ltd. (R & D Jones Ltd.), Cardigan; 1912 sold to Frederick W Horlock, Mistley; 1915 sold to Cotton Powder Co. Ltd., London (William J Douglas); 1920 sold to Bickford, Smith & Co. Ltd.; 1922 sold to Coast Lines Ltd., renamed *Irish Coast*; 1938 sold to Charles S Kendall, Southsea; 1940 sold to Vectis Transport Co. Ltd., Portsmouth (E W Gilbert); 1942 sold to British Iron and Steel Corporation (Salvage) Ltd., Glasgow (Arthur H Turner); 1949 renamed *Arcliff*; 1949 sold to Ministry of Transport, London; 1951 scrapped at Troon.
Truro Trader	1922-1938	100	Built by P McGregor & Son, Kirkintilloch, 1912 as *Inniscroone* for The Coaster Motor Shipping Co. Ltd. (John M Paton), Glasgow; 1918 sold to Henry L Greig, Hull; sold to London and Paris Marine Express Co. Ltd.; 1922 sold to Henry L Greig & Reginald Smith, Hull; 1922 sold to John Johnston, Glasgow; 1922 to Olsen, Johnston & Co. Ltd., Glasgow; sold to Coast Lines Ltd., renamed *Truro Trader*; 1938 sold to Stephen A Portus, Garston Dock; 1939 sold to Wadsworth Lighterage & Coaling Co. Ltd., Liverpool; 1962 scrapped.
Carmarthen Coast	1922-1939	961	Built by Ardrossan Drydock & Shipbuilding Co. Ltd., Ardrossan, 1921 as *Svanfoss* for Otto & Thor Thoresen A/S, Norway; completed as *Langfjord* for Den Norske Amerikalinje A/S, Christiania, Norway; sold to Det Bergenske D/S, Bergen, Norway; 1922 renamed *Nova*; 1922 sold to Coast Lines Ltd., renamed *Carmarthen Coast*; 9 November 1939 sunk by mine laid by *U-24*, 3 miles off Seaham Harbour.
Western Coast	1922-1941	1,390	Built by Caledon Shipbuilding & Engineering Co. Ltd., Dundee, 1919 as *War Leven* for the Shipping Controller, J Moss & Co. Ltd., manager; sold to Moss Steamship Co. Ltd., Liverpool, renamed *Limoges*; 1922 sold to Coast Lines Ltd., renamed *Western Coast*; 1941 to Burns & Laird Lines Ltd.; 1946 renamed *Meath*; 1948 to British & Irish Steam Packet Co. Ltd.; 1952 to Burns & Laird Lines Ltd., renamed *Lairdscastle*; 1958 scrapped at Hendrik-Ido-Ambacht, Netherlands.
Ayrshire Coast	1922-1923 1925-1947	773	Built by A & J Inglis Ltd., Pointhouse, 1922 for G & J Burns Ltd., order taken over by British & Irish Steam Packet Co. Ltd., order taken over by Coast Lines Ltd., completed as *Ayrshire Coast*; 1923 to Burns & Laird Lines Ltd., renamed *Spaniel*; 1925 to Coast Lines Ltd., renamed *Ayrshire Coast*; 1947 to Belfast Steamship Co. Ltd, renamed *Ulster Mariner*; 1955 scrapped at Passage West, Cork.

Eastern Coast	1922-1954	1,223	Built by A & J Inglis Ltd., Pointhouse, Glasgow, 1922 as *Scottish Coast*, renamed *Eastern Coast* before completion; 1954 sold to Donald J Shanks, Hamilton, Bermuda, resold to Hamilton Bermuda Steamship Navigation Co. Ltd., Hamilton, renamed *Pamela Shanks*; 1955 sold to African Coasters (Pty) Ltd., Durban, renamed *Margin*; 1964 scrapped at Durban.
Dorset Coast	1924-1929	483	Built by James Towers Shipbuilding Co. Ltd., Bristol, 1924 as *Reedham* for Walford Lines Ltd., London but completed for Coast Lines Ltd. as *Dorset Coast*; 1929 to Belfast Steamship Co. Ltd., renamed *Logic*; 1935 renamed *Ulster Hero*; 1945 sold to J & A Gardner & Co. Ltd., Glasgow, renamed *Saint Conan*; 1958 scrapped at Dublin.
Victoria	1925-1934	145	Built by W J Yarwood & Sons Ltd., Northwich, 1898 as *Victoria* for Northwich Carrying Co. Ltd., Northwich, Cheshire; 1925 sold to Coast Lines Ltd.; 1934 sold to Kelly's Barges Ltd., Liverpool; 1943 sold to Wadsworth Lighterage & Coaling Co. Ltd., Liverpool; 1962 scrapped.
Scottish Coast	1925-1938	774	Built by A & J Inglis Ltd, Pointhouse, 1922 as *Scottish Coast*, completed as *Lurcher* for J & G Burns, Glasgow; 1925 to Coast Lines Ltd., renamed *Scottish Coast*; 1938 to Belfast Steamship Company, renamed *Ulster Coast*; 1954 sold to Ahern Shipping Co., Montreal, Canada, renamed *Ahern Trader*; 10 January 1960 wrecked at Muddy Hole, Gander Bay, Newfoundland,
Cumberland Coast/ Cambrian Coast	1925-1929 1933-1947	759	Built by Harland & Wolff Ltd., Govan, 1921 as *Princess Dagmar* for M Langlands & Sons, but launched as *Gorilla* for G & J Burns Ltd.; 1922 owner renamed Burns & Laird Lines Ltd.; 1925 to Coast Lines Ltd., renamed *Cumberland Coast*; 1929 to City of Cork Steam Packet Co. Ltd., renamed *Kinsale*; 1933: to Coast Lines Ltd., renamed *Cambrian Coast*; 1947 to Belfast Steamship Co. Ltd., renamed *Ulster Merchant*; 1954 scrapped at Newport, South Wales.
Allegiance	1925-1951	171	Built by W J Yarwood & Sons Ltd., Northwich, 1917 as *Allegiance* for Alfred Cooper, Widnes; 1920 sold to Hansen Shipping Co. Ltd. (Hansen Brothers Ltd.), Cardiff; 1921 sold to John Cockburn & Joseph P Gunn, North Shields; 1925 sold to Coast Lines Ltd.; 1951 sold to Abel Barges Ltd., Liverpool, renamed *Wharfedale*; 1966 scrapped at Preston.
Sutherland Coast	1926-1930	772	Built by Harland & Wolff Ltd., Govan, 1920 as *Princess Caroline* for M Langlands & Sons, completed as *Redbreast* for G & J Burns Ltd.; 1922 owner renamed Burns & Laird Lines Ltd.; 1926 to Coast Lines Ltd., renamed *Sutherland Coast*; 1930 to Burns & Laird Lines Ltd., renamed *Lairdsbrook*; 1960 scrapped at Haulbowline, Cork.

Killarney	1931-1947	2,082	Built by Harland & Wolff Ltd., Belfast, 1893 as *Magic* for Belfast Steamship Co. Ltd.; 1924 to City of Cork Steam Packet Co. Ltd., renamed *Killarney*; 1931 to Coast Lines Ltd.; 1947 sold to Bury Court Shipping Co. Ltd., London, renamed *Attiki*; 1948 sold to Epirotiki Steamship Navigation Co. 'George Potamianos', Piraeus, Greece, renamed *Adrias*; 6 October 1951 wrecked on Falkonera Island, Greece, on passage Crete to Piraeus.
Fife Coast	1933-1940	367	Built by Ardrossan Dockyard Ltd., Ardrossan, 1933; 8 August 1940 sunk by torpedoes fired by E-boats *S-21* & *S-27*, west of Beachy Head, on passage London to Falmouth and Plymouth.
British Coast	1933-1964	889	Built by Henry Robb Ltd., Leith, 1933; 1964 sold to Newfoundland Marine Services Ltd., Saint Johns, Newfoundland, renamed *Newfoundland Coast*; 1979 sold to Labrador Shipping Co. Ltd., Canada; 14 July 1981 wrecked 16 miles west of Providenciales, Turks & Caicos Islands.
Carrick Coast/Zulu Coast	1934-1953	369	Built by Ardrossan Dockyard Ltd., Ardrossan, 1934; 1951 renamed *Zulu Coast*; 7 April 1953 wrecked 2 miles north of Groene River, South Africa.
Atlantic Coast	1934-1962	890	Built by Henry Robb Ltd., Leith, 1934; 1962 to Union Steamship Co. of South Africa Ltd., renamed *Pondo Coast*; 1967 company acquired by Grindrod, Gersigny & Co. (Pty.), Ltd., renamed *Pondo*; 1969 sold to Doride di Navigazione, Palermo, Italy; 1971 sold to Cia. de Nav. Piedramar SA, Panama, renamed *Dona Gracia*; 1973 scrapped at Vado Ligure.
Pacific Coast	1935-1939	1,210	Built by Ardrossan Dockyard Ltd., Ardrossan, 1935; 9 November 1939 gutted at Brest, hulk later towed to Falmouth and scrapped.
Anglian Coast/Griqua Coast	1935-1961	594	Built by S P Austin & Son Ltd., Sunderland, 1935; 1955 renamed *Griqua Coast*; 1961 to Thesen's Steamship Co. Ltd.; 1968 scrapped at Saldhana Bay, South Africa.
Ocean Coast	1935-1964	1,173	Built by Henry Robb Ltd., Leith, 1935 as *Anglian Coast*, launched as *Ocean Coast*; 1964 sold to Anastassios M & Angela Nomikos, Piraeus, Greece, renamed *Effy*; 1967 sold to Titika Cia. Nav. SA, Piraeus, Greece, renamed *Anna Maria*; 8 February 1969 wrecked 10 miles north of Constantza, Romania.
Pembroke Coast	1936-1940	625	Built by Henry Robb Ltd., Leith, 1936; 20 May 1940 sunk by German aircraft at Harstad, Norway.
Devon Coast	1936-1943	646	Built by Ardrossan Dockyard Ltd., Ardrossan, 1936; 2 May 1943 destroyed in aerial attack at Bari, Italy.

Dorset Coast	1936-1943	646	Built by Ardrossan, Dockyard Ltd., Ardrossan, 1936; 12 May 1943 sunk in aerial attack at Algiers; 1946 refloated and sold to Soc. Algérienne de Sauvetage (Zagamé), Algiers, Algeria, renamed *Galatée*; 1949 to Soc. Algérienne d'Armament Zagame & Cie., Algiers; 1953 sold to Cie. Maritime des Chargeurs Réunis, Le Havre, France, renamed *Kaa*; 1955 sold to Isabel Navigation Co. SA (John Manners & Co. Ltd.), Panama, renamed *Isabel*; 1965 sold to Cia. Naviera Viento del Sur, SA (Lam Soon Shipping Co., Ltd., Hong Kong); 1974 sold to Malayan Navigation Co., Penang, Malaysia, renamed *Terang*; 1976 sold to Tat Lee Investment Co. SA, resold to Straits Chartering Agency, Pte., Ltd., Singapore, renamed *Poly I*; 5 August 1976 beached in Gulf of Oman on passage Karachi to Kuwait; declared constructive total loss.
Cornish Coast	1936-1949	219	Built by Ardrossan Dockyard Ltd., Ardrossan, 1936; 1949 sold to M H Bland & Co. Ltd., Gibraltar, renamed *Gibel Musa*; 1954 sold to Leon Farache, Tangier - out of register by 1959.
Antrim Coast	1936-1964	646	Built by Ardrossan Dockyard Ltd., Ardrossan, 1936; 1964 to British Channel Islands Shipping Co. Ltd., renamed *Sark Coast*; 1967 sold to L Raissis, Beirut, Lebanon, renamed *Miltiadis*; 1973 scrapped at Perama, Greece.
Munster	1937-1940	4,302	Built by Harland & Wolff Ltd., Belfast, 1937; 7 February 1940 sunk by mine off Mersey Bar Lightship.
Hampshire Coast	1937-1945	485	Built by NV Industrieele Maat. 'De Noord', Alblasserdam, Netherlands 1937; 1945 sold to Springfjord Shipping Co. Ltd., London; 1946 renamed *Springhaven*; 1947 sold to Havercrest Shipping Co. Ltd., London; 1947 sold to Dundee, Perth & London Shipping Co. Ltd., Dundee, renamed *Gannochy*; 25 February 1958 foundered off Mersey Bar on passage Penmaenmawr to Liverpool.
Norfolk Coast	1937-1945	646	Built by Ardrossan Dockyard Ltd., Ardrossan 1937; 28 February 1945 sunk by torpedo fired by *U-1302*, north-west of St David's Head, Pembrokeshire, on passage Cardiff to Liverpool.
Leinster	1937-1946	4,302	Built by Harland & Wolff Ltd., Belfast, 1937; 1946 to Belfast Steamship Co. Ltd., renamed *Ulster Prince*; 1966 renamed *Ulster Prince I*; 1967 sold to Van Heyghen Frères, Ghent, Belgium, resold to Epirotiki Lines (George Potamianos) Ltd., Greece, renamed *Ulster Prince*; 1968 to Epirotiki Steamship Co. Ltd., Famagusta, Cyprus, renamed *Adria*; 1969 renamed *Odysseus*; 1979 scrapped at Faslane.
Welsh Coast	1937-1955	646	Built by Ardrossan Dockyard Ltd., Ardrossan 1937; 1955 to British Channel Islands Shipping Co. Ltd., renamed *Guernsey Coast*; 6 August 1964 sank in collision 38 miles north east of Cap de la Hague, on passage St Peter Port to Shoreham.
Denbigh Coast	1937-1951 1958-1960	509	Built by NV Industrieele Maatschappij 'De Noord', Alblasserdam, Netherlands, 1937; 1951 to Burns & Laird Lines Ltd., renamed *Lairdsfern*; 1958 to Coast Lines Ltd., renamed *Denbigh Coast*; 18 July 1960 sank in collision in Crosby channel, Liverpool, on passage Manchester to Belfast.

Normandy Coast	1938-1945	1,328	Built by Sir Raylton Dixon & Co. Ltd., Middlesbrough, 1916 as **Lady Cloé** for British & Irish Steam Packet Co. Ltd.; 1938 to Coast Lines Ltd., renamed **Normandy Coast**; 11 January 1945 sunk by torpedo fired by **U-1055** off Point Lynas, Anglesey.
Clyde Coast	1938-1956	511	Built by NV Industrieele Maatschappij 'De Noord', Alblasserdam, 1938; 1956 to Belfast Steamship Co. Ltd., renamed **Ulster Senator**; 1959 to William Sloan & Co. Ltd., renamed **Deveron**; 1963 sold to F C Georgopulos & A N Athanassiades & Co., Piraeus, Greece, renamed **Nissos Delos**; 1966 sold to Dimitrios Argyreas, Piraeus, renamed **Maria**; 1969 sold to Dimitrios Argyreas & Ion S Livas, Piraeus, renamed **Ismini L**; 1972 sold to 'Ismini L' Shipping Co. Ltd., Piraeus; 1973 sold to D Papadimitriou & V Dalabiras, Piraeus; 1974 sold to E Papadimitriou, Piraeus, renamed **Makedonia**; 1979 sold to N Palaeopoulos, Piraeus; 28 September 1979 sank under tow 7 miles off Cape Kiti, Cyprus.
Saxon Queen/Dorset Coast/Matabele Coast	1938 1947-1961	482	Built by NV Boele's Schpsw. & Mch., Bolnes, Netherlands, 1938 as **Saxon Queen** for British Channel Islands Shipping Co. Ltd.; 1938 to Coast Lines Ltd. and then to Plymouth, Channel Islands & Brittany Steamship Co. Ltd., and to British Channel Islands Shipping Co. Ltd.; 1943 to British Channel Traders Ltd.; 1947 to Coast Lines Ltd., renamed **Dorset Coast**; 1951 renamed **Matabele Coast**; 1961 sold to Union Steamship Co. of South Africa Ltd. (Coast Lines Africa (Pty) Ltd.), Cape Town; 1967 scrapped at Durban.
Kentish Coast	1938-1951 1958-1962	459	Built by Werf. Jan Smit, Hgn., Alblasserdam, Netherlands, 1938; 1951 to British Channel Islands Shipping Co. Ltd.; 1958 to Coast Lines Ltd.; 1962 sold to Luigi G Melloni, Savona, Italy, renamed **Melisenda**; 1971 sold to Societa Pimental SpA, Cagliari, Italy, renamed **Monte Carmo**; 1973 sold to Spyridon Karydakis, Greece, renamed **Vanna**; 1974 sold to Pilaros Shipping Co., Greece, renamed **Alekakos**; 1974 sold to Caledonia Maritime Co. Ltd., Limassol, Cyprus, renamed **Aboude** – out of register by 1992.
Mersey Coast	1938-1958 1962-1967	509	Built by NV Industrieele Maatschappij 'De Noord', Alblasserdam, Netherlands, 1938; 1958 to British Channel Islands Shipping Co. Ltd.; 1962 to Coast Lines Ltd.; 1967 sold to Nicolaos Frangos & Sotirios Moundreas, Piraeus, Greece; 1967 sold to D Kontozannis, Piraeus; May 1971 wrecked 9 miles south-east of Ormara on passage from Karachi.

Kerry Coast	1939-1941	1,391	Built by Caledon Shipbuilding & Engineering Co. Ltd., Dundee, 1919 as *War Spey* for Shipping Controller, completed as *Lady Patricia* for British & Irish Steam Packet Co. Ltd.; 1936 to British & Irish Steam Packet Co. (1936) Ltd.; 1938 renamed *Kerry*, owner renamed British & Irish Steam Packet Co. Ltd.; 1939 to Coast Lines Ltd., renamed *Kerry Coast*; 1941 to Burns & Laird Lines Ltd.; 11 March 1944 sank in collision in Mersey, declared constructive total loss; 1945 raised, sold to Henry P Lenaghan & Sons, Belfast, renamed *Bangor Bay*; 1946 sold to Burns & Laird Lines Ltd., renamed *Kerry*; 1947 to British & Irish Steam Packet Co. Ltd.; 1959 scrapped at Passage West, Cork.
Galway Coast	1939-1945	1,302	Built by Clyde Shipbuilding & Engineering Co. Ltd., Port Glasgow, 1915 as *Lady Wimborne* for British & Irish Steam Packet Co. Ltd.; 1936 owner renamed British & Irish Steam Packet Co. (1936) Ltd.; 1938 owner renamed British & Irish Steam Packet Co. Ltd., renamed *Galway*; 1939 to Coast Lines Ltd., renamed *Galway Coast*; 1945 sold to Virtù Steamship Co. Ltd., Malta (Anthony & Bainbridge Ltd.); 1946 renamed *Virtù*; 27 February 1948 ashore off Raz Azzaz lighthouse, Libya, refloated and later scrapped at Tobruk.
Brittany Coast	1939-1946	1,389	Built by Caledon Shipbuilding & Engineering Co. Ltd., Dundee, 1919, as *War Garry* for Shipping Controller, completed for British & Irish Steam Packet Co. Ltd. as *Lady Emerald*; 1936 to British & Irish Steam Packet Co. (1936) Ltd.; 1938 owner renamed British & Irish Steam Packet Co. Ltd., renamed *Carlow*; 1939 to Coast Lines Ltd., renamed *Brittany Coast*; 1946 to Burns & Laird Lines Ltd., renamed *Kildare*; 1948 to British & Irish Steam Packet Co. Ltd.; 1952 to Burns & Laird Lines Ltd., renamed *Lairdsford*; 1960 scrapped at Troon.
Glamorgan Coast	1939-1947	879	Built by Dublin Dockyard Co. Ltd., Dublin, 1920 as *Finola* for Michael Murphy Ltd., Dublin; 1926 Michael Murphy Ltd. acquired by British & Irish Steam Packet Co. Ltd.; 1936 to British & Irish Steam Packet Co. (1936) Ltd.; 1938 owner renamed British & Irish Steam Packet Co. Ltd.; 1939 to Coast Lines Ltd., renamed *Glamorgan Coast*; 1947 to British Channel Traders Ltd., renamed *Stuart Queen*; to Queenship Navigation Ltd.; 1952 to Zillah Shipping Co. Ltd. (W A Savage Ltd.), Liverpool, renamed *Caldyfield*; 1955 scrapped at Preston.
Suffolk Coast	1939-1951	535	Built by N V E J Smit en Zoon's Schpsw., Westerbroek, Netherlands, 1938 as *Marali* for Marcel Porn (Newcastle Coal & Shipping Co. Ltd.); 1939 sold to Coast Lines Ltd., renamed *Suffolk Coast*; 1951 to Tyne-Tees Steam Shipping Co. Ltd.; 1963 sold to Luigi G Melloni, Savona, Italy, renamed *Melania*; 9 February 1970 sank 10 miles south of Livorno, on passage San Antioco to Livorno.

Moray Coast	1940-1954	687	Built by Ardrossan Dockyard Ltd., Ardrossan, 1940; 1954 to British Channel Islands Shipping Co. Ltd., renamed *Jersey Coast*; 1967 sold to Orri Navigation Lines, Jeddah, Saudi Arabia, renamed *Star of Ibrahim*; 1973 sold to Ahmed M Baaboud & Hussan M Fayez & Sons, Jeddah, renamed *Blue Sky*; 9 February 1982 scuttled off Jeddah.
Southern Coast	1943-1955	882	Built by Ardrossan Dockyard Ltd., Ardrossan, 1943; 1955 to Belfast, Mersey & Manchester Steamship Co. Ltd., renamed *Colebrooke*; 1959 to William Sloan & Co. Ltd., renamed *Forth*; 1962 to British Channel Islands Shipping Co. Ltd., renamed *Southern Coast*; 1967 sold to D Varverakis & Chr. Hadjigeorgiou, Piraeus, Greece, renamed *Eleistria*; 1979 sold to Al Rubayia Transport Co., Panama, renamed *Al Rubayia*, resold to Naviglory Ship Corp., Panama; 1985 sold to Al-Rubayah Live Stock Trading & Transportation Co.; 1986 scrapped at Bombay.
Robina	1946-1949	306	Built by Ardrossan Drydock & Shipbuilding Co. Ltd., Ardrossan, 1914 as *Robina* for New Morecambe Central Pier Co. Ltd.; 1922 sold to W A & P Cordingley, Pudsey; 1925 sold to William McCalla & Co., Belfast; 1940 sold to Ulster Steam Tender Co. Ltd., Belfast; 1946 sold to Coast Lines Ltd.; 1949 sold to Southampton, Isle of Wight & South of England Royal Mail Steam Packet Co. Ltd., Southampton; 1953 scrapped at Hendrik-Ido-Ambacht, Netherlands.
Hampshire Coast	1946-1952	1,224	Built by Ardrossan Dockyard Ltd., Ardrossan, 1940 as *Stuart Queen* for British Channel Islands Shipping Co. Ltd.; 1946 to Coast Lines Ltd., renamed *Hampshire Coast*; 1952 to Tyne-Tees Steam Shipping Co. Ltd.; 1959 scrapped at Hendrik-Ido-Ambacht, Netherlands.
Baltic Coast/Cape Coast	1947-1952	1,722	Built by Ardrossan Dockyard Ltd., Ardrossan, 1947 as *Baltic Queen* for British Channel Traders Ltd., completed as *Baltic Coast* for Coast Lines Ltd.; 1951 renamed *Cape Coast*; 13 March 1952 damaged by fire in River Congo, abandoned to underwriters; 1953 sold to Henry P Lenaghan & Sons Ltd., Belfast, renamed *Browns Bay*; 1954 sold to shipbreakers in Ceylon; 1955 sold to Ceylon Shipping Lines Ltd., Colombo, Sri Lanka, renamed *Chilaw*; 1961 sold to Combined Nav. Co. (Panama) Ltd. (United China Shipping Co., Hong Kong), renamed *Combined 1*; 8 December 1961 sank 700 miles north-east of Singapore on passage Kuching to Hong Kong.
Lady Killarney	1947-1956	3,222	Built by Harland & Wolff Ltd., Belfast, 1911 as *Patriotic* for Belfast Steamship Co. Ltd.; 1930 to British & Irish Steam Packet Co. Ltd., renamed *Lady Leinster*; 1936 to British & Irish Steam Packet Co. (1936) Ltd.; 1938 to British & Irish Steam Packet Co. Ltd., renamed *Lady Connaught*; 1940 mined off Liverpool and abandoned to underwriters; 1942 sold to British & Irish Steam Packet Co. Ltd.; 1947: to Coast Lines Ltd., renamed *Lady Killarney*; 1956 scrapped at Port Glasgow.

Devon Coast	1947-1963	972	Built by Burntisland Shipbuilding Co. Ltd., Burntisland, 1937 as **Lottie R** for S & R Steamships Ltd. (Stone & Rolfe Ltd.), Llanelly; 1946 sold to John Stewart & Co. (Shipping) Ltd., Glasgow, renamed **Yewbranch**; 1947 sold to Coast Lines Ltd., renamed **Devon Coast**; 1963 to Queenship Navigation Ltd., renamed **Windsor Queen**; 1965 sold to Progress Maritime Co. SA, Panama, renamed **Elca**; 1967 sold to E Rigas & S Fasoulas, Piraeus, Greece, renamed **Eleni R**; 1973 scrapped at Perama, Greece.
Pacific Coast	1947-1968	1,188	Built by Ardrossan Dockyard Ltd., Ardrossan, 1947; 1968 sold to Kuwait Coast Line Co., Kuwait, renamed **Kuwait Coast**; 1974 sold to Museib Arjumand Zayarti, Abadan, Iran, renamed **Mohamed Nassar**; 1975 renamed **Nassar**; 29 September 1976 wrecked on breakwater at Port Rashid, Dubai, on passage Abadan to Bombay.
Caledonian Coast/ Makalla Coast	1948-1968	1,265	Built by Hall, Russell & Co. Ltd., Aberdeen, 1948 as **Caledonian Coast** for Aberdeen Steam Navigation Co. Ltd., to Coast Lines Ltd.; 1967 renamed **Makalla**; 1968 sold to Alomar Mechanical Engineering Co. (F H Hamza), Kuwait, renamed **Ahmadi Coast**; 1970 sold to Kuwait Coast Line Co. (F H Hamza, A M Khulaib & Mohamed Abdul Aziz Alomar); 1974 scrapped at Cartagena, Spain.
Hibernian Coast	1948-1968	1,258	Built by Hall, Russell & Co. Ltd., 1946 as **Aberdonian Coast** for Aberdeen Steam Navigation Co. Ltd.; 1948 to Coast Lines Ltd., renamed **Hibernian Coast**; 1968 sold to Alomar Mechanical Engineering Co., Kuwait, renamed **Port Said Coast**; 1970 sold to Kuwait Coast Line Co. Kuwait; 1974 scrapped Murcia, Spain.
Damara	1949-1950	1,791	Built by Walter Butler Shipbuilders Inc., Superior, USA, 1942 as **William Bursley** for US War Shipping Administration; 1949 sold to Coast Lines Ltd., renamed **Damara**; 1950 sold to Emilio Canale di Pietro, Genoa, Italy, renamed **Pietro Canale**; 1954 sold to Naviera del Golfo SA, Panama, renamed **Lake Charles**; 1955 sold to Overseas Shipping Corp., Panama; 1956 sold to Caribbean Shipping Corp., Monrovia, ; 1959 sold to Overseas Steamship Corp.; 1962 sold to Marcand Shipping Corp., renamed **Rimandi Mibaju**; 11 May 1964 wrecked on reef off Cayman Islands.
Sark Coast	1950-1952	318	Built by Tees Side Bridge & Engineering Works Ltd., Middlesbrough, 1945 as **LCG (M) 196** for the Admiralty; 1949 sold to Island Shipping Co. Ltd. (British Channel Islands Shipping Co. (Guernsey) Ltd.), renamed **Sark Coast**; 1950 to Coast Lines Ltd.; 1952 sold to Pedder & Mylchreest Ltd., London; 1953 Renamed **Madinina**; 1954 sold to Département de la Martinique (Cie. de Nav. Martiniquaise); 1957 sold to C L Tammis, Kingstown, St Vincent; 13 December 1963 sank off St Vincent.

Adriatic Coast	1949-1968	1,050	Built by Hall, Russell & Co. Ltd., Aberdeen, 1949; 1968 sold to Elias G Spanos, Piraeus, Greece, renamed *Trader*; 1972 to A S Trader Maritime Co. Ltd. (Elias G Spanos), Famagusta, Cyprus, renamed *Ermis*; 1973 sold to Artemission Shipping Co. Ltd. (Tetras Cia. Nav. SA), renamed *Potamia*; 1975 sold to Tamboca Nav. Co. Ltd., Cyprus, renamed *Stella III*; 1980 scrapped.
Baltic Queen	1950	1,791	Built by Walter Butler Shipbuilders Inc., Superior, USA, 1943 as *Gurden Gates* for US War Shipping Administration; 1949 sold to A Coker & Co. Ltd., Liverpool, renamed *Baltic Queen*; 1950 to Coast Lines Ltd., sold to Emilio Canale di Pietro, Genoa, Italy, renamed *Cesare Corsini*; 1953 sold to Marco Proiettis, renamed *Arno*; 1954 sold to Carlo Landi & Co.; 1956 sold to Ferdinando Garre fu Matteo; 1963 sold to P Morfopoulou & A Ermogenis, Piraeus, Greece, renamed *Irida*; 1965 sold to T & G J Moustogiannis, Piraeus, Greece, renamed *O Kalos Samaritis*, resold to Constantinis A Athanassiades & George N Bournias, Piraeus, renamed *Three Stars*; 17 February 1967 damaged by fire off Cape Gata, Cyprus, declared constructive total loss.
Western Coast	1951-1958 1968	791	Built by Goole Shipbuilding & Repairing Co. Ltd., Goole, 1951; 1958 to William Sloan & Co. Ltd., renamed *Tay*; 1965 to Burns & Laird Lines Ltd.; 1968 to Coast Lines Ltd., sold to Melina Corporation of Panama (N C Spanos), Panama, renamed *Charalambos*; 1973 sold to E Proios, Panama, resold to Erika Shipping Co. SA, Famagusta, Cyprus, renamed *Erika*; 14 May 1973 wrecked off Roumbos Island, near Agios Eustratios, on passage Galatz to Hull.
Irish Coast	1952-1968	3,824	Built by Harland & Wolff Ltd., Belfast, 1952; 1968 sold to Epirotiki Steamship Navigation Co. 'George Potamianos' SA, Piraeus, Greece, renamed *Orpheus*; 1969 renamed *Semiramis II*, renamed *Achilleus*; 1970 renamed *Apollon 11*; 1980 renamed *Apollon II*; 1982 sold to Corporacion Naviera Intercontinental de Panama SA, Panama, renamed *Regency*; 1983 sold to Triton Holding Corp. (Passman Shipping Agency SA) Panama; 11 October 1989 wrecked in Philippines.
Herero Coast	1953-1959	493	Built by Schpsw. 'Volharding' Gebr Bodewes, Foxhol, Netherlands, 1950 as *Poseidon* for Kunst & Pekelder, Netherlands; 1953 sold to Coast Lines Ltd., renamed *Herero Coast*; 1959 to Union Steamship Co. of South Africa Ltd. (Coast Lines Africa (Pty) Ltd.), Cape Town; 1967 acquired by Grindrod, Gersigny & Co. (Pty) Ltd., scrapped.

Lancashire Coast/Trojan Prince	1953-1965 1967-1969 1971	1,283	Built by Charles Hill & Sons Ltd., Bristol, 1953; 1965 to Belfast Steamship Co. Ltd.; 1967 to Coast Lines Ltd.; 1968 renamed *Trojan Prince*; 1969 to Belfast Steamship Co. Ltd., renamed *Lancashire Coast*; 1971 to Coast Lines (Services) Ltd., acquired by P&O Short Sea Shipping Ltd.; 1972 to Belfast Steamship Co. Ltd.; 1975 to P&O Ferries Ltd.; 1980 sold to United West Desert for Development de Honduras S de R L, renamed *Paolino*; 1984 scrapped at Salamis, Greece.
Fife Coast/Stormont	1954-1958 1965-1966	906	Built by George Brown & Co. (Marine) Ltd., Greenock, 1954; 1958 to William Sloan & Co. Ltd., renamed *Fruin*; 1963 to Belfast Steamship Co. Ltd., renamed *Stormont*; 1965 to Coast Lines Ltd.; 1966 to Tyne-Tees Steam Shipping Co. Ltd.; 1971 acquired by P&O Short Sea Shipping Ltd.; 1975 to P&O Ferries Ltd.; 1976 sold to Farouk Rassem, W Moukahal & Ahmed Hassan Zeido (United Commercial Co.), Beirut, Lebanon. renamed *Rabunion VII*; 1992 sold to Baraa Z Shipping Co. SARL. (Zeido Hassan Zeido), renamed *Baraa Z*; 1994 scrapped at Tripoli, Lebanon.
Cheshire Coast/Malabar/ Spartan Prince	1954-1965 1970-1971	1,202	Built by Cammell Laird & Co. (Shipbuilders & Engineers) Ltd., Birkenhead, 1954; 1965 to Belfast Steamship Co. Ltd.; 1967 renamed *Malabar*, renamed *Cheshire Coast* and renamed *Spartan Prince*; 1970 to Coast Lines (Management) Ltd.; 1971 renamed *Cheshire Coast*; 1971 to Coast Lines (Services) Ltd.; 1971 acquired by P&O Short Sea Shipping Ltd.; 1971 sold to Amanda Shipping Co. Ltd., Famagusta, Cyprus, renamed *Venture*; 1974 sold to Skiros Shipping Co. Ltd. (Dinami Shipping Agency Ltd.), renamed *Azelia*; 1980 scrapped at Cartagena, Spain.
Essex Coast/ Mountstewart	1955-1957 1965-1967 1968-1969	892	Built by Ardrossan Dockyard Ltd., Ardrossan 1955; 1957 to Belfast, Mersey and Manchester Steamship Co. Ltd., renamed *Mountstewart*; 1960 to Belfast Steamship Co. Ltd.; 1965 to Coast Lines Ltd.; 1967 to British Channel Islands Shipping Co. Ltd.; 1968 to Coast Lines Ltd.; 1969 sold to Greek Currant Producers Line of Panama, Panama, renamed *Evdelos*; 1971 sold to Pounds Shipowners and Shipbreakers Ltd., Portsmouth; 1972 sold to Pothitos Shipping Cia. SA, Mogadishu; Somalia, renamed *Michalis*, to Pothitos Shipping Co., Panama; 1975 sold to Mossel Bay Shipping Co. Ltd.; 1976 sold to Proodos Shipping Co. Ltd. (Prodromos Cia. Financiera Marittima SA),Panama, renamed *Proodos*; 1979 sold to Maritime Commission Inc., renamed *Manuel*; 1980 sold to Basiloos Fottakas de Panagiotis; 1981 sold to Maritime Commission Inc.; 1986 scrapped at Salamis, Greece.

Scottish Coast	1956-1958 1968-1969	3,817	Built by Harland & Wolff Ltd., Belfast, 1956; 1958 to Burns & Laird Lines Ltd.; 1968 to Coast Lines Ltd.; 1969 sold to Kavounides Shipping Co. SA Ltd., Piraeus, Greece, renamed *Galaxias*; 1969 to Hellenic Cruises SA (Kavounides Shipping Co. SA Ltd.), Piraeus, Greece; 1987 sold to Global Cruises SA, St. John's, Antigua & Barbuda; 1989 sold to Princesa Amorosa Co. Ltd. (Louis Shipping Ltd.), Limassol, Cyprus, renamed *Princesa Amorosa*; 2003 scrapped at Mumbai, India.
Cambrian Coast	1957-1971	560	Built by NV IJsselwerf, Capelle a/d IJssel, 1957 as *Jan T* for Rederij Holland NV, Netherlands; 1957 sold to Coast Lines Ltd., renamed *Cambrian Coast*; 1971 to Coast Lines (Services) Ltd.; 1971 sold to W E Dowds Ltd., Newport, renamed *Lorraine D*; 1972 sold to Coastal Motor Ships Ltd., Wallasey; 1981 renamed *Zircon*; 1982 renamed *Glenhaven*; 1988 scrapped at Milford Haven.
Somerset Coast	1958-1959	1,326	Built by Clelands (Successors) Ltd., Wallsend-on-Tyne 1958, as *Somersetbrook* for Williamstown Shipping Co. Ltd. (Comben, Longstaff & Co. Ltd.), completed for Coast Lines Ltd. as *Somerset Coast*; 1959 to Queenship Navigation Ltd., renamed *Richmond Queen*; 1965 sold to Britain Steamship Co. Ltd. (Comben, Longstaff & Co. Ltd.); 1968 to Eskglen Shipping Co. Ltd. (Comben, Longstaff & Co. Ltd.); 1974 sold to Gomba Shipping Ltd. (James Fisher & Sons Ltd.), renamed *Gomba Enterprise*; 1976 to Atlantic Africa Lines Ltd.; 1977: renamed *Atlantic Enterprise*; 20 June 1978 sank at moorings at Bremen, raised and scrapped at Brake, Germany.
Birchfield/Pointer	1958-1965 1968-1971	1,265	Built by Ardrossan Dockyard Ltd., Ardrossan, 1956 as *Birchfield* for Zillah Shipping Co. Ltd. (W A Savage Ltd.); 1958 to Coast Lines Ltd.; 1959 renamed *Pointer*; 1965: to Burns & Laird Lines Ltd.; 1968 to Coast Lines Ltd.; 1970 to Coast Lines (Services) Ltd.; 1971 acquired by P&O Short Sea Shipping Ltd.; 1972 to Belfast Steamship Co. Ltd.; 1975 to P&O Ferries Ltd., sold to Isthmian Navigation Co. Ltd. (Hellenic Mediterranean Lines Co. Ltd.), renamed *Taurus III*; 1976 to Compania Armadora de Sudamerica SA, Limassol, Cyprus; 1981 sold to Thomas Bourtsalas, Eleusis, Greece; 1984 sold to Phalarope Shipping Ltd., Valletta, Malta; 1985 sold to Larnaca Project S de R L (S Ch Jeropoulos & Co. Ltd.), San Lorenzo, Honduras, renamed *Larnaca Town*, renamed *Mina*; 1986 scrapped at Perama, Greece.
Brentfield/Spaniel	1958-1965 1968-1971	1,262	Built by George Brown & Co. (Marine) Ltd., Greenock, 1955 as *Brentfield* for Zillah Shipping Co. Ltd. (W A Savage Ltd.); 1958 to Coast Lines Ltd.; 1959 renamed *Spaniel*; 1965 to Burns & Laird Lines Ltd.; 1968 to Coast Lines Ltd.; 1970 to Coast Lines (Services) Ltd.; 1971 acquired by P&O Short Sea Shipping Ltd.; 1972 to Belfast Steamship Co. Ltd.; 1973 sold to Isle of Man Steam Packet Co. Ltd., Douglas, renamed *Conister*; 1981 sold to Asturamerican Shipping Co. Inc., Panama; scrapped at San Juan de Nieva, Spain.

Tudor Queen	1959	1,029	Built by Burntisland Shipbuilding Co. Ltd., Burntisland, 1940 as *Tudor Queen* for British Channel Islands Shipping Co. Ltd.; 1943 to British Channel Traders Ltd.; 1947 to Queenship Navigation Ltd.; 1959 to Coast Lines Ltd., scrapped at Troon.
Lurcher	1959-1961	859	Built by Scott & Sons, Bowling, 1938 as *Yewmount* for John Stewart & Co. Shipping Ltd., Glasgow; 1947 sold to British Channel Traders Ltd., renamed *Saxon Queen*; 1947 to Queenship Navigation Ltd.; 1959 to Coast Lines Ltd., renamed *Lurcher*; 21 January 1961 sank in collision in the Mersey, later refloated and scrapped at Preston.
Dorset Coast	1959-1971	1,167	Built by Ardrossan Dockyard Ltd., Ardrossan, 1959; 1970 to Coast Lines (Services) Ltd.; 1971 acquired by P&O Short Sea Shipping Ltd.; 1972 to Belfast Steamship Co. Ltd.; 1973 to General Steam Navigation (Trading) Ltd. (P&O Short Sea Shipping Ltd.); 1976 to P&O Ferries (General European) Ltd.; 1978 to P&O Ferries Ltd.; 1979 sold to James S Tyrrell, Arklow, Ireland, resold to James S T Komiros, Egypt, resold to Delta Marine Ltd., renamed *El Hussein*; 1980 to Delta Marine & Trading Ltd., Egypt; 1981 sold to Sayed Mohamed Sadaka Hitfa, renamed *El Kheer*, resold to Naviera Denton Venture S de R L (Nialed Shipping Co. Ltd., Gravesend), San Lorenzo, Honduras, renamed *Denton Venture*; 1982 sold to Intradis Shipping BV, Rotterdam; 1984 sold to Isabella Maritime Co. (Elvira Shipping Agency), Piraeus, Greece, renamed *Ourania*; 1985 scrapped at Bruges, Belgium.
Bison	1961-1972	2,144	Built by Charles Hill & Son Ltd., Bristol, 1961; 1971 acquired by P&O Short Sea Shipping Ltd., to Coast Lines (Services) Ltd., renamed *Norbank*; 1972 to Tyne-Tees Steam Shipping Co. Ltd.; 1975 to P&O Ferries Ltd.; 1976 to P&O Ferries (General European) Ltd., London; 1978 to P&O Ferries Ltd.; 1978 sold to National Suriname Shipping Co., Paramaribo, Surinam, renamed *Flamingo*; 1990 scrapped.
Buffalo	1961-1972	2,163	Built by Ardrossan Dockyard Ltd., Ardrossan, 1961; 1971 acquired by P&O Short Sea Shipping Ltd., to Coast Lines (Services) Ltd., 1972 renamed *Norbrae*, to Tyne-Tees Steam Shipping Co. Ltd.; 1974 renamed *Roe Deer*, 1975 to P&O Ferries Ltd.; 1976 to P&O Ferries (General European) Ltd.; 1977 sold to Harvey Container Ship Ltd., St. Johns, Newfoundland; 1977 to A Harvey and Co. Ltd., St. Johns, Newfoundland, renamed *Newfoundland Container*; 1977 to Newfoundland Container Lines Ltd., St. Johns, Newfoundland; 1978 to Harvey Container Ship Ltd., St. Johns, Newfoundland; 1985 sold to Victory Seaways Enterprises Ltd., Georgetown, Cayman Islands, renamed *Caribbean Victory*; 1986 sold to Renaissance Maritime Inc., San Lorenzo, Honduras, renamed *Lefkimmi*; 1988 renamed *St George*; 1993 sold to International Shipping Corp., Belize, renamed *Container Express*; 1999 scuttled at sea.

Wirral Coast	1962-1971	881	Built by Cammell Laird & Co. (Shipbuilders & Engineers) Ltd., Birkenhead, 1962; 1970 to Coast Lines (Services) Ltd.; 1971 acquired by P&O Short Sea Shipping Ltd.; 1972 sold to James Tyrrell Ltd., Arklow, renamed *Shevrell*; 1973 sold to Usborne & Son (London) Ltd. (Buries, Markes Ltd.), London, renamed *Portmarnock*; 1976 sold to G T Gillie & Blair Ltd., Newcastle; 1977 sold to Taunos Shipping Corp. (Orb Shipping Co. Ltd., London); 1978 sold to Fulpass Ltd. (G T Gillie & Blair Ltd., Newcastle); 1979 sold to Khodor Itani, Beirut, Lebanon, renamed *Nadia I*; 1981 sold to Nadia Hussein Mekkaoui, Beirut; 27 November 1985 wrecked off Lebanon.
Terrier	1963-1971	1,127	Built by NV Scheepswerf van der Werf, Deest, Netherlands, 1957 as *Ebba Ribbert* for Det Dansk-Norse Dampskibsselskab (R A Robbert), Copenhagen, Denmark; 1959 sold to Rederiet Seaway (R Fischer-Nielsen), Copenhagen, renamed *Stege*; 1963 sold to Coast Lines Ltd., renamed *Terrier*; 1970 to Coast Lines (Services) Ltd.; 1971 acquired by P&O Short Sea Shipping Ltd.; 1972 sold to James Tyrrell Ltd., Arklow, renamed *Murell*; 1974 sold to Nobleza Naviera SA, Uruguay, renamed *Quijote*; 1994 sold to Agroindustria Ara Poty Srl, Asunción, Paraguay, renamed *Omar G* – out of register by 2007.
Hadrian Coast	1964-1967	692	Built by Ardrossan Dockyard Ltd., Ardrossan 1941 for Coast Lines Ltd., completed for Minister of War Transport as *Empire Atoll*; 1946 to Ministry of Transport; 1946 sold to Tyne-Tees Steam Shipping Co. Ltd., renamed *Hadrian Coast*; 1948 to Aberdeen Steam Navigation Co. Ltd.; 1964 to Coast Lines Ltd.; 1967 sold to E Daviou, D Agoudimos & A Klissiounis, Piraeus, Greece, renamed *Elda*; 10 January 1970 wrecked near Mehidia, Morocco, on passage Ravenna to Kenitra.
Kentish Coast	1964-1968	498	Built by Ardrossan Dockyard Ltd., Ardrossan, 1946 as *Ulster Duchess* for Belfast Steamship Co. Ltd., to British Channel Islands Shipping Co. Ltd.; 1947 renamed *Jersey Coast*; 1954 to Belfast Steamship Co. Ltd., renamed *Ulster Weaver*; 1964 to Coast Lines Ltd., renamed *Kentish Coast*; 1968 sold to Alomar Mechanical Engineering Co., Kuwait, renamed *Salmiah Coast*; 1970 sold to Kuwait Coast Line Co., Kuwait; 1975 sold to A H G Zaddah, Kuwait – out of register by 1999.
Frisian Coast	1966-1967	592	Built by J Koster Hzn. Scheepswerf 'Gideon', Groningen, Netherlands, 1937 as *Lowick* for Tyne-Tees Steam Shipping Co. Ltd.; 1946 renamed *Frisian Coast*; 1966 to Coast Lines Ltd.; 1967 sold to D Varverakis & Chr. Hadjigeorgiou, Piraeus, Greece, renamed *Agia Eleni*; 1975 sold to Ponga Bros.; 1976 sold to Hamlet Shipping Co. Ltd.; 26 November 1977 stranded in Mandraki Harbour, Rhodes; scrapped.
Novian Coast	1966-1968	507	Built by Smiths Dock Co. Ltd., Middlesbrough, 1936 as *Wooler* for Tyne-Tees Steam Shipping Co. Ltd.; 1946 renamed *Novian Coast*; 1966 to Coast Lines Ltd.; 1968 scrapped at Willebroek, Belgium.

Grangefield	1967-1968	504	Built by NV Scheepswerf Gebroeder van der Werf, Deest, Netherlands, 1954 as *Statensingel* for 'INVOTRA' Invoer-en Transport-Onderneming NV, Rotterdam, Netherlands; 1955 sold to Zillah Shipping Co. Ltd. (W A Savage Ltd.), renamed *Grangefield*; 1964 owner renamed W A Savage Ltd.; 1967 to Coast Lines Ltd.; 1968 to Tyne-Tees Steam Shipping Co. Ltd.; 1969 sold to Transen Shipping Co., Panama; 1973 sold to Trans Sea Shipping Corp., Panama, renamed *Sea Goblin*; 1979 sold to Terra Investment & Trading Co., Panama, resold to Julianna Shipping Co. SA, Panama, renamed *Julianna* – out of register by 1997.
Earlsfield	1967-1969	635	Built by Bodewes Scheepswerven NV, Martenshoek, Netherlands, 1952 as *Coquetdyke* for Coquet Shipping Co. Ltd. (Anthony & Bainbridge); 1956 sold to Zillah Shipping Co. Ltd. (W A Savage Ltd.), renamed *Earlsfield*; 1964 owner renamed W A Savage Ltd.; 1967 to Coast Lines Ltd.; 1969 sold to R S Briggs & Co. (Shipping) Ltd., London, renamed *Katie H*; 1971 to Seabright Shipping Ltd. (Briggs Shipbrokers & Agents Ltd.), London; 7 March 1972 sank in collision 8 miles north of Noord Hinder light vessel on passage Rotterdam to London.
Kelvin	1968	979	Built by A & J Inglis Ltd., Pointhouse, 1955 as *Ulster Premier* for Belfast Steamship Co. Ltd.; 1963 to William Sloan & Co. Ltd., renamed *Kelvin*; 1965 to Burns & Laird Lines Ltd.; 1968 to Coast Lines Ltd., sold to Albaran Bay Corp. of Panama, renamed *Vasilia*; 1972 sold to Hudson K Tannis, Kingstown, St. Vincent, renamed *Alftan*; 1976 sold to Tacamar Panamena SA (Tacarigua Marina SA), Panama, renamed *Tacamar III*; 1982 to Flota Mercante de Quimicos Flomerquim CA (Tacamar Panamena SA), Puerto Cabello, Venezuela, renamed *Canaima*; 1983 scrapped at Cartagena, Colombia.
Talisker	1968	1,016	Built by George Brown & Co. (Marine) Ltd., Greenock, 1955 as *Ulster Pioneer* for Belfast Steamship Co. Ltd.; 1963 to William Sloan & Co. Ltd., renamed *Talisker*; 1965 to Burns & Laird Lines Ltd.; 1968 to Coast Lines Ltd.; sold to Mediterranean Lines Ltd., Haifa, Israel, renamed *Bat Snapir*, to Bat Snapir Mediterranean Lines Ltd., Ashdod, Israel; 1974 sold to Woodbine Shipping Corp. Inc., Panama, renamed *Woodbine*; 1975 sold to Asia Baru Navigation Pte. Ltd., Singapore, renamed *Hong Shen*; 1976 sold to Leong Mee Sendirian Berhad, Penang, Malaysia; 7 November 1988 sank off North Borneo on passage Port Kelang to Kota Kinabalu.
Fallowfield	1968-1971	566	Built by Scheepswerven Gebroeder van Diepen NV, Waterhuizen, Netherlands, 1953 as *Medusa* for Rederij Poseidon (A Kunst & J Pekelder), Groningen, Netherlands; 1954 sold to Zillah Shipping Co. Ltd. (W A Savage Ltd.), renamed *Fallowfield*; 1964 owner renamed W A Savage Ltd.; 1968 to Coast Lines Ltd.; 1971 sold to Arklow Shipping Ltd., Arklow (James Tyrrell), renamed *Arklow Bay*, to Bay Shipping Ltd. (Arklow Shipping Ltd.), Dublin; 22 September 1973 sank 40 miles south west of St Ann's Head, Pembrokeshire, on passage Antwerp to Arklow.

Fernfield	1968-1971	561	Built by Scheepswerven Gebroeder van Diepen NV, Waterhuizen, Netherlands, 1954 to be named **Kelbergen** but completed as **Haaksbergen** for NV Zuid-Hollandsche Scheepvaart Maatschappij, Rotterdam, Netherlands; 1958 sold to Zillah Shipping Co. Ltd. (W A Savage Ltd.), renamed **Fernfield**; 1964 owner renamed W A Savage Ltd; 1968 to Coast Lines Ltd.; 1970 to Coast Lines (Management) Ltd.; 1971 to Coast Lines (Services) Ltd., to P&O Short Sea Shipping Ltd., sold to James Tyrrell Ltd., Arklow, renamed **Shevrell**; 1972 sold to Entreprise de Navigation de L'Isle Inc., Quebec, Canada, renamed **Coudres de L'Ile**; 15 June 1988 sank in collision off Escoumaines, St. Lawrence River, on passage Sept Iles to St. Catherine's.

Coast Lines Ltd. also had the wooden barges **Penhallow** (between 1931 and 1947) and **Penpoll** (between 1932 and 1964) based at Falmouth and the passenger launches **Ganilly** (between 1932 and 1937) and **Polperro** (between 1929 and 1940) also at Falmouth.

The last 'Coast': **Dorset Coast**, owned by General Steam Navigation (Trading) Limited and registered at London, seen on charter to Greenore Ferries at Sharpness in August 1974.

[*Richard Parsons*]

INDEX

Ships within the Coast Lines group with date built in brackets

Fallowfield (1953)	99, 106, 110, 112, 145	*Jersey Coast* (1940)	84, 138
Fernfield (1954)	99, 106, 112, 146	*Jersey Coast* (1946)	144
Fife Coast (1892)	13, 20, 39, 125	*Jersey Queen* (1936)	49
Fife Coast (1933)	31, 40, 41, 51, 60, 61, 78, 134		
Fife Coast (1954)	83, 91, 101, 106, 115, 141		
Finola (1920)	57, 137	*Kelvin* (1955)	109, 145
Fire Queen (1921)	64, 75, 130	*Kelvindale* (1891)	27, 127
Foam Queen (1922)	49	*Kenmare* (1921)	21, 25, 57, 60
Forth (1943)	97, 138	*Kentish Coast* (1908)	6-8, 20, 32, 122
Freshfield (1954)	101	*Kentish Coast* (1938)	54, 55, 60, 65, 79, 91, 97, 106,
Frisian Coast (1937)	106, 144		109, 136
Fruin (1954)	91, 141	*Kentish Coast* (1946)	100, 144
		Kerry (1919)	57, 62, 137
Galway (1915)	137	*Kerry Coast* (1919)	57, 62, 137
Galway Coast (1915)	56, 57, 60, 68, 137	*Kildare* (1919)	137
Ganilly (1922)	39, 51, 146	*Kilkenny* (1904)	125
Glamorgan Coast (1912)	27, 39, 40, 127	*Kilkenny* (1937)	60, 104
Glamorgan Coast (1920)	57, 71, 137	*Killarney* (1893)	25, 32, 39, 73, 134
Glencoe (1846)	35	*Kinsale* (1921)	36, 42, 43, 133
Glengariff (1893)	11, 21	*Kirkcaldy* (1902)	11, 15, 124
Gloucester Coast (1913)	8, 10, 20, 120	*Koolga* (1910)	68, 69
Gorilla (1921)	22, 25, 26, 29, 43, 133		
Gower Coast (1899)	8, 18, 120		
Gower Coast (1911)	9, 20, 39, 123	*Lady Brussels* (1902)	23
Graceful (1911)	8, 118	*Lady Carlow* (1896)	21, 25
Grampian Coast (1936)	51	*Lady Cloé* (1916)	9, 13, 21, 25, 55-57, 65, 136
Grangefield (1954)	106, 110, 145	*Lady Connaught* (1906)	54, 57, 60, 62, 73
Grania (1924)	42, 128	*Lady Connaught* (1911)	33, 46, 54, 138
Graphic (1906)	16, 21, 25, 46	*Lady Emerald* (1919)	13, 21, 24, 57, 137
Greypoint (1905)	65	*Lady Iveagh* (1892)	31
Griqua Coast (1935)	84, 97, 134	*Lady Kerry* (1897)	21, 25
Grouse (1891)	21, 27, 34, 127	*Lady Kildare* (1920)	21
Guernsey Coast (1937)	84, 101, 135	*Lady Killarney* (1911)	73, 74, 79, 82, 86-88, 138
		Lady Killiney (1917)	21, 25
		Lady Leinster (1911)	33, 46, 54, 138
Hadrian Coast (1941)	63, 70, 101, 106, 144	*Lady Limerick* (1924)	28, 47
Hampshire Coast (1911)	12, 29, 30, 50, 119	*Lady Longford* (1921)	28, 47
Hampshire Coast (1937)	51, 54, 57, 68, 135	*Lady Louth* (1906)	47
Hampshire Coast (1940)	69, 79, 80, 138	*Lady Louth* (1923)	28, 32, 47
Harfat (1911)	8, 20, 51, 120	*Lady Martin* (1914)	19, 21, 122
Harlaw (1911)	68, 69	*Lady Meath* (1906)	21
Herero Coast (1950)	82, 93, 140	*Lady Munster* (1906)	33, 46, 54
Heroic (1906)	16, 21, 25, 46	*Lady Patricia* (1919)	13, 21, 24, 57, 137
Hibernian Coast (1946)	70, 79, 94, 100, 109, 139	*Lady Tennant* (1904)	15, 19, 21, 27, 125
Highland Coast (1912)	20, 30, 126	*Lady Valentia* (1920)	22, 25, 131
Hound (1893)	21	*Lady Wicklow* (1895)	21, 25, 26
		Lady Wimborne (1915)	9, 13, 21, 56, 57, 68, 137
		Lairds Isle (1911)	47, 48, 90
Inniscarra (1948)	99	*Lairds Loch* (1944)	105, 108
Innisfallen (1930)	33, 54, 57, 60	*Lairdsbank* (1893)	47
Innisfallen (1948)	71, 81, 111	*Lairdsbank* (1936)	52
Irish Coast (1900)	25, 37, 132	*Lairdsbrook* (1921)	37, 133
Irish Coast (1904)	6, 18, 27, 30, 122	*Lairdsburn* (1923)	31, 47
Irish Coast (1952)	80-82, 85, 86, 89, 90, 94, 102, 105,	*Lairdscastle* (1919)	31, 47
	107-109, 140	*Lairdsfern* (1937)	79, 91, 135
Island Queen (1934)	49	*Lairdsfield* (1953)	113